Divide and Fall?

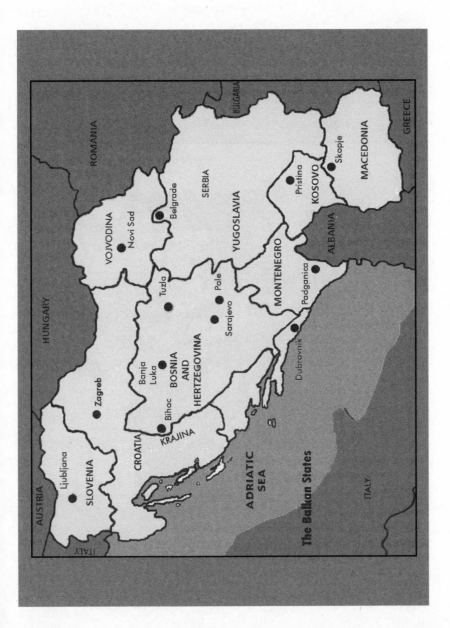

The Balkan States

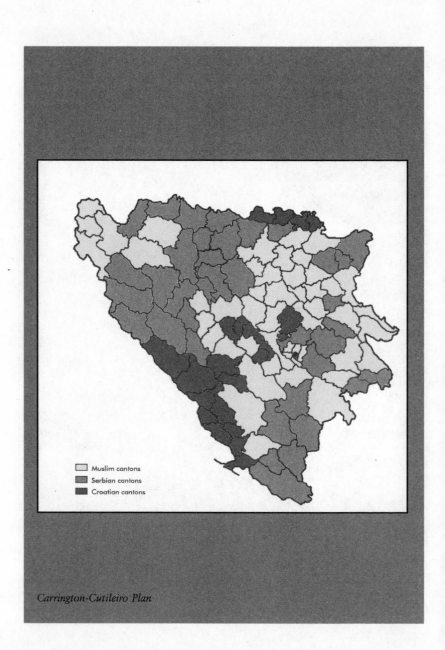

Muslim cantons
Serbian cantons
Croatian cantons

Carrington-Cutileiro Plan

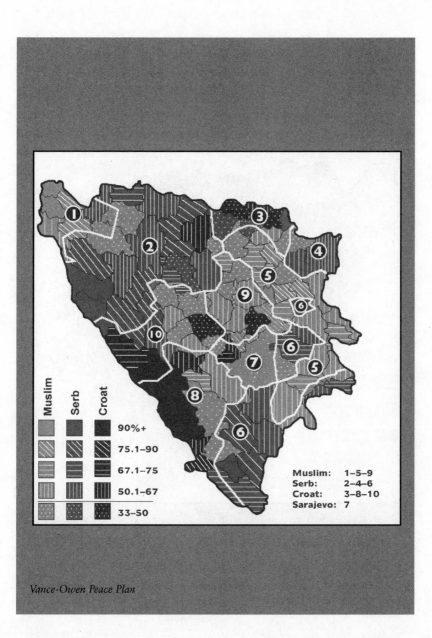

Muslim: 1–5–9
Serb: 2–4–6
Croat: 3–8–10
Sarajevo: 7

Muslim
Serb
Croat

90%+
75.1–90
67.1–75
50.1–67
33–50

Vance-Owen Peace Plan

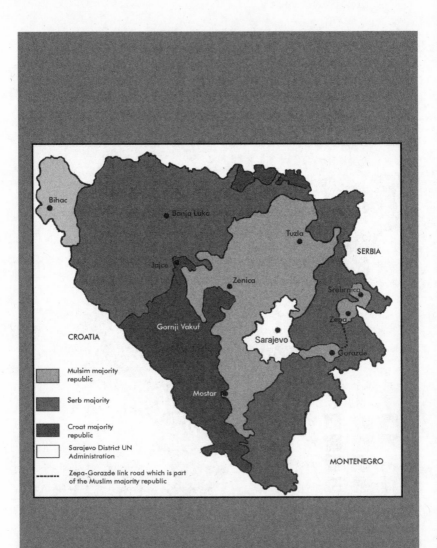

Bihac

Banja Luka

Tuzla

SERBIA

Jajce

Zenica

Srebrnica

Zepa

CROATIA

Gornji Vakuf

Sarajevo

Gorazde

Mulsim majority
republic

Serb majority

Croat majority
republic

Sarajevo District UN
Administration

------- Zepa-Gorazde link road which is part
of the Muslim majority republic

Mostar

MONTENEGRO

Union of Three Republics Plan

Divide and Fall?

Bosnia in the Annals of Partition

———◆———

RADHA KUMAR

VERSO

London · New York

First published by Verso 1997
© Radha Kumar 1997
All rights reserved

Verso
UK: 6 Meard Street, London W1V 3HR
USA: 180 Varick Street, New York NY 10014–4606

Verso is the imprint of New Left Books

ISBN 1–85984–852–4

British Library Cataloguing in Publication Data
A catalogue record for this book is available from the British Library

Library of Congress Cataloging-in-Publication Data
A catalog record for this book is available from the Library of Congress

Typeset by Password Publishing Services, Norwich
Printed and bound in Great Britain by
Biddles Ltd. Guildford and King's Lynn

Contents

Maps

Acknowledgements

This book was written with the support of a fellowship from the SSRC-MacArthur Program for Peace and Security Studies. I would like to thank Shashi Tharoor, David Rieff, Nicholas Rizopoulos and Tozun Bahcheli for commenting on the manuscript, the Helsinki Citizens' Assembly for plunging me into the thick of the Bosnian conflict, Mary Kaldor, Zdravko Grebo, Zarko Puhovski, Sonja Licht, and Konstanty Gebert for helping me to understand Europe and the Balkans, Eqbal Ahmed for helping me to clarify my views on India and Pakistan, Karen AbuZayd, Kris Janovski and Michelle O'Kelly for literally helping me to survive in Sarajevo and giving me crucial insights into the world of international institutions, the Rockefeller Foundation for tolerating my obsession with partition, and my mother and grandmother for much needed support. Needless to say, the shortcomings of this book are my own doing.

Preface

This book is intended to counter the recently revived idea that partition can be a solution to ethnic conflict. Originally a colonial formula, partition assumed two distinct forms after the Second World War: ethnic partition, which was accepted as a compromise formula for decolonization, and ideological partition, which was primarily a means of distinguishing Cold War spheres of influence. Though ideological partition grew in importance during the Cold War, ethnic partition suffered a loss of legitimacy, and has gained a new lease of life chiefly in the wake of the 1995 Dayton Agreement for Bosnia-Herzegovina. Its reappearance in a post-colonial and post-Cold War era is especially curious, given that the disintegration of the Cold War has delegitimized ideological partitions (such as Germany and Korea). Indeed, in the present time the formula is essentially anachronistic.

Partition draws on structures of ethnonational negotiation which were developed under colonialism: because they were rooted in divide and rule policies, when the shift to decolonize occurred it took the form of divide and quit. Herein lies the rub. In the case of Bosnia, the divide and rulers (Radovan Karadzic and Ratko Mladic, Slobodan Milosevic and Franjo Tudjman) are quite different from the divide and quitters (Western Europe and the US, roughly a dozen multinational institutions). Thus, the established process of the shift to divide and quit, which entails the relinquishment of divide and rule, has followed a different trajectory in Bosnia. Though the international community has outlawed divide and rule, its local proponents have not. Whether it is possible to accommodate divide and rule within divide and quit, however, is a moot point. As the following chapters seek to argue, the Bosnian war and the post-war experience of implementing Dayton indicate otherwise.

In fact, the Dayton Agreement was prefaced by a post-Cold War initiative to overcome the troubled history of partition, which dealt with both ethnic and ideological partitions and focused in particular on the unstable ethnic partitions of Ireland and Cyprus, the incomplete ethnic partition of Israel-Palestine, and the partition-in-making of Bosnia-Herzegovina. The brave new post-Cold War world, it seemed for a few giddy years, would redeem its ugly history of war and division. In the immediate aftermath of the Cold War, the US and the UN adopted a new development-centred approach which I have dubbed "renewable peace", because it recognizes that the process of emerging out of partition wars is a slow and difficult one. The concept of renewable peace is based on three key elements: that instead of seeking an overall political settlement determined by conditions of war, the goal is to identify windows of opportunity for peace within an ongoing conflict; that instead of waiting for the end of war before investing in peace, each window of opportunity will be used to initiate programmes which might then widen the terrain of peace (what the Clinton government called the "economic underpinnings of peace"); and that a wider regional responsibility for nurturing the transition to peace – through regional development banks and multilateral peace making – is crucial.

A policy combining these three elements has been deployed to differing degrees in Northern Ireland, Israel-Palestine, Cyprus and Bosnia, and can be said to mark a critical boundary of post-colonial and post-Cold War peace making. While timidity and a lack of political will mean the policy is still inchoate, historically this is par for the course for international policy formation. A comparison of pre- and post-Cold War divide and quit, this book argues, in fact indicates that the revival of ethnic partition theory is not only short-lived but points to a wider process of change in which the deployment of partition as a solution to ethnic conflict will be seen as doing more harm than good, whether in the short or long term.

1

A Lesser Evil

In November 1995, when the Dayton Peace Agreement was signed, few believed that the West would put in an intervening force of some sixty thousand troops only to ratify through peace what the war was fought for: ethnic states. But as the "Dayton process" unfolded, many began to recognize that the agreement, with its formal recognition of Republika Srpska, was essentially a partition agreement with an exit clause – that once a partition could be stabilized, the international community would be able to withdraw from an area into which it was dragged hind foremost. In fact, however, the Dayton Agreement included two exit clauses, as a form of double indemnity. While key aspects of the agreement, such as the creation of two "entities" with virtually separate legislatures, administrations and armies, went towards partition, attempts to bypass its more hostile legacies were made through provisions for a common economic space, arms control and – in a new departure for most international agreements – an emphasis on the role of civil society. Indeed, in a special twist, the Dayton Agreement's clauses on elections put the onus of choosing between partition and reintegration on a shattered and terrorized Bosnian civil society: if the Bosnian electorate (including the Bosnian Serbs) voted out their nationalist, and in some instances criminal, leaders, then the West would support moves towards reintegration. If, on the other hand, the Bosnian electorate remandated ethnonationalist leaders, then the international community would accept partition as the "democratically expressed will of the people".[1]

However, the decision to hold elections in a still very uncertain peace in Bosnia marked the tilt towards partition: as was predicted, the Bosnians remandated their ethnic leaders and Bosnia moved a step forward in the transition to partition. The step remained a very hesitant one: though legislative elections were held, attempts to resettle areas through voter registration, combined with a rise in violence in the run-up to elections, forced the international community to postpone cantonal and municipal elections indefinitely. The mandate for partition was still unclear.

The Bosnian war and the Dayton Peace Agreement of 1995 reignited interest in a theory which had fallen into disuse since the 1970s, that partition could be a solution to ethnic conflict. Only six years earlier, in the immediate aftermath of the fall of the Berlin Wall, the reunification of Germany was hailed both as the triumph of democracy over totalitarianism and as a marker of Europe's potential union. In a flush of enthusiasm, the Western powers expanded the Helsinki Accords of 1975 and proclaimed the end of hostility between NATO and the Warsaw Treaty Organization (WTO).[2] The Conference on Security and Co-operation in Europe (CSCE) was formed, partly as a fulfilment of Mikhail Gorbachev's vision of a "common European house"; its establishment also provided a European context to test NATO and WTO's transformation in a reunited post-Cold War Europe. Almost immediately, however, the communist governments of Poland, Hungary and Czechoslovakia fell and the WTO collapsed. Soon after, the Soviet Union quietly dissolved. Though the WTO's collapse sparked fears that the Western powers would have to assume the role of "the world's policemen", the relative smoothness with which the central European countries achieved independence and the Soviet Union dissolved encouraged hopes that European integration could also be achieved relatively smoothly. The newly created CSCE extended membership to all the nations of eastern Europe and the former Soviet Union, and NATO began to discuss enlargement.

A new spirit of overcoming the legacies of partition infused European politics and could be detected in US foreign policy: through a Swedish-Norwegian initiative, Israelis and Palestinians negotiated a historic accord conceding Palestinian rights to self-rule which was signed in Washington and endorsed by the US; through an Irish initiative, Protestant-Catholic talks yielded new scope to resolve the Northern Ireland conflict and, partly under US pressure, the British government conditionally recognized Sinn Fein as a party in negotiations for Irish self-rule; and the EU and US declared a new resolve to remedy the stalemated partition of Cyprus. Moderate gusts of this spirit reached as far afield as the Indian subcontinent, where UN supported proposals for a common Asian security policy were viewed as a way of getting India and Pakistan to cut back the regional arms race each had waged since the early years of partition. The UN, too, had responded to the disintegration of the Cold War with a sense that it might finally fulfil the role it had originally been founded for but which had been severely curtailed during the Cold War. In 1992, the newly recognized states of former Yugoslavia and the former USSR became UN members. At the same time, the UN's peace-keeping operations dramatically increased. Between 1948 and 1978, the UN had conducted thirteen peace-keeping operations *in toto*, of which five remained operative in 1992. In contrast, between 1988 and 1992 the organization established fourteen new operations; in the first six months of 1992 alone, the peace-keeping budget shot up from $700 million to $2.8 billion.[3] At the same time, the mandate for peace keeping was expanded, moving towards peace enforcement in some areas and peace building in others. Gradually, too, a new doctrine of humanitarian intervention was beginning to emerge.

The first flush of enthusiasm, however, faded as the enormous costs of transformation, integration and peace making became evident. The massive injection of aid, which the West had promised as a kind of cushion to the USSR while it dismantled its Cold War security apparatus and became politically and economically liberalized, was never made. Impoverishment had been one of the causes of the disintegration of the communist bloc; the crisis of state legitimacy which ensued was accompanied by the fragmenting of administrative and political structures and the rise of identity politics. Across most of the republics of the former USSR and east and central Europe, communists turned to mobilizing ethnic constituencies as a way of retaining political power; as economic and social scarcity increased, so did ethnic politics and the variety of forms of ethnic conflict. As the 1980s boom began to take a downward turn in Europe, the US and the Pacific Rim, it began to seem as if a new two-tier Europe was beginning to take shape, whose first tier would comprise the richer nations of west Europe – perhaps expanded slightly eastwards[4] – and whose second tier would comprise the entire, partly imaginary, European house contemplated by Gorbachev.

The image of a reunited Europe began to crack. A flow of economic refugees and asylum seekers from Africa and eastern Europe led many in western Europe to question whether the aim of European integration was misplaced in the first place. Denmark's vote against joining the EU in 1992, followed by the narrow margin in favour of European union in France, strengthened scepticism over Europe's capacity to integrate, and the potential for the rapid growth of ethnic conflict in both the East and South, with the massive refugee movements these would entail, became of increasing concern to security analysts. In 1991, the Pentagon issued a paper arguing that the threat of "new conflicts" in the East and South required new forms of intervention. The new conflicts, it said, would appear as protracted low-intensity wars which would not confine themselves within state borders; on the contrary, they were wars which targeted civilians and created massive refugee movements which could destabilize a widening circle of countries and regions.[5] By 1993, it was estimated that one person in every 130 of world population was displaced due to war.[6]

The term which was increasingly used to describe what fuelled these wars was "ethnic nationalism". Initially, an ethnie was broadly construed as a community which collectively defined itself by language, custom, religion, race or culture; ethnic nationalists asserted the primacy of ethnic identities in creating nation states or governing them. In this sense, ethnic nationalism could be defined as qualitatively different from either the European nationalism of the nineteenth century or the anti-colonial nationalism of the twentieth century: while the latter two inclined to egalitarianism and based themselves on citizenship, the former was hierarchical and placed collective rights above individual ones.[7] However, as ethnic nationalism proliferated it became clear that the wide definition of ethnie was itself problematic as far as the relationship between identity and conflict was concerned.

Historically, in the drive to ethnic war, one form of ethnic identity tended to eclipse the others and that one was religious identity, or as the South Asian term will have it, communalism, that is, ethnic conflict based on religious identity. Though racial identities were adduced in defining the two nations in Palestine, and to a lesser extent in India and Cyprus, the chief determinant was religion: Catholics and Protestants in Ireland, Hindus and Muslims in India, Muslims and Greek Orthodox in Cyprus, and Jews and Muslims in Palestine. In this context, the Yugoslav wars, based as they were not only on dissolving the federation but on redrawing its borders communally – between Slav Muslims, Orthodox and Catholics – brought back a spectre which Europeans thought they had laid to rest, that of religious conflict in Europe. As the aims of the Serbian and Croatian political leadership to divide Bosnia-Herzegovina between them grew increasingly to dominate the wars, a bewildered Europe and the US began to re-examine partition theory at two distinct levels: locally, within nations at ethnic war, and Europe-wide, as a new Berlin wall dividing democracies from ethnocracies.[8]

By the early 1990s, partition was beginning to regain credibility as a solution to ethnopolitical strife, but it was still considered to be legitimate only when achieved by peaceful negotiation. The most commonly cited example of a negotiated and peaceful division was Czechoslovakia's "velvet divorce" of 1992. Though this example was brought up again by Richard Holbrooke in November 1995, when he said on the MacNeil-Lehrer news hour in reply to the question of whether the Dayton Agreement was partition that he preferred to use the example of Czechoslovakia's voluntary dissolution, the fact that Bosnia's communal cartography was drawn by a war targeting civilians rather than an unequal but peaceful negotiation made the comparison invidious. Indeed, the key difference between Bosnia-Herzegovina and the Czech Republic and Slovakia, that the former was ethnically intermixed while the latter were relatively homogenous, meant that the dissolution of the Czechoslovak federation did not require an alteration of internal borders or entail the massive displacement of population, and by 1995 fewer and fewer people referred to the Czechoslovak separation as a context for Bosnia. A closer comparison began to be drawn between Bosnia and the partitions of Ireland, India and Cyprus or the incomplete partition of Palestine, because each involved multi-ethnic and demographically dispersed populations – to varying degrees the ethnic map of each was a checkerboard whose redrawing would entail the massive displacement of people – and each was held to be a pragmatic recognition of irreconcilable ethnic identities.

In fact, the comparison with Ireland, India, Palestine and Cyprus drew attention to a different element of the Bosnian partition process: be irreconcilable ethnic identities what they may, historically the parties at war are generally loath to agree a partition without international mediation. Describing the partition of India in 1947, the former civil servant Penderel Moon summarized the British role in pushing partition through without establishing the boundaries of the new states or planning for the wars which might ensue as "divide and quit".[9] The phrase followed on an earlier description of the partition of Bengal in 1905 as "divide and rule".[10] Both phrases underlined the third party, generally colonial, role in partition and pointed to the fact that decisions to divide are most commonly impelled by considerations which have little to do with the needs or desires of the people who are to be divided. This truism of the history of twentieth-century partitions acquired a new resonance in the Bosnian partition process, which the Dayton Agreement sought to transform into a peacetime, seemingly voluntary, transition, and was given a special twist by the fact that Bosnia was not a colony. A question which arises is whether the thrust towards partition will end in the colonization of Bosnia, a consequence which was partly implied by the Washington Agreement of 1994 under which Bosnia was to confederate with Croatia. Such an outcome would reverse the general twentieth-century process of partition as a means of limited self-determination. However, as this book seeks to argue, it is more likely that the experience of attempting to implement a Bosnian partition in a post-colonial and post-Cold War context will call partition theory itself into question.

Indeed, one of the chief aims of this book is to ask whether partition might be an anachronistic solution to ethnic conflict in these times. Partition has traditionally been linked to empire: though it has recurred as an administrative means of resolving political conflict since the third century, when Diocletian divided the Roman empire along an east-west axis (on a line which ran through the Balkans), it began to acquire its capital 'P' only in the late eighteenth century, through the Russian, Austrian and Prussian partitions of Poland between 1772 and 1918, which can more accurately be described as examples of great power territorial dispositions than of a policy of rule by ethnic or communal division. Divide and rule, in its communal sense, was refined by nineteenth-century British colonialism; paradoxically, the policy developed in an age obsessed with cataloguing ethnic, religious, tribal, linguistic, cultural and civilizational difference, especially in the newly colonized worlds of the East and South. Though such endeavours frequently contributed to superiorist theories of the right to rule, they also contributed to the demarcation of areas of self-rule (for example, in the field of family or personal law, under which different religious groups were bound by their own laws of marriage, divorce and inheritance).

This tangled history continued to dominate partition theory in the twentieth century when, within the British empire, divide and rule began to give way to divide and quit. The shift, which occurred between the two world wars, was itself an important move away from colonialism. While divide and rule had been the dominant motive of partition until the First World War, after the war colonial empires began to be increasingly challenged, and subsequent partitions took place either in the context of devolution (end of empire) or as part of the Cold War policy of zones of influence (Germany, Korea and Vietnam). There were two distinct rationales for the partitions which occurred as a result of the fall of colonial empires: the Wilsonian policy of national self-determination which was put forward as a set of principles on which to base the dismantling of the Ottoman and Austro-Hungarian empires and contain Germany, and the British policy of divide and quit (Ireland, India and, in a delayed response sense, Cyprus and Palestine).[11]

Ironically, the Wilsonian policy had taken a reunited independent Poland as central (this was one of the fourteen points presented by the

US to the Allies in 1918–19). Given that the Poland which came into being was a conglomeration of territories marked by the empires to which they had belonged, whose people were culturally and linguistically different, and which lacked even road and rail connections between the major towns,[12] the extent to which President Wilson equated national with ethnic identity was ambiguous. The fourteen points, in fact, were careful to distinguish between different forms and conditions of self-determination, from independence to limited autonomy.[13] But though they were based on a key distinction between the rights of the colonized and the rights of minorities, their adaptation to a time when the division of the spoils was more important than "the interests of the populations concerned", meant that national or ethnic self-determination – as a value – was more frequently invoked to limit territories than to free them or to unite divided peoples.[14] As Harold Nicolson put it, the fourteen points "were hailed as an admirable method of extracting motes from the eyes of others", but when reference was made to Cyprus, Ireland, Egypt or India, the most fervent British advocate of self-determination felt his ardour cool.[15]

Nevertheless, in the oddly fortuitous manner of much historical change, the Wilsonian principles had an important influence on British colonialism. In the same way as Britain's colonial interests modified its acceptance of principles of self-determination, the extent to which it did accept them altered its colonial practices. The Mandate system, under which Britain ratified its annexations of Cyprus and Palestine, introduced two notional controls: the first that colonial rule was to be time bound, and the second that the goal of colonial rule was to encourage the "autonomous development" of the colonized people towards self-determination. Henceforth, both were touted as constitutive of British policy in the colonies, though the extent to which either was followed varied in relation to internal and external pressures. (Thus, for example, while Home Rule was being negotiated in Ireland, only the most limited measures for representation were introduced in India; while discussions of India's status were under way, Palestine and Cyprus were still in the process of limited representation; while independence was granted to India and discussed in Palestine, Cyprus was still in the preliminary stages of devolution.) Nevertheless, the process by which each colony moved towards independence and partition shared a central problem. The combination of the principles of independence and ethnic self-determination filled a gap in the shift from divide and rule to devolution, which centred on the question of how to satisfy the conflicting loyalties which had been created by divide and rule. What evolved as the two-nation theory, which underlay divide and quit, took ethnic identity as a key determinant of political rights. However, it departed from Wilsonian self-determination in one important respect: it was additionally based on the lesser evil argument, that an ethnoterritorial division may not weed out the problem but it would contain ethnic conflict.

The current version of the argument that partition can be a solution to ethnic wars draws on the British colonial view to argue that partition is still the most satisfactory lesser evil (the greater evil being the continuation of a war until its ethnonationalist ends are fulfilled). Thus, its advocates claim, partition is probably the most humane form of intervention in an ethnic conflict because it attempts to achieve through negotiation what would otherwise be achieved through war; it telescopes the conflict and saves lives. It might even save a country from disappearing altogether.[16] Nor is partition only a temporary means of containing conflict; it can provide a lasting means of containment as existing ethnic partitions show, for example in Ireland, India and Cyprus. Implicitly, both the lesser evil and containment arguments rest on a primordialist and insular reversal of Wilson's principles, which was most succinctly put by Reginald Coupland, the great architect of partition theory in Palestine. Writing in 1937, Coupland argued: "Where the conflict of nationalities has been overcome and unity achieved – in Britain itself, in Canada, in South Africa – one of the parties concerned was English or British, and . . . where that has not been so, as in the schism between the Northern and Southern Irish, or between Hindus and Moslems in India, the quarrel, though it is centuries old, has not yet been composed."[17] In the early years of the Yugoslav wars, the primordialist explanation that these were "ancient Balkans animosities" was commonly advanced, most often as a reason for non-intervention.[18]

The new partitioners, however, reverse the argument and put it forward as the *raison d'être* of intervention.[19]

The intervene-to-partition argument begins, as it were, in the middle: that is, its essential postulates are that the push to intervene occurs only when ethnic wars are so well advanced that ethnic politics set the terms for a negotiated peace. In such a situation, the causes of the war become chiefly of academic interest, as does the question of whether there actually is substantial local support for ethnic states. Thus it is not necessary to deal with these issues in order to provide a stable solution to ethnonationalist wars; a territorial separation of the conflicting ethnic groups will end the war because it will grant through peace the ethnically homogenous states which would otherwise have to be achieved through war. However, in ethnically dispersed states it might be necessary to take military control of the region at war in order to create ethnically homogenous states; the population transfers which will have to take place can then be organized under international supervision. Because ethnic homogeneity will obviate friction, the argument concludes, population transfers will ensure some degree of long-term stability. Alternatively, in areas where demographic dispersion might make ethnic homogeneity difficult, population transfers can contain the risks of renewed or continuing communal conflict by reducing minorities to such a small proportion of the population that they cannot be construed as a threat.[20]

Arguments of this sort claim a hard-headed realism by reference to another argument, that most interventions are guided by self-interest and the less self-interest there is, the more incomplete and potentially damaging the intervention will be.[21] Where there is little self-interest, therefore, it is especially important to limit both the scope and intent of intervention. In this context, intervening to partition provides a clear intent and a limited goal. Indeed, partition can be the most effective form of containment, taking the narrow definition of containment as limiting the spread of a conflict. Despite the claim of realism, however, such an argument more often inclines towards a Lewis Carroll world of selective meanings. Perhaps the most staggering of these is the way it reverses the argument on intervention, which was originally intended to curtail the scope to intervene, by proposing a massive military operation not only to separate the warring factions and stabilize the region, as IFOR was and now SFOR is tasked with in Bosnia, but to seek out, "intern and exchange" entire communities of people.[22]

In this sense the current argument for partition differs radically from divide and quit, and could more aptly be described as "divide and cleanse". Why a democratic country would wish to commit enormous resources to such a dubious end is not considered; in fact, the argument entirely misses the point that the lesser evil doctrine is based on getting out as quickly and cheaply as possible, and conforms as closely to *laissez-faire* as is strategically and morally feasible. Indeed, it was the recognition that this motive superseded all other considerations for the British which had, in the first place, led the local leadership in Ireland, India, Palestine and Cyprus to accept partition as a lesser evil. Ethnic leaders themselves often resisted partition until it became clear that they either had no other options or that the other options were even less satisfactory. Thus it took over a decade for the Zionist movement to accept partition as the only achievable means of self-determination,[23] and the same can be said of the Muslim League. Mohammed Ali Jinnah, regarded by many as the father of Indian partition, died a deeply disappointed man when faced with the results of a partition he had demanded which denied the power sharing he had bargained for.[24]

Similarly, there is little reason to believe that the push to intervene militarily will occur only when ethnic wars are at their peak. Historically, the third-party role has been one of intimate involvement in the ethnonationalist process leading to partition wars, as British policies in Ireland, India, Palestine and Cyprus indicate. Yet when ethnic conflicts reached their peak in these countries, the British showed a marked disinclination to intervene: in fact, they did their best to withdraw as fast as possible. In the case of Palestine, moreover, the British rejected the partition option on the grounds that it would entail a messy military engagement.[25] While there have been limited interventions in Bosnia-Herzegovina, these followed after the international community had been engaged in the region for some time, and the nature of the interventions – first for humanitarian relief and then to deter attacks on some of the safe areas – can be seen as attempts to limit the effects of the partition war rather than aid in the realization of its goals.

Whether there can be a peaceful transition to partition is a moot point. India's political leadership, for example, agreed to partition the country before the spread of large-scale conflict: indeed, the Congress-Muslim League agreement was intended partly to prevent the spread of communal riots from Bengal in eastern India to north-western India, which was also to be divided. Instead, however, the intense war that followed in the areas to be partitioned left over half a million dead in six months, and displaced upwards of fifteen million people. Historically, partition has more often been a backdrop to war than its culmination in peace; though it may originate within a situation of conflict, its effect has been to stimulate further and even new conflict. Moreover, negotiations for partition generally shadow a conflict long before the thrust towards partition becomes evident. Thus, though the British partition of Ireland in 1921 appeared as a late addition to negotiations to end the 1919–21 Anglo-Irish war for independence, partition had been on board since 1912,[26] when it was proposed in response to the government's introduction of the Irish Home Rule Bill that the Protestant majority counties of Antrim, Armagh, Down and Londonderry be excluded from the Bill's purview. This was rapidly followed by a proposal to exclude the entire province of Ulster. Under mounting pressure in Britain, in 1914 the government proposed that Ulster's nine counties could each decide, by vote, whether or not they wanted a temporary, six-year exclusion from Irish Home Rule, an offer which the moderate Irish nationalists were prepared to consider but the Ulster Unionists rejected because they feared that the vote would go in favour of partition only in the four counties where Protestants were in a large majority, losing in the five others.

The moderate nationalist willingness to consider partition divided Irish nationalists and led to the formation of the radical Sinn Fein. Though the Home Rule Bill was enacted in 1914, the outbreak of the First World War suspended its operation and negotiations on self-rule were put on hold until 1916, when the British execution of the leaders of the Easter Uprising triggered an enormous wave of support for Irish independence and made resolution of the Ireland conflict imperative.

In the negotiations which followed, the British government and the Unionists came to an unwritten agreement that both Ireland and Ulster would be partitioned, and that six out of Ulster's nine counties would remain under British rule. The proposal to limit Ulster to six counties (four Protestant majority and two mixed) was made by the Unionists themselves, who had concluded that the inclusion of all nine counties would leave them with far too large a Catholic population. Meanwhile, however, Sinn Fein swept the 1918 Irish polls, formed an Irish Assembly and declared independence. Partly under the pressure of these events, the British proposed the Government of Ireland Bill in 1919, by which Ireland would have two parliaments, one for the southern provinces and one for the northern counties. Both would be joined in a loose federation with Britain, under which Westminster would retain control over foreign affairs, defence, trade, communications and "treason", while all other government functions would be transferred to the two parliaments.

The Bill attempted a peculiar compromise between contending claims for independence and self-determination: it tried to satisfy post-war pressures to embark on a staged withdrawal from empire, but at the same time it purported to accomodate Unionist demands for separation from a self-governing Catholic dominated Ireland under the rubric of self-determination. Its refusal to consider Unionist demands to opt out of devolution by choosing to remain under British rule, however, made it clear that self-determination was part of a package of measures towards withdrawal; self-determination, even when unwanted, could not be considered an "imposition", the government explained. What self-determination comprised was open to question: by including all nine of the northern counties in the jurisdiction of the northern parliament, the Bill offered the Unionists a multi-ethnic Northern Ireland with a 40 per cent Catholic population; in effect, it would institute a form of minority rule which would be open to challenge electorally. The proposal was intended to avert a religion based partition, which might have brought accusations of divide and rule, and was floated with an eye to events within the US, where US participation in the League of Nations was hotly contested by a coalition in which the Irish American organization Friends of Irish Freedom played an important role.

The attempt to move away from divide and rule while avoiding divide and quit, however, proved short-lived. The inherent paradox of conceding a separate parliament to Unionist claims for self-determination while ensuring an electorate in which Protestants constituted a relatively narrow majority moved negotiations towards the further partition of Ulster which had been under negotiation since 1914, and to which Ulster Unionists felt they were morally entitled by their support for the British in World War I. On Balfour's intervention, the Bill was amended in March 1920 so that Northern Ireland would comprise the six counties demanded by the Unionists. Balfour had adduced the 1919 Paris Peace Conference's application of the principle of ethnic self-determination in drawing new borders in central Europe; had they been delimiting the constituency of Northern Ireland, he said, there would have been no question of including "in the Protestant area so large and homogenous a Roman Catholic district as that (say) of the greatest part of Donegal".[27]

Arguing that the Bill was tantamount to a double partition based on religion, of Ireland and Ulster, Sinn Fein rejected it and Anglo-Irish conflict spread across the south, west and north of the country, escalating to guerrilla war with the formation of the Irish Republican Army in the same year. By this point, Sinn Fein itself preferred that Ulster remain under British rule because this would keep the possibility of eventual unification open, whereas a separate Northern Ireland parliament would provide a political and institutional base for partition. Their fears were well-founded: the enactment of the Bill at the end of 1920 in a context of growing communal violence fuelled the physical process of partition and allowed it to institutionalize itself. While the Act continued to be rejected by Sinn Fein and was thus inoperative in Southern Ireland, the Unionists began to prepare for an Ulster parliament, and well before elections were held in May 1921, the interim Unionist government had created and controlled Northern Ireland's institutions of administration, including an armed Special Constabulary for territorial defence which was recruited from men determined to resist the IRA.

Nor did the war end in 1921, when Britain negotiated a treaty with Sinn Fein offering dominion status to Southern Ireland (to be called the

Irish Free State), on condition that they accepted the right of Northern Ireland's parliament to decide whether to secede or enter into a relationship with the Free State in which they would constitute a kind of autonomous province. Under the Treaty, the two houses of Northern Ireland's parliament would have a month to decide. If they decided to secede, a boundary commission composed of representatives of Dublin, Belfast and London would determine the borders between the two parts of Ireland. The treaty included a provision that such a partition could be reversed by a referendum on reunification to be held two years later. Soon after, the Unionist Parliament of Northern Ireland decided to secede, and a boundary commission was established. The decision to accept partition led to a split in Sinn Fein and internecine conflict was added to communal conflict, ending two years later with the suppression of the De Valera led revolt. At which time the British reneged on the promised referendum. In 1925, the Boundary Commission, chaired by the South African jurist Richard Feetham,[28] resolved that the new border would not differ from the old provincial boundaries to any substantial extent; the few adjustments were in Unionist favour. It took, therefore, close on four years of war to achieve the partition of Ireland, and those four years were themselves a culminating phase in a movement towards partition which had begun ten years earlier.

In the course of the decade, communal conflict was entrenched, political movements were fragmented and radicalized, encouraging the rise of armed resistance, and the British were embroiled in a military operation in Northern Ireland which continues till this day. Though the military presence curtailed the toll which continuing communal conflict might otherwise have taken, it also brought the Irish conflict to the heart of Britain as the IRA took to terrorist attacks on London in moves to escalate pressure for a British withdrawal. It is sometimes argued that partition and the subsequent British military presence, costly though it was to Britain, at least contained the Irish conflict and kept deaths to a minimum. But it could also be argued that from the British point of view, independence might have been a more effective form of containment as it would throw the onus of peace onto the Irish; in addition, it might have encouraged regional compromises rather than a religious stalemate which has dominated political life in Northern Ireland for over seventy years.

The enormous difficulties of moving from divide and rule to divide and quit are underlined by the process of partition in India. Britain's first essay at partition in India was, in fact, the division of Bengal in 1905, which led to widespread protest by both Muslim and Hindu Bengalis, in which the newly metropolitan city of Calcutta played a focal role. The move had far-reaching consequences: it transformed the Indian National Congress by giving it leadership of a popular regional movement, while dividing it over whether to continue with its programme of constitutional reform or opt for a boycott of British rule. And it further communalized Indian politics: both the Muslim League and the Hindu Mahasabha were founded in its wake in 1906. In 1912, the British reunited the province in a limited move away from divide and rule; in the same year they had tabled the Bill for Home Rule in Ireland. The reunification of Bengal offered a singular opportunity to revise the ethnic principle underlying divide and rule, but ethnic politics continued to dominate the British "now you see it now you don't" process of devolution of power. The 1909 Indian Councils' Act's extension of a limited number of elected seats to a restricted electorate included the reservation of seats on a communal basis; this was followed in 1916 by the creation of separate Hindu and Muslim electorates in local elections. Significantly, Indian nationalists responded by agreeing that the principle of minority weightage should be substituted for communal representation. The 1916 Lucknow Pact between the Congress and Muslim League proposed a proportionately greater number of seats for Hindus and Sikhs in Muslim majority provinces and for Muslims in Hindu majority provinces.[29]

The end of the First World War and the Paris Peace Conference of 1919 had their own effect in India. In another hesitant step towards devolution, taken in the same year that the Government of Ireland Bill was tabled, the British passed the Government of India Act, introducing limited self-government through a diarchical structure with provincial legislatures, 70 per cent of whose members would be directly elected, while ethnic representation would be assured through separate electorates for Muslims and Hindus (and in the Punjab, Sikhs) on a majority basis. Suffrage remained restricted and the issue of dominion status was postponed. At the same time, the dismantling of the Ottoman empire led a rising pan-Islamic Khilafat movement in India to demand Muslim sovereignty in Arabia, Syria, Iraq and Palestine, and on Gandhi's initiative the Indian National Congress and the Khilafat movement joined in a campaign of non-co-operation with the British.[30] Debate over whether or not to participate in the Council elections split nationalist ranks, but in the 1923 elections both the newly formed Swarajya (self-rule) Party and the Congress did well, the former at the provincial level and the latter at the municipal level.

The limits of the 1919 Act were immediately felt: the newly elected parties' moves towards self-government were blocked or vetoed, and the councils hardly functioned at all. Their failure led to rising communal and political turmoil as voter expectations were disappointed amongst a variety of contending groups and parties. In 1927, the British announcement of the all-white Simon Commission to enquire into reforms briefly united the Congress and Muslim League in a boycott; but the rapprochement broke down in 1928 when the Congress rejected Jinnah's proposal that the Muslim League would give up its support for separate electorates if the Congress would agree to a one-third Muslim representation in the Central Assembly, proportional communal representation in Bengal and Punjab, and the creation of three new Muslim majority provinces of Sindh, Baluchistan and the North West Frontier Provinces (NWFP). Instead, and partly under pressure from the Hindu Mahasabha, the Congress suggested a unitary state with minority representation, including minority weightage.

The boycott of the Simon Commission led the British to revive discussions on dominion status, but negotiations in 1929 for a Round Table Conference to discuss the issue broke down over issues of representation, and there was a renewed upsurge of nationalist agitation and political and communal violence. Though three sessions of the Round Table Conference were held, the first was not attended by the Congress, the second broke down over debates on representation for the smaller minorities, such as Anglo-Indians and Eurasians, and the third was scarcely attended. In 1935, the British passed the Government of India Act, federalizing the provincial legislatures, quantifying ethnic representation along the lines of the Lucknow Pact, and dividing both the Bombay Presidency and the province of Bihar and Orissa to create the majority Muslim state of Sind and the majority Hindu state of Orissa. In the elections which followed in 1937, however, the pact had neither the effect of encouraging communal power sharing, nor of furthering communal divide: the Congress won roughly 40 per cent of the seats to the provincial assemblies, and in the states which were later to be the battlegrounds of partition, the Punjab, Bengal and Sind, it was regional coalitions which formed the new governments. During 1939 and 1940, when Muslim League proposals to push the federal provisions of the 1935 Act a step further towards an eventual federation of Muslim and Hindu majority states began to gain ground, the coalition parties in Punjab, Bengal and Sindh suggested instead a loose federation of seven multi-ethnic regions with minority guarantees and wide-ranging autonomy, under a central government whose powers would be restricted to foreign affairs, defence, customs and monetary policy. The proposals were disregarded by the British government, Congress and the Muslim League alike;[31] the latter's poor showing in the 1937 elections had led it to embark on an energetic organizational programme. In 1942 when, in exasperation with British refusal to set a timetable for self-rule, the Congress announced the "Quit India" campaign, widespread arrests denuded the provincial governments. The Muslim League stepped into the breach and during the Second World War, while Congress leaders bargained for independence, the League unreservedly supported the Allies, as the Irish Protestants had done in the First World War.

For both the Congress and the League, the experience of government under the severely circumscribed mandates imposed by limited devolution meant that individual members' powers resided chiefly in small-time patronage, and though the policy of separate electorates had not so far resulted in the election of communal governments, it progressively steered expectations of patronage in a communal direction. Its effects were bitterly felt between 1945 and 1947, when the British attempted to negotiate an agreement on power sharing between Congress and the League which would allow them to simultaneously withdraw from India and avert a partition war. Negotiations broke down time and time again, basically over two related issues: Congress's refusal to concede the League's claim to be sole spokesman for Indian Muslims, which would by implication transform Congress into a Hindu party, and the League's refusal to enter any federal relationship which would question their right to sovereignty in Muslim majority areas. The extent to which ethnic politics militated against power sharing is evidenced by the fact that Congress and the League came to the verge of agreement on a decentralized federation of Muslim and Hindu majority provinces in 1946, but the agreement broke down when the League refused to allow the Congress to nominate a Congress Muslim member to the transitional government.[32] For the League, the British failure to uphold its rights as sole spokesman was a betrayal of their unreserved support of the Allies during the Second World War; Jinnah announced a League led "Quit India" movement, and in the elections of 1946, the party did very well in the key Muslim majority states of Bengal and Punjab for the first time. The vote was subsequently treated by the British as evidence of the irreconcilability of Hindus and Muslims.

As in Ireland, both independence and partition were hastened by war; after the Second World War a Britain which was economically and morally ravaged by the war could not contemplate the prospect of holding on to a colonial rule which was being increasingly challenged both domestically and by strong Indian independence movements, and the notion of gradual self-government was quickly replaced with a programme for the speedy transfer of power. Though partition was only decided in 1947, it had been proposed on and off from the early years of the century and by the 1940s, British officials, especially in north-western India, were referring openly to Pakistan. The decision to partition India was taken after a year of fruitless negotiations (from 1945 to 1946) for a decentralized federation. When it was finally agreed, the logic of the two-nation theory, that Hindus and Muslims comprised separate nations each deserving their own territories, entailed the partitions of Punjab and Bengal and meant a Pakistan much smaller than the Muslim

League had envisaged. The partition of India was announced within months of a formal agreement, before borders had been finalized and without any consideration of the populations involved. In the six months following the announcement, a partition on paper had to be fought through on the ground before it could be achieved.[33]

In comparison to the partitions of Ireland, Palestine and Cyprus, the 1947 partition of India can be considered successful because neither India nor Pakistan nor Bangladesh seriously challenge each other's right to exist, but much of the evidence indicates that this success has less to do with the ethnic principle than with other factors, among which the distance of the subcontinent from Europe is important. Unlike Ireland, Palestine, Cyprus and Bosnia, the sheer size of the Indian subcontinent meant a dozen or more new states could have been created. Indeed from this point of view, the deployment of the ethnic two-nation theory had the paradoxical effect that the one new state which was created, Pakistan, was unfeasible because it was in two parts, divided by roughly two thousand kilometres of Indian territory. Moreover, the fact that the subsequent separation of these two parts occurred as a conflict between east and west Pakistani regional ethnic identities, resulting in the inde-pendence of Bangladesh in 1971, points to the inadequacies of the ethnic principle in providing solutions. In a profound if horrible way, the con-flict between East and West Pakistan, resulting in the independence of Bangladesh in 1971, ended the partition question because it pointed out that superimposing one overarching communal identity over com-munities of multiple identity did not provide a lasting solution to ethnic conflict; on the contrary, one partition could imply further essentializ-ing partitions. As the case of Kashmir implies.

Since partition, India and Pakistan have engaged in a prolonged con-flict which has twice flared into war over what has been described as being, in a phrase dearer to Pakistani than Indian politicians, "the un-finished business of partition", Kashmir. On ethnodemographic grounds it can be argued that the conflict has continued because the Muslim majority Kashmir valley was retained by India when it should have gone to Pakistan, but following ethnic grounds could well entail a further partition of the state into three – the valley, Buddhist Ladakh and multi-ethnic Jammu – which would not only set the stage for intensified conflict and ethnic cleansing because much of Jammu lies between Pakistan and the valley, but would also end Kashmir as it currently exists.

Significantly, the British rejected the partition option in Palestine in the same years as they espoused it in India. The two reasons they gave for its rejection in Palestine were unfeasibility and the dangers of a military conflict which would involve an expanded British presence. Detailed proposals for the partition of Palestine had been made by the British between 1936 and 1938, and based again on the two-nation theory, but this time with the added dimensions that the European Jews and the Asian Arabs were set apart racially and culturally. In a sense, some form of ethnic partition had been foreshadowed by the 1922 League of Nations' approval of a British Mandate for Palestine and the Transjordan and its ratification by the 1923 Treaty of Lausanne. Under both, the British simultaneously reaffirmed their commitment to the 1917 Balfour Declaration, made when the British annexed Palestine, that the British government "viewed with favour the establishment of a Jewish national home" in Palestine, and committed themselves to defending the civil and political rights of the "non-Jewish communities".

Ironically, the Mandates idea was initially developed under the influence of President Wilson and was intended to represent a departure from empire: indeed, in so far as the Mandate role was to aid Palestinians to become self-governing, the Mandate was really a form of transitional rule towards full self-determination. The Allies had, in fact, fallen out on interpretation of the Mandate, and an American suggestion that an inter-Allied commission visit Palestine to determine "the state of opinion and the soil to be worked on by any Mandatory" ended as a solely US commission. The King-Crane Commission recommended "serious modification" of the programme for Jewish immigration,[34] but President Wilson's influence was dissipated by the US decision to stay out of the League of Nations. The British had interpreted this definition of the Mandate as essentially formal from the start,[35] and their pursuit of quite separate policies in Palestine and the Transjordan infinitely complicated the issue of self-determination, as Palestinians were divided between the two territories and the Transjordan became a semi-autonomous kingdom in 1927.

The pursuit of the Balfour Declaration in Palestine, meanwhile, meant that between 1920 and 1939, the Jewish population of Palestine shot up from roughly a tenth to nearly a third of its total population. The Jewish Agency, which the British had established to plan and oversee immigration, created enclaves of Jewish existence: land aquired by Jews could only be sold to other Jews; Jews could not employ non-Jews. Gradually, the Agency began to acquire powers of government; they not only defined the rights and duties of Jews but also maintained law and order in the Jewish enclaves.[36] Arab resistance mounted and, by the early 1930s, turned from communal rioting to opposition to British rule. In 1936, following a Palestinian general strike, the British appointed a Royal Commission to look into Palestinian grievances, headed by Lord Peel. The Peel Commission Report recommended a partition under which the Jewish state would comprise the northern quarter of Palestine and a large part of its west coast; Nazareth, Bethlehem and Jerusalem would remain under British Mandate; and the remaining two-thirds of Palestine would comprise an Arab state.

Again, partition was linked to devolution and for the same reasons as in Ireland and India, that without partition self-governing institutions would be dominated by one or the other nationality. But what could be argued in Ireland and India fell apart when applied to Palestine. The relatively recent migration of Jews, which was given a fillip by the 1917 Balfour Declaration, meant a particularly piecemeal demographic dispersion in which partition would entail massive and forced transfers of a large proportion of the Palestinian population. For the Zionists, who believed that the declaration of support for a Jewish homeland promised them Palestine, partition was a bitter pill; and when the Peel Commission Report was published in 1937, the Zionist Congress rejected its recommendations, arguing that because the Jewish population of Palestine was still small, the territories it was offered were inadequate.[37] For the Arabs, the Peel Commission recommendations were a clear betrayal of the League of Nations Covenant. In September 1937, an Arab National Conference pledged their opposition to the Report, and rebellion broke out. The British hastily appointed a special committee to look into "the technical aspects" of partition: the 1938 Palestine Partition Commission recommended two possible partition maps. Under the first, the northern quarter which the Peel Commission offered to a Jewish state would be broken up, with the large Arab enclave of Galilee remaining under British Mandate; under the second, the British would retain rule over most of Palestine, the Jewish state would comprise a narrow strip of the west coast and the Arab state would comprise an area of central Palestine. Neither option was really satisfactory, the report concluded, and it would be better to drop the partition option entirely.[38]

Combined with the eastward spread of the Second World War and its threat to British positions in the Middle East, this led to a rapid British reversal of support for a Jewish state, and in 1939, a White Paper laid out a new policy under which the Mandate would be extended and its goal would be an independent united Palestine. The first steps to implement the policy were land reservation for Arabs and a restriction on Jewish immigration; the latter was especially resented as evidence of Nazi genocide mounted, and Palestinian Jews began in their turn to take to rebellion. By the mid-1940s, the Jewish Agency was no longer co-operating with the British Mandate to oversee law and order in the Jewish enclaves; instead there were overlapping Jewish paramilitary forces, a "static force" of settlers, and a field army of the Jewish Settlement Police. As the full extent of the Holocaust began to be known, pressure to open Palestine's doors mounted, and in November 1945, US President Truman appealed to British Prime Minister Attlee to resettle a hundred thousand Jewish refugees in Palestine. With the end of the Second World War and the replacement of the League of Nations by the United Nations, the British had to redefine their Mandate in Palestine.

In 1946, an Anglo-American Enquiry Committee was set up to assess conditions for replacing the Mandate with a trusteeship while planning for a "permanent solution". The Committee rejected early independence for Palestine, and concluded that partition was unfeasible not only because it would entail forcible population transfers but because it could well result in a tiny Arab state, a Jewish state in two parts and three blocs under continuing British administration, resulting in a situation in which one part (the Jewish homeland) would be self-governing while the other would not. The problem of administration would be further compounded by the indefinite economic and infrastructural disruption which the creation of these new territories would entail. Instead, the Committee suggested a trusteeship whose tasks would be essentially the same as those of the earlier Mandate, a proposal which the British government rejected and the British members of the Committe suggested as an alternative that two autonomous Jewish and Arab provinces be formed. The suggestion had the merit of being opposed by both Jews and Arabs; the Arabs on the grounds that this would entrench partition and the Zionists on the grounds that it would create a unitary state with an Arab majority. The latter now took to underground resistance to the British Mandate and henceforth negotiations took place within a context of continuing violence. In 1947, the British referred the dispute to the United Nations; the committee they set up was divided between a minority proposal for a binational federal state and a majority proposal for partition.[39] The Security Council opted for partition, with a special UN administration for Jerusalem and a continuing economic union for Palestine.

The plan required Britain to undertake a substantial part of its implementation but, with a Ministry of Defence forecast that Britain's troop presence would have to be reinforced in the wars which would follow, Britain announced instead that it would withdraw in May 1948. Communal conflict broke out in Palestine and spread rapidly to a civil war in which both sides sought to establish ethnoterritorial control as widely as possible, while the British stood by. In April 1948, the Jewish Agency announced it would declare a Jewish state when the British withdrew in May; within a month they had wrested control of the key areas of Haifa and Jaffa, expelling Arabs from both. War broke out between Israel and the Arab states, resulting in the displacement of some 750,000 Palestinian Arabs, whom Israel refused to repatriate after the war ended. Jordan, meanwhile, annexed the West Bank. What resulted was a kind of skewed partition creating one new state but not the other. (In this sense, the recent Accords can be interpreted as moves to complete the "unfinished business of partition".) Subsequently, there have been three Arab-Israeli wars (in 1967, the Israelis occupied the West Bank), and the issue of territorial feasibility continues to dog the peace process.

The last-minute British rejection of divide and quit in Palestine was probably based more on their desire to rescue relations in the Middle East than a concern not to repeat the effects it had had in the Indian subcontinent. Nevertheless, the refusal to engage in the population transfers, which had been made an explicit part of the partition proposal, because they would have to be forcible should give the contemporary advocates of partition pause. It is sometimes argued in the Indian context that since partition was agreed before major conflict occurred in the north-west, a peaceful transfer of population could have been organized, like the Greek-Turkish population exchange following the 1919–22 war, but though the latter did not take place in conditions of military conflict, it did entail some degree of diplomatic force. Whether even this could have been achieved had the agreement not come in the wake of the dismantling of the Ottoman empire and a war between Greece and Turkey is questionable. Ironically, both of the populations transferred comprised people to whom expulsion was a consequence of defeat – for the Turks the fall of the Ottoman empire and for the Greeks Turkey's victory in the1919–22 war. It is a moot point, too, whether such a transfer could be engineered on a much larger scale. In the Indian case, it is virtually impossible that anything short of force would have persuaded close on sixteen million people to give up home and livelihood.

In many ways, the case of Cyprus offers the most striking parallels to Bosnia and makes the issue of whether there can be any peaceful transition to partition acute. As a British colony, until the Second World War the access of Cypriots to government institutions was limited to representation in the island's Legislative Council on the same basis of separate electorates (Greek Cypriot and Turkish Cypriot) as in Ireland and India. A shift to self-government was briefly considered in the immediate post-war years, at the same time as the British were withdrawing from India and Palestine. In 1949, the British extended the principle of separate electorates to municipal elections, as they had done in India earlier; the elections stimulated rising Greek nationalist claims for unification with Greece (*enosis*), and devolution was again put on hold. With diminishing influence in the Arab world following the Palestine débâcle, and the developing crisis in Suez, British attention turned to Cyprus' potential as a military base.

In 1955, an armed insurrection by Greek Cypriot nationalists (EOKA), followed by severe anti-Greek riots in Istanbul, led the British to convene the London Conference on the future of Cyprus, at which the two-nation theory was expanded under the rubric of "double self-determination" (and independence was made contingent on partition). In the same year, the "Cyprus is Turkish" party was formed. Until this point, the Turkish government had been wary of involvement in Cyprus, in continuation of the Ataturk doctrine of coming to terms with Turkey's imperial history, but now Turkey began to gradually involve itself in Cypriot affairs, partly through British encouragement and partly in response to the increasing mainland Greek presence on the island. By 1957, the proliferation of right-wing Greek Cypriot paramilitaries had led the British to form an Auxiliary Police Force composed chiefly of Turkish Cypriots; soon after, the first communal riots between Greek and Turkish Cypriots broke out. In the summer of 1958, further communal riots led to the declaration of a state of emergency in Nicosia; ethnic cleansing had already begun in the city's mixed neighbourhoods and in scattered villages. The British now proposed that a "condominium" of Greece, Turkey and Britain govern Cyprus; the Macmillan Plan of 1958, as it came to be known, also suggested a form of municipal cantonization, that Cyprus be divided into Greek and Turkish municipalities. In 1960, two years of negotiations on the Macmillan Plan broke down amidst mounting civil and communal unrest, and following the 1959 and 1960 Zurich and London conferences on Cyprus the British withdrew, leaving in place an independent island under a new Cypriot constitution.

Though the British brokered constitution was intended to avert partition, it was based on a kind of minimum compromise which deployed the principle of ethnic representation at every level, creating separate municipalities and providing for ethnic distribution in the civil service, the police and the army. Though Turks comprised some 18 per cent of the population, they were allocated 30 per cent of the jobs. They were also given a right of veto in legislative decisions on elections and taxation. The recruitment of Turkish Cypriots to the civil services and army was slow, and even three years later the quotas were nowhere near being met. Because the constitution was achieved by engaging the moderates on either side while conciliating ethnic nationalists, it stimulated a protracted internecine as well as communal conflict, and in 1963, the first partition boundaries were drawn through the walled city of Nicosia on a "Green Line" dividing Greeks from Turks. This was followed by a Turkish Cypriot declaration of support for partition and the arrival of UN troops in 1964; at a second London Conference on Cyprus, partition was officially considered for the first time, but at the NATO Foreign Ministers' Conference which followed hard on its heels in May 1964, Turkey suggested a binational federation under which Turkish Cypriots would gain 38 per cent of the island. Both meetings proved inconclusive, and in 1966 mounting Greek and Greek Cypriot pressure for *enosis* was followed by a military coup in Greece in 1967, the renewal of conflict in Cyprus and a Turkish Cypriot proclamation of a "Provisional Cyprus-Turkish Administration" (in 1967), to which the Greek government responded by sending troops in to support the radical Greek Cypriot underground.[40] Turkey asked for intercommunal talks, and under US pressure Greece agreed to withdraw its troops.

The talks were led by the then Under-Secretary of State Cyrus Vance, who was to be the UN envoy in negotiations in former Yugoslavia a quarter of a century later. A window of opportunity opened in Cyprus: Archbishop Makarios again renounced aspirations for *enosis*, and Turkish Cypriot leader Rauf Denktash acknowledged that the level of minority weightage offered in the 1960 constitution was unfair, and indeed that the policy of separate municipalities had proved a financial burden on the Turks. The talks, however, broke down on the issue of local autonomy, and in 1973 Makarios said, "We are prepared to accept, to a certain degree, a form of local Government, but not to such an extent that might lead to cantonization or federation. Such a settlement could at a later stage lead to partition." Talks on partition had been held by the Greek and Turkish governments as early as 1969; reportedly, at the NATO Foreign Ministers' meeting in June 1971, the two governments secretly agreed on the terms of division.[41] Alarmed by Makarios's negotiations, the Greek junta engineered a coup in 1974, replacing Makarios with the extremist Greek Cypriot nationalist, Nikos Sampson. In 1974 and amidst rising violence, Turkey invaded northern Cyprus on the strength of its guarantor status, reinforcing the *de facto* partition of the island which still continues.

The policy of mandatory ethnonational representation embodied in the 1960 constitution was actually an expanded version of the ethnic politics which the British had deployed in Cyprus since 1919 for much the same reasons as in India: a complex adjustment of divide and rule to the doctrine of ethnic self-determination which emerged in the immediate aftermath of the First World War. As in India, the policy engendered a process of political development in which it eventually became the rationale for partition,[42] despite attempts to divert it from this course. In this sense, the *de facto* partition of Cyprus can only be described as a partition by default which the UN maintained buffer zone inadvertently aided by reinforcing the division of the island. The conflict following independence in 1960 was compounded by the fact that Turkey, Greece and Britain were appointed guarantors by the constitution. The formal structure that this gave to a wider engagement in Cypriot conflicts drew both the Greek and Turkish armies in, allowing the later international tolerance of Turkey's invasion in 1974 and the partition it ratified. While the number of deaths can be said to have been restricted since then, the division of Cyprus consists of little more than a prolonged stand-off which is not only dependent on the continuing presence of UN troops but remains in a state of constant readiness to erupt. Nor can conflict be contained in Cyprus. How short the fuse to its spread is, over twenty years since partition, can be seen by the August 1996 events in which a violent demonstration between Cypriots could result in Greece and Turkey threatening war. (The costs of containment, therefore, include permanent watchfulness on the part of NATO and the Atlantic allies.)

As the ensuing chapters on Bosnia indicate, the partition wars in former Yugoslavia followed a similar trajectory. Like Ireland, India, Palestine and Cyprus, discussions of partition preceded the outbreak of ethnic conflict in former Yugoslavia, and played point-counterpoint with the course of war in the region. Tito's death in 1980 was followed by intense power struggles both within the communist party and within the federation, which rapidly developed into ethnic nationalist movements for the dissolution of Yugoslavia. The crisis had been accelerated by the withdrawal of international aid to the federation in the 1980s, and was compounded by Yugoslavia's decline in importance as the meeting ground of East and West – a space which was no longer necessary when Mikhail Gorbachev launched the *glasnost* and *perestroika* campaigns. In the 1990 elections, ethnic nationalists won in republican elections across the federation; though intense negotiations were pursued to decentralize the federation, especially by the multi-ethnic republics of Bosnia-Herzegovina and Macedonia, Serbian president Slobodan Milosevic's intransigence undermined them at every stage. As relations within the federation slid into conflict, Milosevic and Croatian president Franjo Tudjman held a series of secret meetings in early 1991, to discuss the partition of Bosnia-Herzegovina between Serbia and Croatia. The European Union (then the European Community), which had accepted the responsibility of mediating a resolution to the deadlocks within the federation in late 1990, now found itself negotiating while war raged.

In the summer of 1991, Slovenian and Croatian declarations of independence were followed by war: though the Slovenian conflict was little more than a skirmish because Slovenia was at one edge of the federation and relatively homogenous, the large Serb population of Croatia ensured a bitter and prolonged war which was bound to spill over into neighbouring Bosnia, with its proportionally even larger and contiguous Serb population. In fact, a cease-fire in Croatia negotiated by Cyrus Vance in December and January 1992 offered a brief window of opportunity to prevent the war from starting in Bosnia: President Izetbegovic appealed at the time for a preventive deployment of international troops, but was told by the EU that Bosnia would first have to apply for recognition. When the EU did recognize Bosnia, in April 1992, it was just as war broke out. The EU negotiations had been complemented by CSCE negotiations to end the conflict: in fact, first efforts to find a solution

were entrusted to the CSCE rather than the UN, in an initiative to
develop the organization as a forum for European reunification, as well
as the umbrella for NATO's transformation in the post-Cold War period. The CSCE, however, swiftly came to grief over the recognition
debate, having opposed the German push for speedy recognition of
Croatia and Slovenia, and the initiative in former Yugoslavia passed to
the UN.

Though UN troops were stationed in Bosnia at the time, their mandate was in the Serb areas of Croatia, not Bosnia. International energies
were, in any case, focused on wresting an ethnopolitical solution to the
conflict rather than intervening to end it: in other words, following the
do-little rationale of lesser evil theory. In all the negotiations which
ensued, one or another form of ethnic separation dominated the search
for a solution. Before the outbreak of war, the EU had hosted talks in
Lisbon at which a new plan for ethnic cantonization in Bosnia was
floated. Though the plan was immediately rejected by what remained
of Bosnia's government (the Serb members having opted out), Serb and
Croat ethnic nationalists pursued it in both negotiations and on the
ground. By the summer of 1992, a three-way partition of Bosnia had
been fleshed out by Serb and Croat leaders, detailed maps of Republika
Srpska and Herceg-Bosna were agreed, including that Sarajevo and
Mostar would be partitioned, and by late 1992, the Bosnians were fac-
ing a two-pronged attack, by Serbs in the north and east and by Croats
in the west and south. The failed cantonization plan was replaced in
January 1993 with an EU-UN plan to create ten ethnically based provinces under a weak federal government. The plan benefited nobody but
the Croats, who stood to gain larger territories than they either controlled or could claim on the basis of ethnic proportionality. Though
the Croat-Muslim conflict had begun the previous autumn, it became
an all-out war in April 1993, when Croats began to seize territories
allocated them under the plan. Conversely, in early 1993, the Serbs
renewed attacks on the eastern Bosnian enclaves of Srebrenica, Zepa
and Gorazde in an attempt to establish claims to the land which the
plan denied them; and later rejected the plan altogether.

By the summer of 1993, when the territory under Bosnian government control comprised no more than scattered enclaves, the US moved closer to a support for the ethnic partition of Bosnia which it had so far opposed. On 22 May, the US, Russia, Britain, France and Spain put forward a Joint Action Plan for a Union of Three Republics, the sealing of Bosnian borders, and the establishment of six "safe areas".[43] The Joint Action Plan was widely seen as a harbinger of the next stage of talks, towards a three-way partition, and hard bargaining began over territorial allocations which continued well into the autumn and was accompanied by fierce fighting. The US, however, was pursuing a two-track policy: while officially they supported the Joint Action Plan, privately they were trying to limit partition by brokering a Muslim-Croat federation. Though these attempts were initially met by the intensification of the Croat-Muslim war, a carrot and stick approach prevailed on Tudjman, and in March 1994, the Croats and the Bosnians signed an agreement to federate Croat and Bosnian held territories and eventually confederate with Croatia. The agreement was viewed as a tacit acceptance of the two-way partition of Bosnia and was immediately followed by a Serb demand for recognition of an independent state (Republika Srpska) and renewed attacks on the eastern enclaves.[44]

Partly for this reason, the Washington Agreement remained chiefly a cease-fire agreement whose civilian implementation of a Croat-Bosniak Federation was contingent on the terms of an eventual peace; at its heart lay the question, if a two-way partition was acceptable, then why not a three-way? The complicated answer – that the international community could not accept the creation of a tiny land-locked Bosnian state which might not be viable and would act as an ongoing spur to Muslim resentment; and that the Croats might expect a quid pro quo in the Serb areas of Croatia – was not calculated to please the Herzegovinians. In fact, though the ethnic power-sharing elements of the Agreement were not implemented, the scope that these offered for the ethnic consolidation of power was fully exploited. This was because, like the 1960 Cyprus constitution, the Agreement mandated ethnic representation at the municipal and regional levels as well as at the national or federation levels, and extended it to the civil and police services – in the case of Cyprus, to the army as well – thus encouraging sectarian appointments.

Both locally and nationally, the more authoritarian sections of the Muslim Party for Democratic Action (SDA) and the Croatian Democratic Union (HDZ) began to dominate political and administrative bodies.

To this extent, the Agreement's incorporation of provisions for local and regional devolution of executive powers succeeded merely in bringing partition to a more intimate stage, as the introduction of separate electorates at the muncipalities' level had done in India and Cyprus. It also undermined the Washington Agreement's other significant provision, to put Mostar and Sarajevo under international administration (a similar proposal for Jerusalem had been made by the UN partition plan for Palestine), so as to dissolve partition at the local level and initiate a process of integration from below. Because the Agreement on Mostar made all decisions dependent on a council of equal numbers of Croats and Muslims, each represented by their own mayors, the EU administration instead found itself a frequent and rather expensive bystander as the ethnic nationalists who partitioned the city consolidated their hold through the provisions of the Agreement.

In 1995, events in Croatia again pushed the pace of events in Bosnia. In May, a successful lightning Croatian army attack on the UN Protected Area of west Slavonia sent a wave of Croatian Serbs into Bosnia. In July, Bosnian Serb forces attacked the Safe Areas of Srebrenica, Zepa and Gorazde: the first two fell in an agonizing fortnight while international troops stood by. As the peace process sank to its nadir, renewed fighting around the Bosnian Safe Area of Bihac and a Serb attack on the Safe Area of Sarajevo brought NATO air strikes against Serb positions. In August, Croatia moved against the UN protected Croatian Serb territories, and one of the worst exoduses of the war began, of panicked Croatian Serbs into Bosnia. In September, a joint Croat-Muslim offensive recaptured hundreds of kilometers of Bosnian-Serb held land in north-western Bosnia, and the division of Federation and Serb held territories began to resemble the 51:49 ratio which the international community had sought to negotiate. Under intense international pressure, the fighting waned and tentative agreements were reached. Bosnia would comprise two "entities", the Muslim-Croat Federation and the Republika Srpska, each with their own parliaments, armies, police forces and law courts. NATO would send a sixty thousand strong force to police the agreement. The stage appeared to be set for partition, but a partition which would be established under international supervision rather than as a result of the divide and rule war fought with Milosevic and Tudjman's support.

There is a peculiar anomaly here. Unlike Ireland, India, Palestine and Cyprus, the attempted Bosnian partition is not a by-product of the colonial shift from divide and rule to divide and quit. Curiously, not only are the divide and rulers (Presidents Milosevic and Tudjman of Serbia and Croatia, Radovan Karadzic, Ratko Mladic and Mate Boban of Bosnia, and a host of attendant radical nationalists) quite distinct from the divide-and-quitters (over time, the EU, UN, NATO, UNPROFOR, IFOR and SFOR), but they remain in an ambiguous relation to each other. On the one hand, it would be relatively easy to quit and let divide and rule have sway; on the other hand, the established logic of the move to divide and quit requires the relinquishing of ambitions to divide and rule. Indeed, the process by which the international community moved towards divide and quit in Bosnia has been one of increasingly outlawing divide and rule, as the Bosnian War Crimes Tribunal's indictments of Karadzic and Mladic, and the Dayton Agreement's provisions for the rights of refugees to return imply.

The Dayton Agreement, like its precursor, the Washington Agreement, was intended to institute a prolonged cease-fire which could result either in a peace based on partition or a peace based on reintegration. To a large extent, the agreement took partition as a *fait accompli*: as the thinking went, a *de facto* partition had already been largely achieved through the infamous policies of ethnic cleansing; the little pockets of multi-ethnic territory which remained would be dealt with through apparently voluntary population transfers and resettlement. However, as post-Dayton developments indicated, partition was far from a *fait accompli*. The second partition which was put on hold by the Washington Agreement hovered in the wings of the Dayton Agreement.

Moreover, as the map of Republika Srpska showed, even the implied partition was unstable. Like Pakistan on the partition of India, the Serb entity was in two parts, connected only by the narrow Posavina corridor which had been disputed since the war began; additionally, the two parts leaned in opposite directions, Banja Luka towards Zagreb and the eastern strip towards Belgrade. Normalization would again pull Banja Luka economically to Zagreb and diminish its links to the east. This might mean a further division of the Republika Srpska, rather like Pakistan and Bangladesh, in which case the Republika Srpska would be reduced to a strip of eastern Bosnia. Banja Luka had, therefore, to be forced to look eastward. But the isolation of Banja Luka could only be maintained artificially, through keeping it in a state of anarchy and mafia rule which could not be self-sustaining – as in Italy or the US – but had to depend on external bulwarks. In effect, this meant that efforts to consolidate a partition would have to either further partition the Republika Srpska or find some way of reconciling ethnic and political partition with shared economic and infrastructural space. The attendant ills of such an effort are horrifyingly demonstrated by the process of implementation of the Oslo Accords in Israel-Palestine.[45]

The Dayton Agreement tries to find a reconciliation by including the contingency clauses of previous partition agreements, which provided for partition as an interim solution offering a breathing space for rationality to return as fear ebbed. Significantly, partition has rarely been seen as anything other than a temporary solution to a crisis, which can be reversed as the crisis recedes. Historically, however, ethnic partitions have rarely been reversed in the envisaged time frame; far from offering a temporary breathing space, the process of partition has inexorably driven communities further apart. Sinn Fein aquiescence to partition of Ireland was on condition that there would be a subsequent referendum on unification; the referendum did not take place, and now unification is no longer an important issue in the new negotiations on Northern Ireland. The Indian National Congress actually believed that the Muslim League would recoil from partition once it realized that an unfeasible "moth-eaten" Pakistan was all that they could get (to use Jinnah's words); when the Muslim League accepted this as a lesser evil, Nehru hoped that a subsequent vote would reverse the partition, though who was to organize such a vote once India and Pakistan were created was unclear; unsurprisingly, no vote took place. Instead, Pakistan was further divided and Bangladesh was born in an even uglier war than that which took place at the partition of India. The proposed partition of Palestine did not even consider creating feasible entities; indeed, the hope was that sheer unfeasibility would bring the two sides to joint arrangements.

While the Dayton Agreement was being negotiated, both the international community and local politicians expressed the hope that economic rationality, tempered with a solid admixture of reconstruction aid, would either make the partition temporary or overcome the hostile legacies which had made ethnic partition undesirable. As pressure mounted against the acceptance of the 1996 elections as a mandate for partition, more emphasis was put on the reintegration option of the Dayton Agreement: that economic interests and the provisions for a common economic space would erode the partition lines by making them irrelevant. It was argued that the partial partition which the Dayton Agreement partly accepted was only a means of buying time for Bosnia to undergo this process, but historical experience would suggest that the failure to carry out a timely and substantial injection of aid only hardens ethnic divisions. The hope that economic interests would militate against ethnic boundaries which the Dayton Agreement expresses was also voiced in India, Ireland and Palestine, but in each case the aid requirements had not been met and economic rationality had not sufficed of itself. Indeed, partition more often hampered post-war development: attempts to build economic co-operation and encourage cross-cultural exchanges in South Asia were successively impeded by deadlock on the status of Kashmir. Irish nationalists and UN mediators in Palestine both hoped that a geographical and infrastructural thrust towards economic union would gradually dissipate the horrible aftermath of partition; indeed, the UN proposals for partitioning Palestine were explicitly grounded on the hope that economic union would compensate for the stray and disparate territories being proposed. Instead, however, partition's legacies thwarted economic union and kept both Ireland and what was left of Palestine in poverty.

In the run-up to the Dayton Agreement, many talked optimistically of a "mini Marshall Plan" which the West was offering to help build peace, though the experience of fundraising towards this eventuality had so far been dismal. However, few asked whether the Marshall Plan was the appropriate historical example to look to, and indeed the Bosnian experience raises questions about whether there would have been a Marshall Plan at all if Germany had not been the key division of a Europe entering the Cold War. In hindsight, it seems as if the colonial experience would have been a better pointer for Bosnians to interpret Western promises of reconstruction aid. When the question of reconstruction aid came up before the Select Committee on Cyprus, Roy Hattersley, then the Minister of State for the Foreign and Commonwealth Office, was quite clear that most institutions, including the UN and EEC, would not provide the substantial aid that was required until they were convinced that stability had been restored, and this could only occur through "a political settlement" (the British government was prepared to offer aid to the tune of around £750,000).[46] The British government, he said, had learnt from past experience that "imposed solutions . . . from the time of Derby and Disraeli onwards [had] not been a great success". A long-term solution could only "come about if it is acceptable to the people of Cyprus themselves and therefore springs from the discussion held by the representatives of the people of Cyprus". These were Mr Clerides for the Greeks and Mr Denktash for the Turks.[47] Significantly, they are the two representatives in talks today.

If the lessons of these examples for Bosnia are noteworthy, it may be that Bosnia will in fact constitute a turning point in partition theory. Though divide and quit was a motive in the British support for partition in Ireland, Palestine and India, the only partition in which it worked as a means of getting out quickly was in India.[48] From the sequence of events in Bosnia, it seems clear that European and US leaders, and with them the rest of the international community, were prepared to accept the partition of Bosnia if this would curtail Western intervention in the conflict and limit the terms of Western involvement in the region. But as the partition process unfolded, it began to be recognized that divide and quit might actually mean divide and be forced to stay. The September 1996 elections were intended to mark the transition to a peaceful partition but, as the August 1996 pre-election events showed, they accelerated the renewal of low-level conflict and made dramatically evident that partition was still incomplete on the ground. Close to half the population of Bosnia remained refugees: ethnically homogenous territories could only be created if they were refused repatriation to the towns and villages they were driven from, in the same way as Israel refused to repatriate Palestinians. The refugees became the key constituency in the elections which were held under the terms of the Dayton Accord. Ironically, they continue to be used both to further and to challenge ethnoterritorial consolidation, as the Serb manipulation of voter registration and the Bosniak threat of election boycott showed.[49]

Both IFOR and Carl Bildt's Office (risibly named the "Office of the High Representative") made no secret of their concerns that elections were one factor in what they feared would be a rapid slide towards war. Unlike Somalia or Rwanda, Bosnia was a high-profile intervention because the Bosnians are European, not only in "soft" cultural terms, but geographically and strategically. So far, the West had not been able to walk away from this war, and each half-hearted intervention, however delusory, led to an expansion rather than curtailment of involvement. Though the EU withdrew from Mostar in December 1996 and IFOR subsequently gave way to a smaller "stabilization force", SFOR was still larger than UNPROFOR had been, and the international peace-keeping mandate was extended by another year and a half to summer 1998. Whether the extension would allow SFOR to stabilize a partition, which had begun to fall apart even under the gaze of IFOR, becomes critical in the light of the fact that international policy in Bosnia came to divide and quit without having set the terms for divide and rule. This meant that the issue of when to quit would become critical in a way which was not the case in Ireland, India, Palestine or Cyprus. There the actual or potential conflicts arising from partition were set against the greater good of withdrawal by the colonial power. In Bosnia, on the other hand, the fact that foreign powers entered only to divide and quit meant that their withdrawal would be contingent on ensuring that partition brought peace. This left the critical question of what would happen in Bosnia wide open.

2

Divide and Rule

The war in Bosnia began with an episode of the kind which has commonly prefaced the outbreak of communal violence in India. On 1 March 1992, as a Serbian Orthodox wedding procession wound its way through the old Muslim section of Sarajevo known as Bascarsija, the wedding guests brandished Serb flags. This was interpreted by the Muslims present as an act of deliberate provocation at a time when the republic had just held a referendum on independence, in which the majority of Bosnian Croats and Muslims had voted for independence while the majority of Bosnian Serbs had boycotted it. Unidentified gunmen opened fire on the procession killing the groom's father-in-law and wounding an Orthodox priest. The Bosnian Serb leader Momcilo Krajisnik, then Speaker of the Bosnian Parliament, declared the shots "a great injustice aimed at the Serb people", and overnight, barricades went up all over Sarajevo.[1] Barricades had gone up only a few days earlier, after the referendum, but had been dismantled by the police. This time joint patrols of the Bosnian police and the JNA persuaded Sarajevans to dismantle the barricades.

Less than a month later fighting began in the Bosanska Krajina, in a border town called Bosanski Brod which had been previously used by the JNA (Yugoslav National Army) to launch attacks on the Croatian border town of Slavonski Brod (which housed a JNA barracks). Known as the Krajina, the Bosnian-Croatian border divided a large swathe of Serb-populated territory which was settled as the Austro-Hungarian barrier to the Ottoman empire beween 1578 and 1881. In the early communal hagiology of the war, radical Serbs created an imploding symbol of the Krajina as both the defence of Christendom against the Orient and the defence of Western democracy against the Nazis. How that symbol imploded is one of the strands of the partition process in Bosnia. Significantly, Slavonski and Bosanski Brod lie on the north-central border, an area which is a junction point of Serbia, Bosnia and Croatia, and adjoin the Posavina corridor which is the key connection between western and eastern Serb held territories.

From the border, conflict spread to Bijeljina and Zvornik, towns which formed crucial links between the majority Serb communes in the north-west (whose population was 63 per cent Serb, 15 per cent Muslim and 9.5 per cent Croat according to the 1981 census)[2] and the west bank of the river Drina, which continued down to eastern Bosnia and the bor-der with Serbia. The effort to establish contiguous Serb-held territories was, therefore, a primary aim in all that followed. On 1 April, one of Serbia's most infamous paramilitary groups, Arkan's Tigers, led by a former sweetshop owner who was also said to have been a hitman em-ployed by the Ministry of the Interior[3], moved into Bijeljina. They had been in Eastern Slavonia the previous year, where they had pioneered "ethnic cleansing", the term which was first used in May to describe the pattern of mass murder and forced expulsion which grew to character-ize the war in Bosnia.

The strategy of Arkan's Tigers, which was adopted by other Serb paramilitaries, was to surround a village or small town,[4] enter it, block off the entrances and exits, go from house to house ordering people onto the main street, separate the men from the women and children, and allow the latter to leave the village after robbing them. The houses would then be plundered and destroyed, generally by fire. Some of the men would be murdered, others put to forced labour or herded into makeshift prison camps. The paramilitaries would come equipped with a list of prominent local Muslim community leaders: they would get one of their prisoners to point them out and they would be the first to be killed.[5] Eyewitness accounts of communal wars in India tell a similar tale of organized terror with armed bands going from house to house

and village to village, often armed with electoral registers and generally
with a local informant in tow.[6] Those armed groups, however, were
more often an *ad hoc* lumpen conglomeration, unlike Arkan's Tigers
who made an easier transition from small-time mafia to paramilitary
and who have remained a force throughout the war and into the post-
war peace.

Though the war in Croatia had demonstrated JNA complicity with
Serb paramilitaries, and Bosnia itself had suffered the destruction of a
mosque in Trebinje during the shelling of Dubrovnik by JNA reservists
from Montenegro in November 1991, President Izetbegovic appeared
to believe that the JNA would behave differently in Bosnia and asked
them to defend Bijeljina against Arkan's Tigers.[7] At this stage, the chief
threat appeared to be from Croatia; already by early February, the
Bosnian region of western Herzegovina was being mobilized along ethnic lines. The spillover of the war in the Croatian Krajina, initially
through a series of small clashes between Serb and Croat refugees and
local militias, had rapidly caused an ethnic build-up and barricades had
gone up in Mostar; a Tudjman supported coup in the Bosnian HDZ,
which replaced the more moderate Stepan Kljuic with the militant nationalist Mate Boban, both exacerbated ethnic tensions and might have
inclined Izetbegovic to believe that the JNA, in its own interests, would
defend the borders of Bosnia-Herzegovina.[8] Perhaps he was also influ-
enced by the fact that the local JNA commander had supported Bosnian
territorial integrity and had helped curb the outbreak of violence in
Sarajevo on 1 March. The JNA moved into Bijeljina on 3 April, but the
violence continued unabated, and on 4 April Ejup Ganic, the Defence
Minister, and the Croat members of the coalition government pressu-
rized President Izetbegovic into calling for a mobilization of the territorial
defence. The Serb nationalist members of the Presidency, Nikola Koljevic
and Biljana Plavsic, resigned in protest at the mobilization and on 5
April, Serb paramilitaries laid siege to the Sarajevo Police Academy.

Though most accounts of the wars in former Yugoslavia take either
the primordialist position, that religious enmity runs so deep in the
Balkans that little will change it,[9] or that communalism was chiefly a
rhetorical device (and, therefore, did not seriously affect the course of

the war),[10] historical accounts of the Bosnian war indicate that communal categories gained in potency – especially via the Serbs and Croats – as Yugoslavia hurtled from economic to political disintegration.[11] The rise of the nationalists was also a crisis of communist government, and its effect was to accelerate the fragmentation of most institutions of governance, from the civil service to the army and the police. Paramilitaries like Arkan's Tigers had already begun to undermine police and army functions in Serbia and Croatia (starting with Kosova and Knin) in the late 1980s, and had begun to move into Bosnia in the early 1990s. Contemporary accounts indicate the Bosnian government was in complete disarray when the war began.

On the same day as paramilitaries laid siege to the Police Academy, a small demonstration appealing against ethnic conflict, which started out in the west of the city, became a procession of thousands streaming across the Vrbanja bridge into the majority Serb inhabited area of Grbavica to show that the city "belonged to all the people". As the crowd moved uphill towards the Police Academy *en route* to Grbavica, Serb paramilitaries opened fire and a young woman was shot. The crowd turned back to the Parliament building, where a hastily formed National Salvation Committee began intensive discussions with the People's Assembly on the demand for fresh elections. On 6 April, the day the EC recognized Bosnia, discussions were still going on about whether or not to hold fresh elections when Serb snipers opened fire on the Parliament building from the Holiday Inn.

The call for fresh elections was especially significant. The first free elections in Bosnia, on 9 November 1990, had brought in a coalition government formed by three ethnic and communally based parties, the Muslim Party of Democratic Action (SDA), the Serb Democratic Party (SDS) and the Croatian Democratic Union (HDZ), who between them won 202 of the 240 seat in the two houses of parliament.[12] All three had been founded in the summer: the SDA in May, as a "political alliance of Yugoslav citizens belonging to Muslim cultural and historical traditions",[13] and the SDS and HDZ in July 1990. Both of the latter were Bosnian branches of parties formed in Croatia, and as such they underline the way in which diaspora nationalism can influence native ethnonational consolidation, especially when the diasporas are contiguous. The SDS was founded by Croatian Serbs in the Krajina region and the Bosnian Croat HDZ was a branch of the ruling party of nationalist Croats. SDA leader Alija Izetbegovic was guest of honour at the SDS founding congress and, at a memorial meeting for Second World War victims, Izetbegovic and the radical Bosnian Serb leader, Radovan Karadzic, had pledged that "blood must never flow down the Drina river ever again".[14]

The SDS branch was especially active in the eighteen Serb majority communes adjacent or close to the twelve Serb majority communes in the Croatian Krajina, and the founding of a Bosnian branch of the HDZ in western Herzegovina can be seen as at least partly a counter to the SDS. Though the three parties formed a joint front against the communists, they were already divided over power sharing: the SDS and the HDZ wanted ethnonational parity, while the SDA preferred the majoritarian democratic system of one man one vote.[15] The election law which was formulated took an intermediate position between the two: it accepted an ethnic principle but made it proportional. The bicameral Assembly's election results were: "to reflect ethnically, within fifteen percentage points, the population as a whole". The candidates' ethnic identity was listed on ballot papers alongside their party affiliations.[16]

The 1990 election results have been widely seen as a vote for ethnic nationalism and as evidence that the Muslims, Croats and Serbs put communal or ethnic identities above secular or pluralistic ones, but the results were more mixed than this. In parallel elections, Serbia and Croatia had voted overwhelmingly for the ethnonationalist leaders Slobodan Milosevic of Serbia and Franjo Tudjman of Croatia. In comparison in Bosnia,[17] though the extremist Radovan Karadzic had been voted in chiefly by the Serbs, nationalist Croats had voted for the relatively moderate Stepan Kljuic, and the Bosnian Muslims were divided between ethnic and secular identity. The north-western Bosnian Muslim leader Fikret Abdic, who had once headed the Yugoslav agro-industrial company *Agrocomerc*[18] and who was known as a pragmatic Yugoslavist, got more votes than anyone else (beating Alija

Izetbegovic by over 150,000 votes). Though this entitled Abdic to become president he traded the presidency to get an ally, Alija Delimustafic, made Interior Minister and Izetbegovic became president. According to Delimustafic ethnic patronage now became common and the administration began to be "Lebanized" with the police, in particular, being segmented along ethnic and communal lines.[19] Internal dissension began to snowball to political disintegration: In February 1991, the SDA and the HDZ proposed that parliament declare that republican laws held precedence over federal laws and, in April, the SDS riposted with a proposal to divide Bosnia into ethnoeconomic regions, with each "nation" administering its economic and political interests, and declaring a "Serb Community of Krajina" in western Bosnia.[20]

The proposal followed earlier meetings between Presidents Milosevic and Tudjman in January (which continued through March), at which they discussed dividing Bosnia between Serbia and Croatia. In its turn, the discussion was prompted partly by negotiations over the possible secession of Slovenia and Croatia, and by the search for a quid pro quo for the displacement of population entailed in establishing an ethnic state in Croatia, but it was also spurred on by the conflicts between Serbs and Croats in the Croatian Krajina, which had begun during the late eighties and were spiralling into war.[21] The process of ethnic build up in Croatia was an early warning of what could happen in an even graver way in Bosnia. As the HDZ rose in prominence during the late 1980s, the majority Serb areas of the Krajina prepared to secede from Croatia, with political support and arms supplied by Serbian president Milosevic. In June 1990, the newly elected HDZ government proposed amending the Croatian constitution to assert the sovereignty of the Croatian nation (implying also a rejection of the two constituent nations formula of Yugoslav Croatia); in July, the SDS rejected the proposal and said they would call for political autonomy if Croatia seceded from Yugoslavia and, in August, the SDS held a referendum in which Croat residents of the Krajina were not allowed to vote. The referendum ratified a "Declaration on the Sovereignty and Autonomy of the Serb People".[22] Tensions continued to mount and, when the Croatian legislature called for secession from Yugoslavia in February 1991, clashes between the

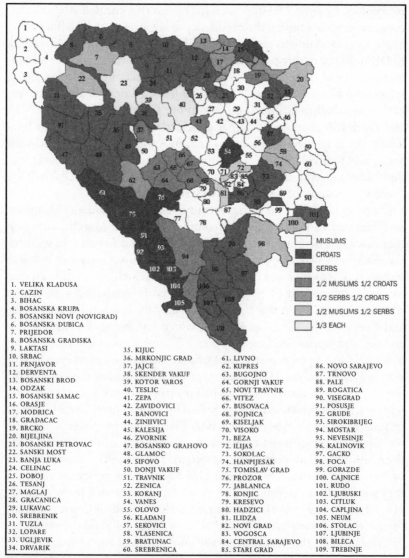

MUSLIMS
CROATS
SERBS
1/2 MUSLIMS 1/2 CROATS
1/2 SERBS 1/2 CROATS
1/2 MUSLIMS 1/2 SERBS
1/3 EACH

1. VELIKA KLADUSA
2. CAZIN
3. BIHAC
4. BOSANSKA KRUPA
5. BOSANSKI NOVI (NOVIGRAD)
6. BOSANSKA DUBICA
7. PRIJEDOR
8. BOSANSKA GRADISKA
9. LAKTASI
10. SRBAC
11. PRNJAVOR
12. DERVENTA
13. BOSANSKI BROD
14. ODZAK
15. BOSANSKI SAMAC
16. ORASJE
17. MODRICA
18. GRADACAC
19. BRCKO
20. BIJELJINA
21. BOSANSKI PETROVAC
22. SANSKI MOST
23. BANJA LUKA
24. CELINAC
25. DOBOJ
26. TESANJ
27. MAGLAJ
28. GRACANICA
29. LUKAVAC
30. SREBRENIK
31. TUZLA
32. LOPARE
33. UGLJEVIK
34. DRVARIK

35. KIJUC
36. MRKONJIC GRAD
37. JAJCE
38. SKENDER VAKUF
39. KOTOR VAROS
40. TESLIC
41. ZEPA
42. ZAVIDOVICI
43. BANOVICI
44. ZINIIVICI
45. KALESIJA
46. ZVORNIK
47. BOSANSKO GRAHOVO
48. GLAMOC
49. SIFOVO
50. DONJI VAKUF
51. TRAVNIK
52. ZENICA
53. KOKANJ
54. VANES
55. OLOVO
56. KLADANJ
57. SEKOVICI
58. VLASENICA
59. BRATUNAC
60. SREBRENICA

61. LIVNO
62. KUPRES
63. BUGOJNO
64. GORNJI VAKUF
65. NOVI TRAVNIK
66. VITEZ
67. BUSOVACA
68. FOJNICA
69. KISELJAK
70. VISOKO
71. BEZA
72. ILIJAS
73. SOKOLAC
74. HANPIJESAK
75. TOMISLAV GRAD
76. PROZOR
77. JABLANICA
78. KONJIC
79. KRESEVO
80. HADZICI
81. ILIDZA
82. NOVI GRAD
83. VOGOSCA
84. CENTRAL SARAJEVO
85. STARI GRAD

86. NOVO SARAJEVO
87. TRNOVO
88. PALE
89. ROGATICA
90. VISEGRAD
91. POSUSJE
92. GRUDE
93. SIROKIBRIJEG
94. MOSTAR
95. NEVESINJE
96. KALINOVIK
97. GACKO
98. FOCA
99. GORAZDE
100. CAJNICE
101. RUDO
102. LJUBUSKI
103. CITLUK
104. CAPLJINA
105. NEUM
106. STOLAC
107. LJUBINJE
108. BILECA
109. TREBINJE

Fig. 2.1 *Bosnia-Herzegovina – ethnic distribution in 1991*
Source: Organization for Security and Co-operation in Europe (OSCE).

armed police of Croatia's Ministry of Internal Affairs (MUP) and Serbian police reservists broke out, which JNA troops quickly joined in support of the Serb reservists. In April 1991, the five republican presidents agreed that the negotiations over Yugoslavia's structure were fruitless, but a proposal to hold republic-wide referendums on independence was stymied by Milosevic's argument that every major ethnic group in each republic should hold a separate referendum, which Izetbegovic opposed on the grounds that it "could cause an explosion that could blow Bosnia-Herzegovina to smithereens and that in the future people would be shooting at each other from windows . . . the people of Bosnia-Herzegovina are mixed up like corn and flour."[23]

War was precipitated soon after by the Slovene and Croatian declarations of independence at the end of June. The Slovene war ended ten days after it had begun, principally because Slovenia was at one edge of Yugoslavia and its population was ethnically homogenous. In contrast, the war in Croatia was intense not only because of the large Serb population but also because they were concentrated in areas adjoining the multi-ethnic republic of Bosnia – with an even larger number of Serbs – and Serbia proper. In May 1991, when Croatia held a referendum on independence, the Croatian Serb SDS held a separate referendum and declared themselves an autonomous region of the Yugoslav federation. Alarmed by the threat of war in Croatia, and what such a war might spell for Bosnia, President Izetbegovic toured Western Europe and the US to ask for the preventive deployment of UN peacekeepers, but was turned down.[24]

Within three weeks of the outbreak of war the Dutch, who were then holding the European Community (EC) presidency, suggested that the option of negotiated internal border changes be explored because the Serb political leadership and the JNA "would not tolerate" an independent Croatia with an 11 per cent Serb population. EC support for changing internal borders, they added, could be justified on the grounds that the provisions of the Helsinki Act included the right to self-determination of national minorities within republics as well as of the republics themselves. At the same time, it was clear that:

this option would entail daunting problems. In the first place it is impossible to draw Yugoslavia's internal borders in such a way that no national minorities would remain. Many minorities reside in relatively small pockets or even in isolated villages. On the other hand it cannot be denied that, if the aim is to reduce the number of national minorities in every republic, better borders than the present ones could be devised.[25]

The Dutch proposal was rejected by the other eleven EC member states not only because of the problems which the Dutch had anticipated, but also because "it was out of date to draw state borders along ethnic lines".[26] Two months earlier, in May 1991 – in a last-ditch effort to stave off the Slovene and Croat declarations of independence – the EC had pledged its support to a unified Yugoslavia and offered it the carrot of a $4.5 billion aid package.[27] Nevertheless, the conflict developed along the lines sketched by the Dutch. Though President Izetbegovic had manifested his commitment to rescuing Yugoslavia from disintegration by a series of confederalist proposals, it began to be rumoured that he was prepared to restructure Bosnia on ethnic lines. Less than ten days after he and Macedonian President Gligorov had suggested a "Community of Yugoslav Republics",[28] it was reported that at a mini-summit in Split on 12 June 1991, he had discussed plans to either divide Bosnia into ethnic cantons or restructure it as a union of three constituent nations with Presidents Milosevic of Serbia and Tudjman of Croatia.

President Tudjman later admitted he had suggested the latter plan but Izetbegovic had categorically rejected it.[29] President Izetbegovic himself appears to have been deeply divided between his desire for a Muslim nation and his adherence to a united Bosnia within some form of Yugoslavia. In July 1991, on a visit to Turkey, Izetbegovic asked if Bosnia could join the Organization of Islamic Countries, fuelling SDS fears that he wanted Bosnia "to become an Islamic republic".[30] In the same month, the SDA split and a small number of deputies, led by Adil Zulfikarpasic, a Swiss businessman who had returned to Yugoslavia for multi-party elections and had financed the SDA at its founding, and Muhamed Filipovic formed the Muslim Bosniak Organization (MBO), which appears to have inclined towards a pro-Serb strategy. Between July and August, the MBO held a series of meetings with President Milosevic of Serbia and SDS leader Radovan Karadzic, at which they negotiated a Muslim-Serb accord to preserve Bosnia's territorial integrity within Yugoslavia. Known as the Belgrade Initiative, the agreement was touted in the Serbian media, but was apparently rejected by President Izetbegovic as favouring the Serbs not only in Bosnia but in Croatia, which was already at war.[31]

Despite this rejection, the Abdic-Zulfikarpasic-Delimustafic-Filipovic policy of pragmatic appeasement appears to have prevailed in the autumn of 1991. In September, President Tudjman put out feelers via the Croats in the presidency to see if the Bosnian government would bring the Bosnian territorial defence into the Croatian-Yugoslav war to open a second front against the Serbs, but Interior Minister Delimustafic had agreed to let the JNA use northern and western Bosnia as resource bases for attacks on the Croatian national guard.[32] The policy seems to have been ineffective from the start. The Bosnian Serbs began declaring Serb "autonomous regions", first in the western and south-eastern Serb majority areas and then in a narrowing spiral of smaller and smaller pockets such as the Romanija mountainous region east of Sarajevo. In September, the SDA accused the SDS of violating the governing coalition agreement. Matters came to a head in the 14–15 October parliamentary session, in which the successful secession of Slovenia and the secession war in Croatia led to a debate on the eventual secession of Bosnia if Yugoslavia disintegrated: SDA and HDZ deputies proposed a memorandum on the sovereignty and neutrality of Bosnia, the SDS deputies walked out, and the remaining deputies adopted the memorandum. The memorandum was again an attempt to find an intermediate position between being part of a Serb dominated Yugoslavia and being torn apart by moving too quickly to independence, but the SDS was in no mind to appreciate the attempt. On 9–10 November, the SDS retaliated with a referendum in which only Bosnian Serbs could vote, and they voted to remain with Yugoslavia.[33]

HDZ support for the sovereignty and neutrality of Bosnia appears to have been so much lip service, for in the same month a "Croatian Community of Herceg-Bosna" was declared in the thirty Croat majority communes of western Herzegovina and central Bosnia, and a "Croatian Community of the Bosnian Sava valley" was declared in the eight Croat majority communes of northern Bosnia. HDZ leaders explained that this was primarily a protective measure against SDS pressure for Bosnia to remain in Yugoslavia: these communes would only recognize a government committed to independence,[34] but in December, the SDS leader Nikola Koljevic and the HDZ leader Franjo Boras began a series of talks about an ethnoterritorial division of Bosnia. The aim of the talks, according to Boras, was to prevent a war by mutually agreeing to a division, and in late November, the two visited President Tudjman to lobby his support for the idea. According to Stipe Mesic: "The talk was about creating ethnically clean areas. In other words, the problem of Muslims had to be solved, since it was obvious that Boras and Koljevic had already agreed on the borders among themselves."[35]

International mediation played point-counterpoint to this process. In September 1991, the EC formally accepted responsibility for mediating the conflict and set up a Peace Conference for former Yugoslavia. Its chair, Lord Carrington, had served during the 1938 discussions of partition of Palestine and had been part of a mission to South Africa during discussions of a possible partition of that country; as British Foreign Secretary, he had subsequently steered Zimbabwe to independence and democracy in 1980. In the early months of the Peace Conference, Lord Carrington's efforts were to avert partition wars by combining decentralization with the protection of minority rights, but he soon moved to combining decentralization with ethnic power sharing (building on the trend of the 1990 election), an approach previously adopted by the British in India in the years before partition, and tried again in Cyprus in the constitution of independence, in both cases with the dismal consequences described in Chapter Three. In the case of Bosnia, the approach was further muddied by its tentative and staggered application, first to the whole Yugoslav federation and then in isolation to the republic of Bosnia-Herzegovina. Indeed, the effort to combine ethnic politics with decentralization was made in Bosnia just as it began to be given up in Yugoslavia; while in May–June 1991, the

EC and the US had affirmed their support for a unified, perhaps confederal, Yugoslavia, after the outbreak of war attention turned increasingly to the issue of recognition of its republics as independent states.

Thus EC negotiations for a Bosnian confederation of ethnic nations took place at the same time as the EC gave up attempts to prevent the Yugoslav federation from dissolving, and implied that the EC might do as little to prevent Bosnian disintegration as it had done to prevent that of Yugoslavia. In November 1991, the EC asked a five-member judicial commission, headed by Judge Robert Badinter of France, to draw up the conditions which each republic would have to satisfy for recognition as an independent state, chiefly on human rights and minority rights protection. In the same month the EC, meeting in the Hague, secured an agreement to cease fire in Croatia. The agreement was an impetus to the push for independence; both Austrian and German leaders, then the most open supporters of Slovenian and Croatian independence, argued that European recognition of the two republics as sovereign states could prevent the further outbreak of war. In fact, the agreement did not bring about an immediate cease-fire; instead, conflict intensified as Serb and Croat leaders jockeyed to improve their bargaining power through territorial control.

While the Badinter Commission was still at work, Germany announced at the EC Foreign Ministers' meeting on 16 December that it would unilaterally recognize Slovenia and Croatia on Christmas day.[36] In the nine-hour debate which followed, Lord Carrington argued that:

> early recognition would torpedo the (peace) conference. And that if they recognized Croatia and Slovenia, then they would have to ask all the others whether they wanted their independence. And that if they asked the Bosnians whether they wanted their independence, they inevitably would have to say yes, and that this would mean a civil war (in Bosnia).[37]

The same points were made by Cyrus Vance, the UN negotiator, and President Izetbegovic had already cautioned against early recognition,[38] as had a series of Conference on Security and Co-operation (CSCE) meetings throughout 1991. UN Secretary-General Perez de Cuellar, French and US Presidents François Mitterand and George Bush, and British Prime Minister, John Major had already written to German Chancellor Helmut Kohl stressing the probability of war in Bosnia if Germany went ahead with recognition.[39] The EC debate was resolved only when Germany reminded Britain that it had acceded to Britain's demand that the social chapter of the Maastricht Treaty be dropped.[40] In a compromise formula, the EC announced that applications for recognition would be decided on 15 January 1992, and meanwhile, the Badinter Commission would assess the applications. Germany then decided to recognize Slovenia and Croatia anyway on 18 December 1991.[41] On 3 January 1992, the November cease-fire agreement was expanded into a comprehensive truce by Cyrus Vance. The truce was to be monitored by the UN not the EC, and it comprised three major elements: a separation of the forces and deployment of UN peace-keeping troops; a time bound demilitarization of the warring region (now divided into four sectors and termed UN Protected Areas); and a gradual normalization pending negotiations over the area's political status. By this time, thousands had died, some 700,000 people had become refugees, and Croatia had suffered enormous physical damage.

Meanwhile, the Bosnian government prepared for independence. In December President Izetbegovic applied to the EC for recognition but in January, he was told that the "expression of the (people's) will" for an independent state was not "fully founded". Recognition might still be possible, the Badinter Commission advised, if Bosnia held a referendum under international supervision.[42] At the same time, though the Badinter Commission had said that Croatia did not meet the human rights' standards for recognition, the EC decided to recognize Slovenia and Croatia. The decision was so controversial that it was openly criticized by the wider European organization of which EC states were members, the CSCE, on the grounds that it:

> was destabilising to those it left behind. This was apparent in press coverage of Yugoslavia on the very day that Croatia and Slovenia were recognized –

15 January 1992 – which indicated that "secret" talks were taking place between Serbia and Croatia, along with ethnic Serb leaders from Bosnia-Herzegovina, to divide Bosnia-Herzegovina between them as a way of resolving their own differences.[43]

The SDS was quick to to strike: in the same month, while continuing to remain in the Bosnian government, the SDS declared a Serbian republic of Bosnia-Herzegovina, proclaiming it part of the Yugoslav federation. On 25 January, the SDA and HDZ announced that the referendum on independence which was required by the EC for recognition would be held at the end of February, and the SDS called for a Serb boycott; Serbs were warned that those who voted would be considered traitors, and in several Serb majority areas, local SDS officials prohibited the setting up of polling stations and refused to release voter lists to the Election Committee until Serb names had been excised. In Banja Luka, "more radical than thou" Serbs formed their own assembly and proposed that the Bosanska Krajina join with the Kninska Krajina to form an autonomous territory of the Yugoslav federation.[44]

On 21 February, a week before the referendum, the EC sponsored Lisbon Conference hosted talks led by Lord Carrington and Ambassador Cutileiro on Bosnia-Herzegovina at which the major topic was the possible cantonization of the republic into three ethnoterritories. Cantonization had become something of a buzz word following the Milosevic-Tudjman talks of early 1991: in October, the moderate Croat nationalist Kljuic had repeated Tudjman's proposal for ethnic cantonization, and in January 1992, the militant Serb nationalist Karadzic was talking about Bosnia as a "Balkan Switzerland".[45] The Serb, Muslim and Croat delegations to the Lisbon Conference came equipped with copies of the Swiss constitution, as had Greek and Turkish Cypriots, Sinhalas and Sri Lankan Tamils, and Indians and Kashmiris before them.

Why the Swiss constitution became the model for ethnonationalists is a question which is dealt with later, but one response to cantonization proposals is germane here. When a Swiss constitutional model was proposed by Tamil Federalists in Sri Lanka in 1956 during a constitutional conflict over whether the Sri Lankan state would be unitary or federalized along ethnic lines, it was an independent candidate from a region with a large Tamil population who pointed out that such a model could not work in the demographically dispersed conditions of Sri Lanka. "Let the Federals produce a map of Switzerland. Does it make as ridiculous a map as the one of Ceylon produced by them? Does not even commonsense suggest to them that there should be geographical continuity among the cantons of the various states?"[46]

The map which was produced by the Lisbon discussions would have drawn a like howl from our 1956 interlocutor. None of the three ethnic groups had contiguous territories, but the Muslim cantons were the most scattered.[47] It seems Radovan Karadzic also proposed partitioning Sarajevo – on a "green line" as had been deployed in the partition of Cyprus' capital, Nicosia – but this was not accepted.[48] President Izetbegovic agreed in Lisbon to the formation of ethnically based territorial units in Bosnia – not yet partition but a step in its direction – but when details of the Lisbon agreement, including the map, were leaked in Sarajevo, there was such an immediate outcry that he withdrew from the agreement. While Izetbegovic announced his withdrawal in Sarajevo, Radovan Karadzic and Josip Manolic (a Tudjman aide representing the Bosnian Croats) held a secret meeting in Graz at which Karadzic told Manolic that any agreement would have to include Serb control of the northern corridor. Apparently, this was the first time that Bosnian Serb and Croat leaders had pored over the map together. There were extensive discussions on population transfers.

In the event, populations were transferred by force rather than agreement. When the EC recognized Bosnia on 6 April, following an overwhelming vote in favour of independence,[49] Arkan's offensive to create contiguous Serb territories gained momentum. On 8 April, Serb paramilitaries and JNA forces massed outside Zvornik began shelling the town from inside Serbia, and on 9 April, Arkan issued an ultimatum to the majority Muslim population of Zvornik (60 per cent) to surrender. The next day Zvornik fell. Arkan's Tigers moved on to Srebrenica, where the town's Muslim leaders were urgently negotiating with local Serbs for an agreement which would protect the town, but the Tigers' arrival disrupted the negotiations. The Tigers encountered their first resistance in Srebrenica when a Muslim militia, led by a policeman named Naser Oric who had once been in Milosevic's bodyguard, succeeded in routing them at the end of April.

At the same time as the Tigers moved towards Srebrenica, Serb forces began shelling Sarajevo. The shells fell as Easter was celebrated by the representatives of four faiths in a bid to resist the growing communalization of Bosnia: the Fransciscan monk, Marko Orsolic, the Serbian Orthodox priest, Krstan Bjelajac, the Sarajevo Imam, Ibrahim Seta, and the Jewish community president, Ivan Ceresnjes.[50] While Sarajevo was being shelled, Momcilo Krajisnik slipped into the city to propose to Izetbegovic that the Serbs would stop the war if he would agree to partition Sarajevo into twin cities. This push for a two-level partition, of the cities and the country, was to characterize the war for the next three and a half years. In this context, the partition process in Bosnia can be most closely compared to that in Cyprus, where too the first boundary of partition was drawn in the capital – the "Green Line" in Nicosia which Karadzic had cited as precedent for the division of Sarajevo during the Lisbon talks. Paradoxically, though the partition of Sarajevo remained a major goal throughout the war, this emphasis was to result in the eventual downfall of Serb war aims.

By the beginning of May 1992, Serb forces had begun establishing a northern corridor by consolidating their hold on Brcko and Doboj. "Bureaux for Population Exchange" began to be set up all over northern Bosnia, which functioned for the most part as extortion dens. Muslims and Croats not only had to pay in hard currency to be allowed to leave, but had to sign over properties and assets. Refugees were packed into sealed trains at Doboj and sent to Zagreb. Where the population was highly dispersed, they were driven out one by one. On 2 May, Serb forces turned their attention to Sarajevo. Serb troops moved from the surrounding Vraca and Trebevic mountains into Grbavica, but this first attempt at forcibly partitioning Sarajevo was half-hearted as they lacked the infantry. Nevertheless, they got to the suburbs of Grbavica, Mojmilo and Nedzarici, and cut Dobrinja off from the rest of the city (the suburb suffered a siege within a siege for the best part of the war). These areas now constituted the inner-city front lines and became a *de facto* partition of the city, albeit only of areas at its periphery.

By this point, the recognition of Bosnia-Herzegovina, pushed through on US initiative, meant that the JNA was now a foreign force in Bosnia.[51] As it was, its presence in Bosnia had been hugely swelled by the withdrawal of JNA troops from Croatia. Initial trust in the JNA because of the record of its local commander, General Kukanjac, had been dissipated by the joint attacks made by JNA troops and Arkan's Tigers in the eastern enclaves; now the very weak local territorial defence blockaded the JNA barracks in the Sarajevo suburb of Lukavica, both to prevent it from becoming the seat of attacks on Sarajevo and to ensure that the arms stored there were not handed over to Bosnian Serb forces. The JNA riposted by taking President Izetbegovic hostage at the barracks in return for the safe passage of JNA troops out of Sarajevo under UN escort. As the convoy was about to leave the barracks the then head of UNPROFOR, General Mackenzie, was radioed by the UN that Ejup Ganic, Acting President in Izetbegovic's absence, had ordered that the agreement on safe conduct apply only to the JNA commander General Kukanjac. President Izetbegovic countermanded Ganic's order and the convoy started out, but after the president's vehicle was out of sight the Bosnian militia halted the rear vehicles and began to remove the weapons they carried. Though General Jovan Divjak, the deputy commander of the Bosnian territorial defence (a Serb who chose to remain with the Bosnian government) arrived at this point and ordered that the convoy be allowed to continue, the shaky chain of command paid little heed to his order and the convoy was finally allowed to pass only after Izetbegovic returned and talked to the troops.

An odd story attaches to Ganic's acting as president in Izetbegovic's absence. While Izetbegovic was being held, Fikret Abdic made a sudden appearance in Sarajevo, walking into the television studio which functioned for the moment as the communications link between Ganic in Sarajevo and Izetbegovic in Lukavica, as the government lines were down. Abdic's appearance was interpreted by Ganic and Kljuic as an attempted palace coup: Izetbegovic would disappear and Abdic would be waiting conveniently in the wings. Izetbegovic appears to have concurred in this reading of Abdic's appearance, for when he was told of it he hastily appointed Ganic Acting President. After Kukanjac left, the RSA became the chief Serb force in the region, with Ratko Mladic, who had proved his Serb loyalties in Croatia, as its commander.[52]

On 6 May, a second secret meeting between Serbs and Croats took place at Graz airport, this time between Karadzic and the maverick Croat leader Mate Boban. A former clothing-store manager, Mate Boban had emerged through Tudjman's patronage as the *de facto* leader of the Croats, eclipsing the more moderate HDZ leaders Kljuic and Boras. Karadzic and Boban had detailed discussions on Croat and Serb territories in Bosnia. The SDS had initially planned that the south-western boundary of their greater Serbian state would lie along the Neretva river, partitioning Mostar and bringing east Mostar into Republika Srpska. But Karadzic agreed to Mate Boban's suggestion that instead the main street running through Mostar, Marshal Tito Street, should be the boundary of the Croatian territory of Herceg-Bosna, and also agreed that Herceg-Bosna would comprise the Croat-majority coastal areas, an adjoining Serb majority area, Kupres (which was 51 per cent Serb), and the mixed Muslim-Croat central Bosnian areas. The talks were deadlocked on the very issue which was to remain unresolved in the war, the northern corridor comprised by the Posavina and Brcko regions which linked the Bosnian side of the Krajina with eastern Bosnia, but, in an agreement prefiguring the eventual agreement after four years of war, Karadzic and Boban decided they would accept international arbitration for the region around Kupres and seven towns in the Posavina.[53]

Soon after, the JNA withdrew from the east bank of Mostar, and on 17 June, Croatian forces, comprising units of the Croatian military which had originally entered Bosnia in pursuit of the Croatian-Serb war, the Croatian Defence Council (HVO), the progenitor and military arm of Herceg-Bosna, and the paramilitary arm of the radical nationalist Croatian Party of Rights (HOS),[54] drove the Serbs out of Mostar. How far they had to use force is debatable, given the Karadzic-Boban agreement. The HVO now began to consolidate its hold on territories, with cash and *matériel* support both from its parent HDZ and from other supporters in Croatia. The first small steps towards integration with

Croatia had already begun: the Croatian dinar had replaced the Yugo-slav currency in some parts of Herzegovina by 1991, partly because the Bosnian state had no currency and partly because the choice of cur-rency used marked ethnonational affiliation. On taking over Mostar, Boban dismissed almost all the Muslims in public life and replaced them with HDZ members loyal to his hardline nationalism, mounted road-blocks around the city, and curtailed Muslim movement both into and out of Mostar. In Sarajevo, the flourishing black economy based on the siege of the city was further ethnicized when Croatian hardliners took control of the neighbouring town, Kiseljak (41 per cent Muslim and 52 per cent Croat before the war began), through which humanitarian aid convoys were routed. Within months of the start of the humanitarian effort, Kiseljak had gone from nondescript to prosperous. Under the Karadzic-Boban agreement, Kiseljak was one of the mixed Muslim-Croat towns of central Bosnia which was to go to Herceg-Bosna, and Kiseljak Croats now became allies of the Serbs in perpetuating the siege of Sarajevo.[55]

As war intensified in Bosnia, criticism of the European peace negotia-tions mounted both in Western Europe and the United States. By the summer of 1992 the US, while continuing to hold off from an active role in the negotiations, was arguing that the international community should support the legitimate government of Bosnia-Herzegovina and those representatives of Bosnian Serbs, Croats and Muslims who stood for a multi-ethnic Bosnia, and should ostracize the "terrorist wing" of the SDS.[56] In July and August, Roy Gutman and Ed Vulliamy's electrify-ing reports of SDS operated concentration camps in Bosnia brought public dissatisfaction with the negotiations to new heights; within the US, the disclosure that detailed accounts of ethnic cleansing had been available to Western governments and the UN long before the Gutman and Vulliamy reports appeared raised something of a furore in the Sen-ate. The staff report to the US Senate Foreign Relations Committee on 18 August 1992, which made the disclosure, added that had the US and UN responded to these reports many lives might have been saved. The report, however, also said that by this point ethnic territories had al-ready been created; the implication that its criticisms were *post facto* placed added question marks on the issue of intervention.[57] In fact, however, the report assumed that the chief point of the war was to fulfil the aim of a Greater Serbia; the Croat nationalist aims which the Karadzic-Boban agreement exemplified were not taken into account.

Yet by the autumn of 1992, there were three armies in Bosnia: the RSA (Republika Srpska Army), the HVO (Croatian Defence Committee) and the ABH (Army of Bosnia-Herzegovina). On 25 October, a gangland fight over a gasoline consignment in Prozor sparked war between the Muslims and Croats. Local units of the HVO and the ABH sprang to the defence of their (ethnically bound) mafiosi and there were gun battles in the streets. A resultant breakdown of communications between the HVO and the ABH led both to desert their positions at Jajce which was surrounded by Serb forces but not in any danger until 29 October, when forty thousand panicked Muslims and Croats poured out and the Serbs walked in. Two days earlier, an SDS proposal to create a confederation of "three territorially distinct states based on ethnic or confessional principles" had been rejected by the international mediators, Cyrus Vance and David Owen, on the grounds that:

> Such a plan could achieve homogeneity and coherent boundaries only by a process of enforced population transfer – which has already been condemned by the International Conference, as well as by the (UN) General Assembly . . . Furthermore, a confederation formed of three such states would be inherently unstable, for at least two would surely forge immediate and stronger connections with neighbouring States of the former Yugoslavia than they would with the other two units of Bosnia-Herzegovina.[58]

Sarajevo at this point was like a film splice of *Casablanca, The Third Man* and *The Chess Players*. Small-time arms dealers, spies, paramilitaries, black marketeers and journalists crowded the Holiday Inn; the city's intelligentsia met the RSA siege with infuriating (and calculated to infuriate) insouciance by day and feverish partying by night. In the Presidency, Izetbegovic bore the mien of an eighteenth-century regent who watched helplessly while his people died and his land trickled away. With its own world of soldiers and bureaucrats, the UN was sequestered in a building closer to the airport than the city centre from which it made forays into the maze of Balkan politics – generally in armoured vehicles. (Though UN troops had been stationed in Sarajevo following the Vance plan for the embattled areas in Croatia, their mandate did not cover Bosnia; it was only five months after the war had begun that UN troops were tasked first with keeping the airport open for the humanitarian airlift and then with protecting road convoys of aid.[59] Their limited mandate was a source of considerable scorn which was exacerbated by the sequestered way in which they lived.)

Elsewhere, story piled upon story in a crescendo: the Bosnian army was gaining and the siege of Sarajevo was about to lift; Karadzic would never give up Sarajevo because he wanted to return as conquering hero to the city which disdained him; NATO was about to intervene to save Europe's Bosnia; Europe did not care because Bosnia was Muslim but the Islamic countries would supply it arms; to circumvent this the US was going to weigh in on Bosnia's side; but did the US like Izetbegovic? In an odd foreboding that it was its arts which would save Sarajevo, cultural production multiplied. A series of independent radio stations, newspapers and journals were launched; with gas lamps, the theatres ran to full capacity; posters and wall art appeared on the streets. In the ruins of the Public Library an old violinist played "the Sarajevo suite" every evening; not far away, an engineer opened a soup kitchen for children and fed the leftovers to aging musicians, painters and writers. Sarajevo, they said, and not wryly, was going to be the cultural capital of Europe, the city which had repulsed war simply by its spirit. What everybody believed was that the war would soon be over, and in favour of a multi-ethnic Bosnia.[60]

The war, however, was about to enter a new phase. Thanks to the Karadzic-Boban agreement, by winter 1992, the RSA and HVO had no more territory to fight over but both had unfinished business with the ABH. As the war between the Muslims and Croats intensified and the war between the Muslims and Serbs continued, the Bosnian government itself began to become ethnically divided. Logically, the "war cabinet" began to be dominated by the SDA, and within the presidency relations between even the more moderate HDZ members and the SDA became so strained that Bosnian Prime Minister Akmadzic, a Croat, protested that he, rather than Foreign Minister Silajdic, should address the UN Security Council on 6 and 7 February 1993.[61] As a joint RSA-HVO attack on the ABH intensified, the more moderate Serbs and Croats in the government began to be marginalized from the process of political and military decision making, and additional obstacles to international negotiations reared. The SDA began to be seen as a culprit in this process; privately, international mediators and UNPROFOR commanders responsible for humanitarian aid had long criticized the Bosnian government for being neither grateful enough for aid nor willing enough to compromise for peace,[62] but now the mediators began to actively canvass opposition to the government. According to David Owen, the international mediators had regarded President Izetbegovic as intransigent for some months. In December, meeting Fikret Abdic for the first time, Owen was struck by his criticism of Muslims who "blocked" compromises with Serbs and Croats, and urged him to join the Bosnian Presidency and pull his weight at their meetings.[63]

In early January 1993, Cyrus Vance and David Owen presented a plan (which they had been working on for four months) to create ten ethnically based provinces or cantons under a weak federal government:[64] the plan benefited nobody but the Croats, who stood to gain larger territories than they either controlled or could claim on the basis of ethnic proportionality. The plan itself was based on a note by the then UN representative Martti Ahtisaari, circulated in October, which laid out five constitutional options for a Bosnian settlement for the ICFY to choose from. The options were: a centralized state; a centralized federal state with "significant functions carried out by between four and ten regions"; a loose federal state of three ethnic units, not geographically continuous; a loose confederation of three ethnically determined republics with significant independence, possibly even on security issues; and a Muslim state with the Serb held territories seceding to the FRY (Federal Republic of Yugoslavia) and the Croat held territories seceding to Croatia. According to David Owen, he and Cyrus Vance chose the second option as the negotiating basis of the Vance-Owen Peace Plan, both as the best compromise solution and because it: "promised the most stable form of government, since much of the predicted intercommunal friction could be kept from the central government by giving the provinces competence over the most divisive issues, for example, police, education, health and culture, while depriving them of the right to be a state within a state."[65] The plan was intended to forestall partition by scattering the cantons so that three ethnoterritories could not be formed, but in a war situation its other key elements, the devolution of most civil powers to cantons, including policing, and the acceptance of the ethnic principle – at military, territorial, administrative and political levels – brought the conflict to more intimate levels. David Owen later remarked that he and Vance had been careful not to label any of the provinces Serb, Croat or Muslim, but the fact that the military arrangements envisaged by the plan were that RSA troops would withdraw to Banja Luka, Bijeljina and east Herzegovina, and HVO troops would withdraw to the Posavina (each nationalist party then having its own armed wing) made the ethnic principle clear. Moreover, by 14 January Owen was exploring the possibility of a territorial exchange between the SDS and the HDZ, by which the Bosnian Serbs would gain the Posavina corridor to link their eastern and western territories, and the Croats would gain territory linking Bihac to Livno, thus controlling Bosnian territory all along Croatia's eastern border.

In effect, the proposal conceded the aims of Republika Srpska and Herceg-Bosna for a tripartite partition of Bosnia. When Izetbegovic rejected the proposal, Owen suggested that the Bosnian government be given control over Brcko, but this meant the Croats would have to give up territory above the Sava river for a Serb corridor, which the Croats were only prepared to do if they could control the border between the Croatian and Bosnian Krajina. This, however, meant that the Croatian Krajina SDS would be cut off from supply lines from Serbia through Bosnia: while privately Karadzic and even Milosevic were ready to cede the Serb claims in Croatia which this implied, they could not be seen to be party to it.[66] Owen omits to mention that the "swaps" he was so blithely attempting to arrange would entail the massive displacement of populations (the territory linking Bihac and Livno was 95 per cent Serb, the Posavina was majority Croat) and gave a fillip to the ongoing process of ethnic cleansing. Though the Bosnian government, which had presented a proposal for thirteen multi-ethnic regions which would "dilute Serb majority areas" in December,[67] protested that the plan was a prelude to ethnic partition (because the weakness of the federal government meant the provinces would be effectively self-governing), in March, Izetbegovic accepted it, arguing in Sarajevo that he was doing so because he was confident the Serbs would reject it. Under US pressure, Vance and Owen had adjusted the peace plan so that Brcko would be part of Tuzla province (that is under Bosnian government control), an arrangement to which the SDS could not possibly agree.[68]

By March 1993, when the Bosnian government reluctantly accepted the Vance-Owen plan, the SDS rejected any form of centralized government, arguing that all that was needed was a central co-ordinating body. As far as the Serbs were concerned, the Vance-Owen peace plan demanded large territorial concessions at a time when the only areas remaining as obstacles to Serb territorial ambitions were the eastern enclaves of Srebrenica, Zepa and Gorazde. Under the Vance-Owen plan, all three were in Muslim majority Tuzla province, a jagged area curving around Serb majority Pale province, which was itself in three pieces dotting eastern Bosnia. A Serb acquiescence to the plan would mean effectively giving up Greater Serbia, and early 1993 appears to have seen a two-pronged Serb strategy to acquire east Bosnia through negotiation and force. At the same time as Srebrenica was being attacked, Bosnian Serbs were demanding a territorial exchange in the negotiations which would allow them to link Zvornik and Sekovici.[69]

Srebrenica had remained a thorn in the RSA side since April 1992, when the local Muslim militia had driven Arkan's Tigers out. Commanded by Naser Oric, the militia had conducted periodic raids into Serb territory since. The Serbs held Oric responsible for a massacre near Bratunac in December 1992, and in January 1993, when the militia killed Serb villagers and burnt their villages in a raid on Serb positions to the north, Serb forces retaliated with an onslaught in which thousands of Muslim villagers fled to Srebrenica town, doubling its population in days. Surrounded by Serb forces who blockaded aid convoys, Srebrenica began slowly to starve. In March 1993, in an attempt to draw international attention to the plight of Srebrenica, the Bosnian government announced it would accept no more aid for Sarajevo while Srebrenica starved. On 11 March, the new UNPROFOR chief, General Morillon, went to Srebrenica to negotiate the opening of aid routes. Naser Oric, who had been told by Ejup Ganic to keep General Morillon in Srebrenica until he had provided some guarantees of security, had mobilized Srebrenica's women and children to surround Morillon and hold him hostage. The gallant general, it seems, was quite independently moved by the plight of Srebrenica and he succeeded in persuading the Serbs to allow aid in, though he had to go to Belgrade to do so.

The first convoy to come in was besieged by women and children desperate to leave the town, and the UN High Commission for Refugees (UNHCR) found itself a reluctant assistant to ethnic cleansing.[70] The next day, when General Morillon attempted to return to Srebrenica, he was halted again by women and children, this time Serb, at Zvornik. Two weeks later in April, the Serbs issued an ultimatum that if the Muslim militia did not surrender and the Muslims leave Srebrenica, they would attack the town. Though the UNHCR began to evacuate Srebrenica, the Serbs shelled it on 12 April. Oric's forces were outgunned, and on 14 April the local authorities smuggled a message to UNPROFOR headquarters in Belgrade that the Bosnian defence was about to collapse, and requested the UN to broker a surrender. The request placed the UN in a quandary as Srebrenica was in a Muslim canton under the Vance-Owen plan, and the UN feared pressure for military intervention would mount if the UN was seen to broker the surrender of an area which had been internationally allocated to the Bosnian government. On 16 April, the UN Security Council declared Srebrenica a "safe area" and the surrender was produced as an agreement to disarm as part of the process of rendering Srebrenica safe. The agreement, however, had been made between Ratko Mladic, the commander of the RSA, and Sefer Halilovic, the commander of the ABH; Oric's militia, which had fought its own guerrilla war to defend Srebrenica, felt betrayed by the agreement and a small band of his men remained in the town.[71]

Mladic's acquiescence to the agreement, it seems, had been secured through the intervention of President Milosevic, who was both anxious to avert further sanctions on rump Yugoslavia and convinced that the cantonization plan would provide a peacetime breathing space in which the internationally demonic image of the Serbs could be gradually erased and the Republika Srpska could thereby gain international acceptance. Pragmatically, Milosevic had ascertained from Owen that, under the plan, federal decisions could be made only through consensus and so the SDS could veto any decision going against their plans for a Serbian state.[72] With this in mind, Milosevic persuaded Radovan Karadzic to sign the Vance-Owen Peace Plan on 2 May, but on 6 May the Serb Assembly rejected it.

Though the Vance-Owen plan (see frontispiece maps) did not initiate the Croat-Muslim war, there is little doubt that the Croats saw a sympathetic view taken towards their territorial ambitions in it. By the end of April, there was all-out war between the HVO and the ABH. Meeting David Owen on 21 April, Croatian Defence Minister, Gojko Susak, said that the Croats were beginning to prefer an alliance with Serbs to one with Muslims; on the same day, RSA commander Ratko Mladic told Owen that the Serbs would defend Croats in the Mostar region, the heartland of Herceg-Bosna.[73] Some of the nastiest fighting of a nasty war now began in central Bosnia. In Kiseljak, Croat militiamen entered Ahmici, the only Muslim village in the area, slaughtered dozens of villagers and set it on fire, ostensibly to deter the wave of Muslim refugees from Srebrenica from seeking shelter in Kiseljak. In Travnik, the HVO demanded that the ABH disarm and disband on the grounds that Travnik was in a Croat governed province under the Vance-Owen plan, and in Zenica, which was an ABH stronghold, talks between the Muslim mayor and the local HVO commander broke down when the HVO started shelling from the surrounding hills.

The Bosnian fight back began in central Bosnia with troops composed of refugees. The Third Corps of the ABH formed two new brigades, of men driven from north and east Bosnia, the Seventeenth "Krajiska" Brigade in Travnik and the Seventh Muslim Brigade in Zenica. The Krajiska Brigade was led by Colonel Mehmet Alagic, a refugee from the Kozara mountains in north Bosnia; the Seventh Muslim Brigade was agressively Islamic, arguing that Bosnian adherence to the principles of multi-ethnic tolerance had led to the destruction of Muslims, and it was now time for Bosnian Muslims to defend themselves as Muslims rather than Bosnians. Within Zenica, the Seventh Brigade made periodic attempts to Islamicize daily life, smashing alcohol shops and destroying pigs.[74] Ironically, the Zenica municipality had sought to be declared a "peace zone" in early 1992.[75]

By the summer of 1993, the territory under government control was a smattering of isolated enclaves, none viable without the life support of international aid,[76] and arguments for the establishment of safe areas began to become compelling. On 6 May, the UN passed Resolution 824 (1993) extending the safe areas to Sarajevo, Tuzla, Zepa, Gorazde and Bihac, but on 13 May, the French circulated a 'non-paper' to the US, Britain and Russia in which they suggested that any ideas of reconquering territory around the enclaves or providing them with complete armed protection be given short shrift; instead the safe areas should function as "sanctuaries". With the example of Srebrenica before them, the US voiced concerns that the safe areas could become euphemisms for giant refugee camps; at the same time, the situation on the ground led them to conclude that the Vance-Owen plan was unfeasible; as the Serbs extended their domination over eastern Bosnia it became more and more evident that only defeat could lead them to relinquish these territories.

The US now moved closer to support for the ethnic trifurcation of Bosnia in an initiative involving Russia, France and Britain initially, and, when other members of the European Union protested at the 'Great Powers' reference, Spain. On 22 May, the US, Russia, Britain, France and Spain put forward a Joint Action Plan for a union of three republics, the sealing of Bosnian borders, and the extension of the UN mandate to include the protection of the six safe areas (the UN subsequently extended UNPROFOR's mandate by Resolution 836 of 4 June, and requested 7,600 additional troops). In the aftermath of the Bosnian Serb rejection of the Vance-Owen peace plan, President Milosevic had announced he was sealing the border between Bosnia and Serbia, but he continued to stall the stationing of international monitors on the border, fearing, Owen suspected, that they would hamper his control over aid to the Croatian Serbs. The Joint Action Plan was widely seen as a harbinger of the next stage of talks towards a three-way partition.

Though he complained bitterly at what he saw as the US's volte-face, Owen appears to have had no qualms about swinging rapidly to a pro-partition position himself, for at the end of May, he told the British Foreign Office that he planned to sound out Tudjman, Izetbegovic and Milosevic on the possibility of redrawing the borders between Croatia, Bosnia and Serbia. And in June, the international mediators, by dint of sustained pressure, had re-established a form of the pre-war presidency structure (in a move to counter Izetbegovic's growing inclination to one-man rule). Fikret Abdic was appointed a member of the presidency and was a part of the Geneva talks.[77] Though Owen mentions his December 1992 meeting with Abdic only in passing, the "Abdic factor" appears to have been actively pursued by international negotiators in the interim. Already by spring 1993, rumours of an imminent Abdic led coup in the Bosnian government were rife, to the point that even new refugees to Sarajevo were discussing whether he might not be a more useful (because internationally favoured) leader than Izetbegovic.[78] The seamy side of Owen's Balkan odyssey was beginning to emerge.

Its first sign was that the international community now chose to preside over partition negotiations in which the territorial control exercised by rebel Serb and Croat leaders was acknowledged as giving them parity with Bosnia's official leaders (now almost all Muslim). Meeting Presidents Milosevic and Tudjman between 9 and 11 June, Vance and Owen turned to reviving the Carrington-Cutileiro proposal for a Bosnian confederation of three ethnic cantons.[79] On 11 June, the Serbs presented a map for a Union of Three Republics in Bosnia, giving the Muslims less than 24 per cent of the country's territory, but were told that 30 per cent was a minimum requirement. In Washington, President Clinton announced that the US would accept partition as long as it was freely accepted by the parties themselves. In Geneva, Owen was told by US ambassador Victor Jackovitch that Silajdic and Ganic could live with the new proposals, even the map (with some qualifications).

On 22 June, Owen suggested to the EU Foreign Affairs meeting that the Carrington-Cutileiro plan for a three-part confederation and cantonization should be reconsidered, and on 23 June, Owen and Stoltenberg had a meeting with Presidents Bulatovic (of Montenegro),

Tudjman and Milosevic at which nine constitutional principles for a Union were formulated. Owen then wrote to Izetbegovic about the meeting (why Izetbegovic was not present is not explained). Izetbegovic's response to the proposals was that the public were not ready to face the fact "that partition had taken place on the ground" and he would need to discuss the issue before he could agree to negotiate. Owen interpreted this response as a demand for more territory for the Muslim republic, and on 9 July, he and Stoltenberg persuaded Tudjman and Milosevic to "try and get" 30 per cent of the country's territory for the Muslims. On 12 July, Izetbegovic said he was ready to attend the talks. On 27 July, Karadzic presented a map under which the Serb republic would have 54.3 per cent of Bosnian territory, the Muslim republic (to which the Bosnian government was reduced by implication) would have 28.4 per cent and the Croat republic would have 17.3 per cent.

On 28 July, Boban countered with a map giving the Serb republic 52 per cent of Bosnian territory, the Muslim republic 26.7 per cent and the Croat republic 21.3 per cent.[80] The 30 per cent which Owen believed was the US bottom line, was finally made up by the Croats agreeing to "give" the Muslim republic Stolac. On 30 July, Owen and Stoltenberg announced that a map had been agreed, but this announcement, like the previous announcement on the Vance-Owen plan, proved to be premature. By 20 August, the mediators had carved a rough agreement on the boundaries of the three republics, and it had also been agreed that Sarajevo would be placed under UN and Mostar under EU administration, but Brcko and the eastern enclaves remained sticking points. The Bosnian republic remained fragmented, with Bihac isolated in the northwest and the three eastern enclaves connected only by one road.[81] Nevertheless, the agreement was put to the vote: the Serb assembly voted fifty-five to fourteen in its favour, the Croat assembly was overwhelmingly in its favour (with only one dissenting vote), and the Bosnian parliament (which was the only legitimate body of the three) voted to continue negotiations on the plan.

By early September, the Bosnian government was reduced to such shrifts as asking whether their acceptance of Republika Srpska's right to secede might secure larger territory for the Muslim republic; flush with power, the Serb leadership suggested that if an agreement on the proposed territorial allocations was implemented, then perhaps some territorial adjustments could be discussed two years later. Following this, President Izetbegovic signed a declaration with the Serb leader Momcilo Krajisnik, who had first attempted to negotiate the partition of Sarajevo with him, that the three republics would hold referendums on whether to remain in federation or secede after two years, providing they had agreed on a territorial division. Apparently, the declaration was protested by Foreign Minister Haris Silajdic on the grounds that it would lead to ethnic partition and the creation of a purely Muslim state; and by the Croats on the grounds that the Serb leadership might adduce it as a precedent for a resolution of the Krajina conflict.[82] At the same time, the Bosnian Serb leadership was confronted by a challenge from within: the militias which ran Banja Luka staged an uprising on 10 September, demanding that the seat of Serb government move from Pale to Banja Luka, that an enquiry be made into corruption (this was a veiled attack on Radovan Karadzic, who had recently been accused of making off with goods to the tune of 300 million German marks), that local regions control their own economies (Banja Luka, the most prosperous of the Serb regions, was effectively feeding the Pale government), and that there be new elections to the Serb Assembly. The uprising fizzled out as quickly as it had arisen, but it underlined the rifts which a self-governing Serb republic might face.[83] Significantly, the leaders of the uprising did not receive the kind of international attention that Abdic had earlier received from Owen and was to have again, though a recognition of the rifts within the Bosnian Serb leadership might have had a positive impact on the negotiating process.

Meanwhile, after close on a month of hectic negotiations over some 2–3 per cent of Bosnian territory, a map giving 53 per cent of Bosnia to the Serb republic, 17 per cent to the Croat republic, and 30 per cent to the Muslim republic was agreed during talks on the British ship HMS Invincible, on 20 September 1993. The Muslim republic would have access to the sea through Neum and the use of the port of Ploce. The northern corridor linking the two Serb territories would centre on Brcko. Sarajevo would be placed under UN administration for a two-year interim period and Mostar would be under EU administration. Two days later, Izetbegovic turned down the plan: he was concerned about the eastern territories. Meeting on 27 September, the Bosnian assembly endorsed his decision, believing that under the influence of sanctions, domestic pressures on Milosevic would lead him to pressurize the Bosnian Serbs to compromise. The Bosnian Serbs and Croats, however, interpreted the new formula of a union of three republics as tantamount to a recognition of a three-way partition, and Boban and Karadzic confidently styled themselves Presidents of Herceg-Bosna and Republika Srpska. At the same time, Fikret Abdic began negotiations with the Bosnian Serbs and Croats to establish his independent control over Bihac.

This was perhaps the finest hour of Owen's odyssey: some nine months of political finagling (he first met Abdic in December 1992) had at last yielded a concrete result. Abdic was expelled from the Bosnian presidency, and war broke out in Bihac between Muslims loyal to Abdic and Bosnian government forces.[84] On 21–22 October, on the joint initiative of Presidents Tudjman and Milosevic, Abdic signed separate agreements with the HDZ leader, Mate Boban, and the SDS leader, Radovan Karadzic, under which an "Autonomous Province of Western Bosnia" was established by the self-styled presidents of Herceg-Bosna, Republika Srpska and the "Autonomous Province of Western Bosnia". The agreement with Mate Boban specified that the Croatian paramilitary HVO units in Bihac would "remain incorporated into the armed forces" of Abdic's province, while the agreement with Radovan Karadzic called upon the Bosnian government to recognize Bihac as an autonomous province of the Muslim republic proposed by the EU, and to set up a boundary commission to establish the borders between Bihac and Republika Srpska.[85]

Bosnia was now about to enter its third year of war. While communal cartographies were being negotiated, the real process of establishing them on the ground through mass murder and forced expulsion was in full sway. Though Presidents Tudjman and Izetbegovic had signed an agreement for a cease-fire between the HVO and the ABH in September, the war between Croats and Muslims in central Bosnia – which had grown partly as a consequence of the cantonal maps drawn by the Vance-Owen plan – intensified in October. The fighting was now concentrated in areas where the issue of who would control the multi-ethnic cantons was still to be resolved.

In the town of Vares, whose pre-war population had comprised equal numbers of Muslims and Croats, and a Serb minority which had fled when the war first broke out, both Croats and Muslims had worked hard to preserve communal peace, even through the summer of 1993 when the Croat-Muslim war was far advanced. But the town's resources were first strained by waves of Croat refugees from surrounding towns and villages, and then cracked under the communal pressure the Croats brought with them. Refugees accused the local Croat leadership of collaborating with the enemy from whom they themselves had fled, and the Vares Croats began to divide. In October, an armed HVO unit from Kiseljak arrived in Vares and first jailed and then replaced the town's Croat mayor and police chief. The town's Muslims were rounded up and their houses were raided and plundered. Within a few days almost all of them had left. Surrounded by ABH controlled territory, the Croats could not defend Vares. On 3 November, the HVO evacuated Vares' Croats, and on 5 November, the ABH Seventh Brigade, itself formed of refugees, walked in. The town's Muslims returned and now a wave of Muslim refugees replaced the Croat refugees who had earlier flooded the town. The entire town of Crna Rijeka in northern Bosnia, which had been cleansed by Serbs, was resettled in Croat homes in Vares.[86] A new demographic engineering, using refugees, had begun.

On 7 November, the foreign ministers of Germany and France, Klaus Kinkel and Alain Juppe, wrote to the president of the EU Foreign Affairs Council, Willy Claes, arguing that the Muslim majority republic should comprise at least one-third of Bosnia's territory (that is, that the 30 per cent negotiated by Owen was too little). Privately Owen argued that "doing a deal" to reunite Sarajevo under Muslim control was more important than seeking an extra 3 per cent territory, as Sarajevo was the economic and political hub of Bosnia.[87] In December, the EU presented an Action Plan with a new map which provided the proposed Muslim republic with expanded territory to link the eastern enclaves of Gorazde and Zepa, and a corresponding link for the Croat republic of territory between Jajce and Gornji Vakuf (which was to be supplied in exchange for territory between Zenica and Sarajevo). This would allow the Muslim republic 33.5 per cent of Bosnian territory and the Croat republic 17.5 per cent. Though the Plan was following through on the proposal for a Union of Three Republics (see frontispiece maps), it also set the lines for a tripartite partition.

Certainly, the view that partition might now be internationally acceptable was one factor in the HDZ and SDS rejection of the Plan's other proposal that Sarajevo be reunited under a two-year UN administration and Mostar be reunited under a two-year EU administration (to which the Serbs and Croats had agreed in earlier talks in August 1993).[88] Though joint agreements on overall territorial allocation were made at the presidential level, between Izetbegovic and Tudjman, and Tudjman and Milosevic, the proposal for reunifying Sarajevo and Mostar had to be agreed by the local HDZ and SDS leaders, Mate Boban and Radovan Karadzic. In other words, Tudjman and Milosevic might well have been able to deliver on the overall agreement – as they later did, by withdrawing substantial financial and military support – but that still left the problem of local control unresolved.

According to David Owen, though he and Thorvald Stoltenberg argued that the EU should not foreclose the possibility that an agreement to divide Sarajevo and Mostar would bring a speedy end to the war, the EU was committed to reunifying both. Whether this was because the EU leaders recognized that the issue of local political disintegration was key to a substantive peace is unclear; more likely, they were concerned that as divided cities, Sarajevo and Mostar might assume the same political potency that the divided Berlin had had. By this point, Sarajevo had become a telling symbol of international inadequacy: indeed, the way in which Sarajevo rose above the banality of evil is one of the great achievements of its people and of the international artists and journalists who supported them. The beginning of 1994 saw a flurry of international activity devoted to the lifting of the siege of Sarajevo and its demilitarization under a UN administration. Touted as a "Sarajevo first" policy, which sought an approach "from below", the policy was held to reverse earlier assumptions that peace could be achieved by an agreement between Milosevic, Tudjman and Izetbegovic, that is, "from above"; instead, it suggested that a more fruitful approach might be to begin with Sarajevo, and if the siege of Sarajevo could be lifted, then an overall settlement might ensue.

However, this from below element of the policy remained inchoate, and subsequent events imply it was largely rhetorical. While negotiations on a UN administration for Sarajevo wound on, the ABH embarked on its own campaign to lift the siege and attacked Grbavica on Christmas day in the Orthodox calendar. The communal tones which had shadowed the war from the first ethnonationalist victories were now the loudest ones.

3

Divide and Quit

Though the European Union Action Plan appeared to mark the lowest point of European policy towards Bosnia, in which the divide and rule aims of Milosevic and Tudjman were accepted despite the terrible war of attrition each had waged to achieve them, 1994, in fact, constituted a turning point in Western policy which was marked by a gradual shift from divide and rule to divide and quit policies: that is, it marked a move away from letting domestic actors set the terms of negotiation and a move towards enlarging the role of European institutions in establishing a peace based on partition. The shift was brought about chiefly on US initiative. While publicly lending support to the tripartite partition of Bosnia which was implied by the EU plan for a Union of Three Republics, the US had pursued a two-track policy since the autumn of 1993, seeking at the same time to control or limit the partition process bilaterally. Beginning in August 1993, Charles Redman, the US special envoy to Bosnia, held a series of meetings aimed at brokering a Muslim-Croat federation. The idea was first discussed by Redman, Bosnian Prime Minister Haris Silajdic, and Croatian Prime Minister Mate Granic. Silajdic and Granic both expressed an interest in the proposal, and in September 1993 the two came to a rough agreement on a federation, but the agreement had little chance of being mooted while the Croat-Muslim war worsened. US pressure on Croatia to stop supporting the Croat offensive in Bosnia had grown sharper as Tudjman resisted it and, in the late autumn, Redman had begun to threaten sanctions against

Croatia. In December 1993, the US ambassador to Croatia, Peter Galbraith, was told that: "Mate Boban would be taking, as it was put to me, a long vacation."

In Bosnia, Haris Silajdic and Ivo Komsic of the Bosnian-Croat Peasant Party began working on a federation structure which incorporated several elements of the Vance-Owen plan, including ethnic cantonization. The limits of agreement, however, were soon revealed: at a 9 January 1994 meeting in Germany, when discussing a Croat-Muslim Treaty of Co-operation, including the confederation option, when the Bosnian leaders asked the Croat leaders to agree to demilitarize central Bosnia, the answer was no.[1] Ten days later, Tudjman and Milosevic agreed to formally recognize each other's new countries; significantly, Bosnian Serbs and Croats followed suit with an agreement to place liaison officers in Pale and Mostar, respectively proclaimed the capitals of Republika Srpska and Herceg-Bosna. Neither Bosnian Croats nor the Croatian government were ready as yet to give up the Tudjman-Milosevic partition plan. At the end of January, Silajdic complained to the UN that the Croatian army continued to engage in the Bosnian Croat-Muslim conflict, and UNPROFOR estimated that there were anything between 3–5,000 regular Croatian army troops in Bosnia.[2] On 3 February, the UN gave Croatia a two-week deadline to pull its troops out of Bosnia and implied that failure to do so would be met with the imposition of sanctions against Croatia, but by 18 February no troop withdrawals had taken place. Sanctions were not imposed, partly to give US diplomacy a chance. While Komsic presented the federation proposal to a special Croat assembly called in Bosnia, which was attended by Croats from all over former Yugoslavia (and some from abroad), Redman and Galbraith pressed Tudjman to support a Croat-Muslim federation with the option of confederation with Croatia.[3] In return, the US would support Croatian applications for membership in European institutions, and would mobilize aid for Croatia, especially for its army.

The offer proved sufficiently tempting: at the end of February, four days of proximity talks in Washington yielded a "Framework Agreement for the Muslim-Croat Federation", and a preliminary agreement that the new federation would confederate with Croatia. A cease-fire took force across central Bosnia and UNPROFOR troops began to be moved to the Croat-Muslim frontlines. Though the Framework Agreement was presented as an opening for an overall peace and a rejection of partition – it was open to the SDS to join, and both Redman and Bosnian opposition leaders expressed the hope that the kind of pressure which was exerted on the Croats to bring them into a federation could now also be applied to the Serbs – the SDS interpreted it as a sign that the international community was ready to accept a two-way partition of Bosnia and demanded recognition of Republika Srpska.[4]

The SDS were not far from the truth. Though there was a formal difference between the Framework Agreement and the EU Action Plan for a Union of Three Republics, in that the former ratified ethnic units at the cantonal rather than republican level, the substantive difference between them was that the former was signed by two ethnic parties while the latter had depended on agreement by all three ethnic parties. The Framework Agreement created a federation of two constituent nations, Croats and Muslims (now named "Bosniaks"); Herceg-Bosna would be formally dissolved, but the federation would have the right to confederate with Croatia. The Serb controlled territories were not mentioned because the SDS was not a party to the agreement; in effect, this let them out of the new constitutional arrangements of Bosnia-Herzegovina and allowed them, by implication, to choose their own constitutional arrangements. But the Serb controlled territories were still not linked to each other: the Brcko corridor was still very narrow, and the three safe areas of Srebrenica, Zepa and Gorazde divided the eastern crescent of Serb held territory. The SDS appears to have assumed that the Framework Agreement was an implicit recognition of their right to the eastern enclaves, and had they waited for the international negotiations to wend their way, they might have been proved right. But they moved to take the areas by force and prolonged the war by another eighteen months.

In the same month as the Framework Agreement was signed, a series of events forced an agreement to lift the siege of Sarajevo. On 4 February, Serb snipers killed ten people in the government controlled Sarajevo suburb Dobrinja. On 5 February, a bomb in the crowded Sarajevo marketplace killed 49 and wounded 200. That morning Karadzic had told UNPROFOR General Bo Pellnas that the SDS would accept a UN administration in Sarajevo if the city and its environs were demilitarized, and the next day he promised General Rose, now commanding UNPROFOR in Bosnia, and UN Special Envoy Yasushi Akashi that the RSA would remove its heavy weapons from around Sarajevo as a part of the demilitarization of the area.[5] Convinced that he was on the verge of sealing a cease-fire and weapons withdrawal plan, Rose persuaded the British to oppose a Franco-American initiative for a NATO ultimatum to the Serbs at the North Atlantic Assembly meeting on 9 February, on the grounds that an ultimatum would set back the agreement. The British were alone in their opposition, however, and NATO issued an ultimatum to the RSA to withdraw their heavy weapons to a twenty kilometre distance from Sarajevo (an "exclusion zone") within ten days. The ultimatum also called on the Bosnian government to place any heavy weapons they had in the exclusion zone under UNPROFOR's control, and threatened air strikes against either party for failure to comply.

Playing good cop to NATO's bad cop, Rose arranged a meeting between Bosnian and Serb military commanders on the same day as the NATO ultimatum, and elicited a verbal agreement from the latter to withdraw their heavy weapons from Sarajevo. The attempt to help save SDS face, however, was interpreted by Serb leaders as a sign of weakness. In the ensuing UNPROFOR-RSA negotiations on where the heavy weapons were to be located, the RSA turned down all Rose's suggestions and were finally allowed to choose their own locations, most of which were in the same places from which Sarajevo had been attacked. Four days before the NATO ultimatum was due to expire, British Prime Minister John Major went to Russia to canvass Yeltsin's support against the ultimatum. On 17 February, Yeltsin appealed to the Bosnian Serbs to pull back their heavy weapons and guaranteed to place Russian troops in those areas from which they pulled back, and Russian officials met with Bosnian Serbs in Pale. Karadzic and Mladic agreed both to withdraw their heavy weapons and to allow a UN administration for Sarajevo, and four hundred Russian troops were moved from eastern Slavonia to the hills surrounding Sarajevo (not even a tenth of the 4,600 troops that UNPROFOR estimated would be required to truly secure freedom of movement for Sarajevans).[6] The UN line on negotiations had triumphed over the NATO initiative on peace enforcement, but at the cost of indefinitely postponing peace in Bosnia. The positioning of UN peacekeepers along the Sarajevo confrontation lines ended by reinforcing the *de facto* partition of the city in Bosnian Serb favour. The Serbs viewed the Russian troops as temporary guardians of their heavy weapons rather than confiscators.[7]

The US and Russian initiatives in the negotiations signalled a new division of responsibilities under which the US was primarily responsible for making the Croat-Muslim federation work, and the Russians were responsible for pushing the Serbs to agree to the putative partition they were being offered.[8] By the end of March, Charles Redman and Vitaly Churkin were convinced that a comprehensive peace settlement could be achieved by extending the Sarajevo cease-fire model, the separation of forces and the withdrawal of heavy weapons to the whole of Bosnia-Herzegovina. Like Carrington, Cutileiro, Owen, Vance and Stoltenberg, they had misread the signs. Moving on the assumption that the creation of the Muslim-Croat Federation meant an implicit recognition of Republika Srpska's right to the eastern enclaves, the Serbs started shelling Gorazde in early April. Of the three eastern enclaves, Gorazde was the most strategically important to the Serbs because it straddled the main road connecting the Serb towns of Visegrad and Foca, and Serb attempts to construct a bypass linking the two towns were hampered by ABH raids from inside the enclave. (Throughout the war Bosnian army attacks were geared primarily to obstructing Serb and Croat offensives to consolidate a partition.)

Despite reports from UN Military Observers in Gorazde that the enclave was in a precarious situation, General Rose played down what was happening. On 7 April, a report by the Military Observers was leaked. The report protested official UNPROFOR statements on the situation. "From the BBC World Service news of 5 April we heard 'An UNPROFOR assessment said that it was a minor attack into a limited area'. We again do not concur with that position. It is a grave situation. It needs to be realized that the city centre of Gorazde is just three kilometres from the

Bosnian Serb army front line."[9] Though the UN Security Council demanded that the attacks cease and NATO warned of air strikes on Serb positions, the attacks continued. Air strikes were ordered but they were so limited as to be counterproductive. Three bombs were dropped on 10 April and three more on 11 April. The Serbs retaliated by seizing 150 UN personnel on Mount Igman and shelling Tuzla, and continued the assault on Gorazde. On 15 April the Bosnian defences collapsed, and by 16 April, the Serbs controlled the strategic heights around Gorazde. Concerned both by what was being done to a UN safe area and by the possibility that the RSA shooting down of a British jet might lead to more severe air strikes against them, Vitaly Churkin brokered an agreement between Akashi and Krajisnik that there would be no more air strikes if the RSA would stop shelling Gorazde, pull their troops back to a distance of three kilometres from the town centre by 18 April, and release the UN hostages. Karadzic, however, was in Banja Luka when the agreement was made, and when he came back on 17 April he succeeded in persuading Akashi to grasp at the straw of an offer that the Serbs would allow medical evacuation from the enclave as sufficient proof of the SDS's intention to comply with the other conditions of the Akashi-Krajisnik agreement. On the same day, the RSA entered Gorazde and occupied the right bank of the river Drina. General Rose now committed the unpardonable: he evacuated UN military personnel but left UN civil personnel to their fates. On 19 April, Bosnian Serb forces stormed the UN weapons' collection point at Sarajevo's Lukavica barracks and seized eighteen anti-aircraft guns. NATO issued an ultimatum that the RSA would face further air strikes unless there was an immediate cease-fire, troops were pulled back to a three kilometre distance from the centre of Gorazde by midnight on 23 April, and heavy weapons were withdrawn to a distance of twenty kilometres from the town by midnight on 26 April. But on the 23rd, when the RSA had still not complied with the cease-fire order and had not even begun to withdraw its troops to the specified three kilometre distance, Akashi refused to authorize air strikes (under the UN-NATO agreement, air strikes could not be ordered without Akashi's authorization) on the grounds that UNPROFOR and Bosnian Serb leaders had reached an agreement to

cease fire and allow UN troop deployment in Gorazde, and were
beginning to withdraw their heavy weapons.

At the same time, in a move widely seen as pre-empting the NATO
ultimatum, General Rose dispatched 150 Ukrainian peacekeepers to
Gorazde. The Ukrainians were supposed to be followed by British and
French contingents, but the French were suddenly ordered not to go by
the French Defence Ministry.[10] It seems the French wanted a more aggressive mandate than the international community was prepared to
consider; the countermanding of their troop dispatch, however, was
subsequently used to justify UN procrastination over air strikes. Without substantial ground troops to take on the protection of the enclave,
the air strikes would have had little more than a symbolic effect, it was
argued, and the French had the largest number of ground troops in the
vicinity. If they were unwilling to send in their ground troops, then
there was no point in ordering air strikes.[11] In Gorazde, the British and
Ukrainian peacekeepers administered an agreement along the lines of
the Srebrenica agreement: the demilitarization of the enclave and the
interposition of UN troops between the RSA-ABH front line and the
town. Following the US and Russian initiatives a Contact Group was set
up to mediate the Bosnian conflict, which was composed of the Foreign
Ministers of France, Germany, Russia and Britain, the EU Commissioner
for Foreign Affairs, and the two Co-Chairmen of the ICFY Steering
Committee.

Meanwhile, Sarajevo was enjoying an interregnum from war. For the
first time in two years, a tram line was reopened and there were traffic
lights on the main street, Titova. Shops and restaurants sprang up and
the black market boomed. International agencies which were
headquartered in Zagreb began talking of moving their offices to
Sarajevo, on the premiss that the summer was going to comprise a transition to peace. It was as if the Croat agreement to enter into a federation
had made a rump Bosnian state more feasible and thus had made a
separate Serb entity more acceptable. Indeed, a tacit acceptance of a
two-way partition was expressed by the Bosnian Ambassador to the
UN, Muhamed Sacirbey: "the Serbian forces that have undertaken the
destruction of the historical three-way ethnic partnership must under-

stand that they cannot choose to be a separate entity in a partitioned Bosnia-Herzegovina and still expect to participate as a constituent partner in the rest of Bosnia-Herzegovina."[12] Indications were, however, that the federation might be more formal than substantive. Though President Tudjman had, by signing the Framework Agreement, formally renounced the Herzegovinian claim to found a Greater Croatia for the Croats, his own beliefs made it impossible for him to implement the agreement he had signed.

The Agreement actually offered Croatia an expanded sphere of power by creating an option for the putative Muslim-Croat Federation to confederate with Croatia. But this would entail accepting a large Muslim population within the sphere of power, a move which the avowedly anti-Muslim Tudjman continued to resist. The option of confederation, in fact, constituted a catch for Croatian nationalists: in order to expand their power in the region, they would also have to relinquish their claims to membership in an ethnically and religiously pure *Mittel Europa* in favour of a Balkans or south-east European association, an offer which the EU had made and continued to make and which the HDZ saw as a ploy to resurrect former Yugoslavia.[13] Indeed, one of the ironies of the Framework Agreement was that many opposition figures feared that, without a parallel confederation between Bosnia and the rump Yugoslavia, Bosnia ran the risk of becoming an unwelcome and progressively radicalized semi-colony of Croatia in which a *de facto* partition between Croat and Muslim dominated territories would be maintained. The complicated ethnic division of powers under the 54-page draft constitution of the federation which was negotiated in early March, with the incorporation of the cantonal provisions of the Vance-Owen plan,[14] was already beginning to show that its chief effect would be to further a peace-time process of ethnic cleansing and tripartite partition: in fact, the two-month interim period between its drafting and formal signing was used by both Croat and Bosnian nationalists to consolidate their positions. By early May, Bosnian and Croat representatives were negotiating hotly on territorial-cum-population exchanges to establish contiguous ethnoterritories within the federation;[15] it seems President Tudjman was

insistent that Croat cantonal borders be agreed before the draft constitution was signed.[16]

Meanwhile, a Bosnian acceptance of Republika Srpska was foreshadowed by rumours that the government was discussing a proposal to
claim the rump-Yugoslavian region of Sandjak, which was predominantly
Muslim, as an exchange for the secession of Bosnian Serbs. With the
promise of peace in the federation territory, the return of refugees was
a key issue from two points of view: throughout the war refugees had
been used to settle areas under one or another authority, in order to
strengthen SDS, HDZ and even SDA control, but the hot negotiations
on territorial and population exchanges implied both that the process
of ethnopolitical resettlement would intensify and that the Bosnian government – which had been unable to engage in ethnic resettlement to
the extent that the HDZ or SDS had because of its military weakness –
would now play an active role in it. At the same time, the Bosnian
government was under different pressure: the majority of Muslims had
traditionally lived in the towns and constituted the professional class
without which Bosnia could not rebuild itself. This class had, however,
been the most secularized in Tito's Yugoslavia and would not return to
towns which had become "Muslim". To encourage them to return, the
multi-ethnic character of pre-war Bosnian towns had to be restored.
This made Mostar and Sarajevo key to the success of a federation agreement, but any attempt to unify either town or to return it to its pre-war
inhabitants was stymied by its symbolic value as capital of a new ethnic
state.[17]

By the time the Washington Agreement for the establishment of a
Muslim-Croat Federation were signed on 10 May 1994, it was clear
that Mostar would be a major sticking point for the Federation. The
Agreement included Mostar being placed under EU administration for
an interim two-year period; though it was originally envisaged that
Sarajevo would be placed under similar UN administration, the fact that
it was the capital of Bosnia meant that such an agreement would be
tantamount to a government abnegation of sovereignty, and it was decided
that the UN would instead appoint a Senior Civil Officer, who would
deal primarily with the restoration of utilities. The EU administration

was to reintegrate Mostar under "a single, self-sustaining and multi-ethnic administration",[18] and on 23 May, the UN secured an agreement on freedom of movement in the Mostar region which permitted them to embark on a first stage of demilitarization – and amounted chiefly to stationing UNPROFOR checkpoints between Bosnian and Croat ones – but did not permit residents of Mostar to move between east and west. In west Mostar, Croat leaders protested both agreements, and the Bishop of Mostar wrote to Owen and Stoltenberg arguing that Mostar was a majority Croat populated town which was a part of Catholic Herceg-Bosna. The people, he said, did not want an EU administration.[19]

The Federation agreement was followed by renewed fighting between Bosnian government and Bosnian Serb forces, and between 6 and 8 June another round of international negotiations yielded a one-month cease-fire agreement. Like countless other agreements, it was violated within days of being signed. By the end of June, it was clear that any hopes that the Serbs would enter the federation on the same terms as the Croats were dead: instead, the Federation constitution was beginning to be viewed primarily as an interim wartime arrangement to form a joint front against the Serbs until territorial divisions were agreed. Already, most of the conflict was in areas from which, under the Contact Group map, the Serbs were to withdraw.[20] The agreement also meant that Bosnians might now finally have a land route open through which to get arms (though the Croat practice of levying a fee of 25–40 per cent of the goods rather limited the arms they were able to bring in). One of the first acts of the federation was to launch an offensive against Fikret Abdic's forces in Bihac, in which the HVO units which had been pledged to him by Mate Boban in October 1993 now fought alongside the ABH against him. The offensive routed Abdic, but made thousands of his Muslim supporters refugees in the Serb populated area of Croatia which was under UN protection.

At the same time, the ethnic principle which informed the constitution, from the naming of two "constituent nations" of Bosniaks and Croats to the allocation of political and executive positions, had a series of immediate consequences. The failure to name the Serbs as a constituent nation led the Serbs within the federation to conclude that they had been consigned to second-rate citizenship (as the federation's use of the term "others" would imply),[21] and many Serbs who had braved the most intense years of the war in order to show their adherence to a multi-ethnic Bosnia now began to leave the federation. The issue also created significant dissension within the SDA between a Silajdic led faction, which argued that the SDA should maintain the values of a secular Bosnia, and an Izetbegovic led majority, which argued that the experience of the war showed that it was vital to build a strong Muslim identity.[22] Politically, the ethnic allocation of seats in a constitution which was chiefly a wartime stand-off between recently embattled parties increased rather than decreased the strength of ethnic nationalists. In the assembly elections of 22–23 June, the SDA and HDZ pushed out most of the smaller and non-ethnic political parties;[23] the moderate Croat leader, Ivo Komsic, who had been a key figure in the negotiations for a federation, was more or less retired and an HDZ leader, Jadranko Prlic, who had been prominent in west Mostar during the Croat bombardment of Muslim populated east Mostar, became Deputy Prime Minister of the federation, while the more moderate Croat nationalist Kresimir Zubak became Vice-President.[24]

Ironically, Prlic had opposed the Federation agreement as constituting a betrayal of Herceg-Bosna. Radical nationalist Croat participation in the federation had, in fact, been given impetus by a split between the Croats of Herceg-Bosna, who enjoyed Tudjman's patronage, and the Croats of northern and central Bosnia, who saw their only safety lying in an integrated Bosnia; the first proposals for a unified country had been made in the autumn of 1993 at an assembly convened by Croats living in the Posavina corridor. Tudjman's signature on the federation agreement, in this context, reinstated the Herceg-Bosna HDZ and sealed the federation's fate as an interim wartime arrangement; moreover, according to independent Croat analysts, Tudjman was "not only seeking to secure the territories on which local Croat officials (would) exercise authority, (but) also seeking to settle accounts in advance for the time when the state being created today begins itself to disintegrate".[25] In other words, Tudjman was playing the waiting game which Milosevic could not play without abandoning the Krajina Serbs.

International negotiators now came closer to a two-way partition. On 6 July, the Contact Group presented a map dividing Bosnia between the federation and a Bosnian Serb entity with 51 per cent of Bosnian territory for the Federation (the sum of the 33.5 per cent and 17.5 per cent agreed under the Joint Action Plan negotiations, to go to the Bosnian and Croat Republics respectively), and 49 per cent of Bosnian territory to go to the Serb entity. The map preserved the eastern enclaves and at the end of July, the Federation, Croatia and rump Yugoslavia accepted it, but the Bosnian Serbs rejected it. Under last-minute pressure by Milosevic, Bosnian Serb leaders agreed that as a compromise, Republika Srpska would treat the Contact Group plan as a starting point for nego-tiations, but the compromise was rejected by the Serb Assembly in Pale. On 3 August, after a Milosevic directed media blitz against them, the Bosnian Serb Assembly rejected the plan for a third time, and on 4 August, the rump Yugoslavia announced they were going to close the border between Serbia and Bosnia and impose an embargo on Republika Srpska. For the first time since the beginning of the war, despite resolu-tions to seal Bosnia's borders from late 1992 on, Milosevic allowed the stationing of international monitors on the Serbian and Montenegrin borders with Bosnia. On 23 September, at the request of the Contact Group, the UN Security Council imposed wide-ranging sanctions against the Bosnian Serbs; on the same day, they eased the sanctions against the rump Yugoslavia as a reward for the closing of the borders.[26] The Bosnian Serbs retaliated with a rampage of ethnic cleansing in Banja Luka and Bijeljina,[27] pushing both houses of the US Senate to resolve in mid-October that if the Bosnian Serbs did not accept the Contact Group plan within two weeks, President Clinton should move to lift the arms embargo against the Bosnian government.[28]

Cold-shouldered by Serbia, Bosnian and Croatian Serbs moved closer together. In October, an ABH offensive on Serb held territories between Bihac and the central Bosnian towns of Bugojno and Gornji Vakuf was initially successful, but in early November, war broke out again in Bihac following a joint attack on the enclave by Bosnian Serb forces and rebel Muslim supporters of Fikret Abdic, supported by Croatian Serbs from across the border. Though the attack was resisted by the ABH Fifth

Corps, with support from Bosnian Croat troops as well as regular Croat army troops, the Serb attack succeeded in regaining most of the territory of the enclave within ten days. Some 400,000 people were besieged, aid convoys were refused admittance, and two Bangladeshi peacekeepers died because they were denied access to medical attention. On 18 November, Croatian Serb aircraft flew from the Udbina airstrip of the Croatian Krajina (a UN Protected Area) to drop napalm and cluster bombs in south-west Bihac, and on 19 November, they bombed north of Bihac. On the same day, the UN Security Council extended the mandate to defend the safe areas to cover air strikes on targets in Croatia, and asked UNPROFOR to plan how they might be strengthened.[29] On 21 November, NATO air strikes began, first on the Udbina air strip and then on three other sites around Bihac. Stung by the débâcle of their token air strikes over Gorazde in the spring, NATO had proposed on 7 October that there should be a rapid response to attacks on the safe areas, no advance warning of air strikes, and each strike should be against a minimum of four targets.[30] While the Serbs warned of an all-out war if the air strikes continued, a debate broke out among members of the international community over the extent to which Serb forces had encroached on the enclave (and therefore whether and what kinds of air strikes were appropriate): it was suddenly discovered that no one was clear about whether a map of the safe area had ever been agreed.[31]

On 24 November, the Serbs resorted to the policy tried and proved in Gorazde, taking some 250 UNPROFOR personnel hostage (mainly the French around Sarajevo) while advancing to within 1.5 kilometres of the centre of Bihac town. By 30 November, almost 450 peacekeepers were being held by the Serbs, while NATO and the UN debated whether to seek a Srebrenica or Gorazde type agreement for Bihac, under which it would be left in the same vulnerable position as the former two, demilitarized and surrounded by Serb held territory. The UN added threats of a pull-out and Croatia's defence minister, Gojko Susak, warned that Croatia would enter the war unless the international community took firm action to stop the Serb offensive.[32] The international community seemed to have sunk to its nadir. NATO suspended its flights over Bihac, the US said that an acceptance of the Serb right to secede would not constitute "appeasement" if Bosnians and Croats agreed to it, and the Contact Group followed through with the concession that the Serbs could amend the maps presented by the Contact Group. On 1 December, UN Secretary-General Boutros Boutros-Ghali said that, in his view, the safe areas could not be defended by force; their safety depended on the mutual agreement of warring groups. On 3 and 4 December, on a visit to Pale, US envoy Charles Redman indicated that the Contact Group might mediate an exchange of the eastern enclaves for land around Sarajevo and Bihac.[33] If Bihac could be linked by land to western Herzegovina, then it would not only be a feasible part of the federation, but would make a valuable separation between Croatian and Bosnian Serb territory.

The Serbs, however, redoubled their attacks on Bihac. On 8 December, surface-to-air missiles were fired into the town, and on 12 December, they launched a mortar and rocket attack which wounded four Bangladeshi peacekeepers. By this time, Bihac had been totally cut off from any aid for close on a month and UNHCR warnings of a humanitarian disaster were frantic. Within the US, the near total rout of the international effort in Bosnia led to mounting pressure for a UN withdrawal, which was given impetus by a French threat of unilateral pull-out. The televised humiliation of French personnel by the RSA soldiers who had taken them hostage had caused considerable outcry in France, but it seems the French threat was a ploy to elicit a more aggressive peace effort. At a NATO meeting on 12 December, French Defence Minister Leotard said the French had decided that a UN withdrawal would "encourage Muslim governments and Russia to enter the war on opposing sides and would disgrace the UN"; additionally, it "would bring Islamic forces into the area". Instead, UNPROFOR should strengthen its position by establishing a protected ground corridor for the delivery of aid from Split to Sarajevo, troops should be moved to provide better security for the Sarajevo airlift, and there should be an overall redeployment of troops all over Bosnia from the traditional peace-keeping interpositions to more defensible positions. The French proposal was opposed by the British.[34]

The winter of 1994 was dominated by two conflicting last-ditch efforts: the first, mediated by former US president Jimmy Carter, to wrest a cease-fire; and the second, a joint initiative of Bosnian and Croatian Serbs, to join their territories by conquering Bihac before the UN mandate in Croatia expired in March 1995. Tudjman had threatened that the mandate would not be extended, and the Croatian army was by now both trained and equipped to reconquer the Krajina without too much difficulty. Despite the ongoing war in Bihac and west central Bosnia, both the Federation and the Serbs agreed to a four-month cease-fire on 20 December, but this had little more than symbolic meaning as most prior cease-fires had also been agreed for the winter months when the climate slowed much of the fighting. Carter had attempted to transform this cease-fire into a separation of forces agreement, but the Bosnian government feared that the interposition of UNPROFOR on the front lines would impose a *de facto* partition of the sort which had occurred in Cyprus, and demanded the SDS accept the Contact Group map as a negotiating point, which they refused to do.[35] The Croatian Serbs and rebel Muslims were not bound by the cease-fire agreement and attacks on Bihac continued through the winter.

Meanwhile, political conflict within the Federation mounted. Though the European Union administration in Mostar had formally commenced in May, its head, Hans Koschnik, had sought to work through consensus between the *de facto* administrations of Mostar West and East.[36] The attempt was a failure: in the four months of its administration, the EU had been unable either to extend freedom of movement between western and eastern Mostar, or to curb the continuing eviction of Muslims by the local authorities of Mostar West. In part, the problem lay with the EU administration's adoption of the federation constitution's ethnic allocation of power. Mr Koschnik's Advisory Council was composed of five Croats, five Bosniaks, three Serbs, one Jew and one Woman [sic].[37] The HDZ authorities of Mostar West represented an entrenched group of paramilitaries, arms dealers and money launderers, and when, in exasperation, Koshnik issued an edict at the beginning of November forbidding the evictions of Muslims from Mostar West, their response was to threaten EU officials. On 4 November, a paramilitary leader shot his Uzi into the air outside the hotel Aero (where a large number of

EU officials stayed). When the WEU police arrested him, the local authorities demanded his release and accused the WEU police of manhandling him, the local police prevented the WEU police from searching his car, and in the end he was not only released, but allowed to keep his gun. In any case, the WEU police presence was largely symbolic: they numbered roughly 60 (the EU administration's eventual goal was to bring the muster up to 200), and did not have the co-operation of the local police.[38]

A spate of reports about the "Islamicization" of the ABH and the Bosnian government's ties to Iran (which had supplied them with both cash and *matériel*) did little to calm the tension. At the Parliamentary Assembly session on 7 November, Prime Minister Silajdic devoted a considerable portion of his speech to refuting charges that Bosnia was becoming an Islamic state, or that the army was being communalized. In February 1995, reports of the presence of Iranian and Afghan *mujahedeen* in Zenica started a debate within the Bosnian government, in which the Presidency was split between those who protested that Bosnia's only hope was to preserve a secular and multi-ethnic army and those who said they "had to tolerate the *mujahedeen* because of the money coming in from fundamentalist countries". Though HDZ and SDA leaders had agreed on 5 February to submit problems within the Federation to an international arbitrator, preferably appointed by the US, and a retired US general had been appointed to help unify HVO and ABH units into a single army, the Deputy Prime Minister and Defence Minister of the Federation, HDZ leader Jadranko Prlic, threatened that the Federation would fall apart if the *mujahedeen* were not expelled.[39]

By the spring of 1995, it had become clear that Bosnia was again sliding into full-scale war. The weapons exclusion zones were being violated and fighting between Bosnian government and Serb forces had been intense around Sarajevo. On 1 May, the cease-fire expired and the RSA began shelling Bihac again. In a sudden attack, the Croatian army attacked west Slavonia and captured it, sending thousands of Croatian Serbs fleeing to Bosnia. The attack had been planned some time before but had been scheduled for the autumn so as to avoid a falling off in summer tourism; the RSA shelling of Bihac, however, forced the pace of the attack on west Slavonia, because Croatia feared that if Bihac fell, the Krajina Serbs would have a rail link through to Belgrade.[40] On 7 May, the RSA shelled Sarajevo, killing nine people. On 24 May, the Serbs seized heavy weapons from the exclusion zone around Sarajevo, and General Smith threatened air strikes if they were not returned by noon the next day. When the deadline passed without compliance, NATO bombed the Serb headquarters in Pale. The Serbs fired a shell into Tuzla's main street, killing seventy-one people. There was a second round of NATO bombing, of ammunition depots in Pale. The Serbs then took French peacekeepers hostage. [41]

The election of Jacques Chirac as France's Prime Minister in May signalled a shift in what had hitherto been a kind of minimal West European consensus on Bosnia. Chirac argued for a more robust approach to the UN mandate. After hundreds of UN peacekeepers were taken hostage in May, France pushed for the creation of a "Rapid Reaction Force" which would respond more aggressively to Bosnian Serb fiats. In fact, UN Secretary-General Boutros Boutros-Ghali had proposed a similar force in 1992, but at the time the proposal had been supported only by the French; in 1995, after a series of humiliations to UNPROFOR troops, the French proposal was supported by most of the West European countries. The force was to comprise some 10,000 troops; 4,000 French, 4–5,000 British and the remainder Dutch, Belgian and German. In late June, the US committed itself to providing $50 million towards the costs of the Rapid Reaction Force (it was estimated the Force would cost $700 million per year),[42] but while the Rapid Reaction Force was being assembled, the RSA began to mass around Srebrenica. Though the build-up to the Serb assault on Srebrenica took a few weeks, the assault itself took only days and the consequent ethnic cleansing was brutally quick.

On 24 June, the Serbs threatened to "demilitarize" Srebrenica, but UNPROFOR did not take the threat seriously. On 6 July, the RSA began shelling the enclave and the commander of the Dutch battalion stationed at Srebrenica asked for NATO planes to be held in readiness for air strikes, but his request was turned down by General Janvier in Zagreb. Apparently, the UN "believed that the Serbs only wanted to take a small part of the enclave in the south", where government troops were said to be concentrated. On 8 July, the RSA moved against UN observation posts in Srebrenica and forced the Dutch to withdraw, and on 9 July, while refugees from surrounding villages flooded the town, the Serbs took thirty peacekeepers hostage. The UN again turned down requests for close air support from the Dutch battalion commander, and on 10 July, when a fourth request was made, General Janvier is reported to have said in a staff meeting, "Gentlemen, don't you understand? I have to get rid of these enclaves."

At one a.m. on 11 July, the Dutch commander was informed that air strikes had finally been ordered, and he persuaded the Srebrenica authorities to evacuate soldiers and civilians from areas that would be targeted. In the early hours of that day, a column of about twelve thousand men moved out of the town to the north, where they ran the gamut of Serb guns. The air strikes did not take place and thousands of the men in the column were killed or captured. It seems Janvier had advised NATO to be on stand-by but had not ordered air strikes. When air strikes were finally ordered in the afternoon, the pilots were told only to fire at tanks or artillery seen firing. After hitting two tanks, the NATO aeroplanes withdrew. The Serb forces threatened to kill Dutch peacekeepers and the Dutch government asked NATO to suspend the air strikes. Srebrenica fell at six p.m.[43] On July 12, 1,500 Serb troops marched into the town, backed by tanks and under the supervision of Ratko Mladic, the commander of the Bosnian Serb forces. The Bosnian men of military age were separated from the others, taken away and massacred. The UN Secretary-General, Boutros Boutros-Ghali, ruled out air strikes and the UN spokesman, Alexander Ivanko, announced that the most the UN had been able to negotiate was that a Dutch soldier be allowed to travel on each bus, to "monitor human rights abuses".

Britain, who had troops in neighbouring Gorazde, responded with warnings of withdrawal, while France pushed for troop reinforcement to recover Srebrenica. (The Bosnian government had already called for its recovery.) The UN Security Council demanded the return of Srebrenica but stopped short of supporting the French proposal.[44] In the US, pressure for lifting the arms embargo intensified.[45] The next day, as refugees began to surge into Tuzla, reports of the carnage of male civilians in Srebrenica began to be made. France said it was ready to commit an additional 2–4,000 troops (its share of the Rapid Reaction Force which was to be in place in another week), on condition that the US would provide close air support and transport helicopters. Zepa was already being targeted as the "next" safe haven on the Serb list of attack. Meanwhile, UNPROFOR began to discuss "regrouping" its forces: with the fall of Srebrenica and heavy pressure on Zepa, it was not clear whether the UN could protect the remaining safe areas. Zepa was the most lightly guarded of the safe areas, with only seventy-nine Ukrainian peacekeepers. UN military officials began to state that the eastern enclaves were undefendable; they had been able to survive thus far only because of Serb acquiescence. In an illuminating aside, a British officer said that Gorazde was less likely to fall than Srebrenica or Zepa, because it "was never demilitarized" as the other two had been when they were declared safe areas, implying that the international community would not act to save Zepa.[46]

In fact, Western governments had concluded some months before that the eastern enclaves were an obstacle to a settlement. Muhamed Sacirbey and the US ambassador to the UN, Madeleine Albright, had discussed a possible territorial exchange in April 1995; it seems the Bosnian government and ABH leadership both saw the enclaves as a strategic burden. According to General Delic of the ABH: "Each of our offensives in other parts of the country ran the risk of having the Serb aggressor make a move on Srebrenica and Zepa." The Sacirbey-Albright discussions envisaged an UNPROFOR withdrawal to central Bosnia (the "troop regrouping" which was also discussed within the UN), which would allow NATO air power to act as a deterrent to RSA attacks on the enclaves; discussions of a territorial exchange would take place within this context and, by implication, would be followed by a transfer of population. But the Western governments preferred to leave it to the UN to float the idea behind the scenes, and the Bosnian government could not be part of a negotiation which gave up the eastern enclaves without a fight.[47]

On July 14, the Serbs encircled Zepa and began shelling the three UN observation posts there. The Ukrainians had already been told not to resist: the Serbs had 450 Dutch troops at their mercy in Srebrenica, together with some 62 Dutch hostages. In Gorazde, fearful Bosnian army troops seized UN weapons; Mladic had named Gorazde as third on his list. In Sarajevo, the Bosnian government called for the resignation of UN Special Envoy, Yasushi Akashi and threatened they would not extend the UN mandate, which was due to expire in November. In London, NATO allies met to discuss the French proposal, largely in relation to Sarajevo, Tuzla and – perhaps – Gorazde. Zepa had already been given up, though it had not yet fallen. On 15 July, the Bosnian Serbs pushed past UN observation posts into the Zepa enclave. They were met by some resistance from Bosnian troops who had seized the weapons of the Ukrainians. In Paris, European officials said there was "little prospect" of military intervention to save Zepa. The Dutch hostages remained a primary consideration, though, in a show of confidence, the Serbs announced they had released fifty of them that day.[48]

As the Serbs pressed forward in Zepa, they seized Ukrainian peacekeepers and threatened that they would kill them if NATO carried out air strikes. Meanwhile, the European Union negotiator who replaced Lord Owen, Carl Bildt, went to Belgrade to negotiate the release of the Dutch troops and to gain access to the detainees from Srebrenica (it was estimated that some twenty thousand men were missing).[49] The next day, 17 July, the British said they were not convinced of the feasibility or even urgency of the French proposals for Gorazde, and the French said that they too had given up any ideas of intervening in Zepa. President Izetbegovic announced that he would begin negotiations with the Bosnian Serbs for the safe evacuation of Zepa civilians.[50] On 18 July, Bosnian army troops in Zepa adopted an RSA tactic for the first time since the war began, and seized Ukrainian peacekeepers, threatening they would be used as human shields unless NATO launched air strikes. In Washington, the Senate began debating a bill tabled by Republican leader Bob Dole, to unilaterally lift the arms embargo, despite White House warnings that this would mean a UN withdrawal and a rift among NATO allies. The US administration began to study options for a more aggressive air campaign, complemented by the French proposals for troop reinforcements and a Rapid Reaction Force.[51]

On 19 July, the Bosnian Serbs announced that Zepa town had fallen, and paraded two Bosnian municipal representatives who had surrendered on Serb television. The Bosnian government denied the report and the UN said that about a thousand Bosnian army troops were continuing to fight, probably in the mountains ringing the town. On 20 July, the mayor of Zepa appealed for international intervention to save Zepa, and the Bosnian Serbs brought sixty buses to the outskirts of the town, to transport the women and children out. Men and boys aged between fifteen and fifty-five would be detained, they said. Meanwhile Krajina Serbs and Fikret Abdic's troops attacked the Bosnian government's Fifth Corps, who were holding Bihac, a move which military analysts saw as attempting to consolidate Bosnian and Krajina Serb communications and supply lines before the Croatian attack on the Krajina began.[52] The Croatian government warned the UN that if Bihac's status was threatened, Croatia would intervene.[53]

In Washington, administration officials said the US would not support the French proposal for a Rapid Reaction Force as it would involve the use of US ground crews. In London, the British suggested that the Serbs be threatened instead with massive air strikes if they attacked Gorazde. At the same time, the French and the British began to work on a plan to open the supply route to Sarajevo over Mount Igman.[54] On 21 July, the allies unfolded a plan for a sustained air campaign if the Serbs attacked Gorazde: air strikes would first target Serb air-defence systems, advancing Serb troops, and their communications and supply lines, and then would strike at a number of Serb military targets across Bosnia. (The Serbs had already started shelling Gorazde – along with Zepa, Sarajevo and Bihac – but this was not taken to constitute an attempt to conquer the enclave. Signs of an attack would comprise the massing of troops and movement of heavy weapons.) The plan was vociferously opposed by Russia, but the London meeting also reached the key decision to abandon the dual-key system under which the UN Special Envoy, Yasushi Akashi, had the authority to decide whether or not to launch air strikes. Henceforth, the decision would be taken jointly by the

UNPROFOR commander for Bosnia-Herzegovina (instead of the head-quarters chief in Zagreb) and the NATO commander.

Five days later, however, NATO officials announced they had agreed that any air strikes campaign would begin only after UN officials had given the go ahead.[55] On the same day, the Serbs released 308 Dutch peacekeepers, many of whom corroborated refugee accounts of RSA supervised genocide in Srebrenica. The Dutch Defence Minister, Mr Voorhoeve, was reported as saying, "Of course, in the last several days we felt that our freedom of speech was constrained by the fact that there were so many Dutch military still in the hands of the Bosnian Serb military. Fortunately, they are free now, and our freedom of speech is restored."[56] In Geneva, the Islamic conference declared that they would unilaterally lift the arms embargo.

On 22 July, President Franjo Tudjman and President Izetbegovic agreed in a meeting with US ambassador Peter Galbraith that Croatia would militarily assist the Bosnian government to retain Bihac,[57] and would seize towns and villages just across the border to ease pressure on the enclave.[58] The next day Croatian artillery began to move into range of Serb supply lines in the region. In London, European and US officials and diplomats admitted that the fact that the threat of retaliatory air strikes was limited to an attack on Gorazde might be construed by the Bosnian Serbs "as a green light" to attack other areas with impunity.[59] RSA shelling and sniping had killed 140 people and wounded 722 in Sarajevo in the past three weeks. On 22 July, two French peacekeepers were killed in an attack on Sarajevo. On 23 July, 800 British and French soldiers moved towards Mount Igman in the first stage of the attempt to secure supply routes into Sarajevo. On 25 July, Zepa fell after holding out for eleven days, and the War Crimes Tribunal indicted Radovan Karadzic and Ratko Mladic for the crimes committed in Srebrenica.[60] The next day, the US Senate voted for the US to unilaterally withdraw from the arms embargo. The vote still had to go through the House and then to the President. The UN Commissioner for Human Rights, Poland's former prime minister, Tadeusz Mazowiecki, resigned in protest at the international community's failure to save Srebrenica and Zepa.[61]

Seeing that international frustration with the Serbs might have reached its zenith, and emboldened by its successful capture of the enclave of Western Slavonia in May, Croatia began an attack on the Krajina border, severing supply routes between Knin and Bosnian Serb controlled territory on 28 July, and the next day, when the Bosnian Croat forces were massed on the western border of Bosnia, it was reported that the US and European governments "felt unable to deliver an unequivocal message to Croatia not to attack the Krajina."[62] While Croat forces attacked Serbian villages on the Bosnian border, the US and Russia launched an eleventh-hour initiative to secure an agreement under which the Krajina would be autonomous and would have its own flag, currency, parliament and police force, and its citizens would be entitled to dual nationality, but the Croatian Serb leaders – in vainglorious folly – turned down the proposal.

On 4 August, Croatian forces bombarded villages along the entire ninety-mile Krajina. Knin was hit by over 1,500 shells. Like the RSA, advancing Croatian army troops attacked UN observation posts and seized UN peacekeepers, on several occasions using them as human shields. In Washington, White House and Pentagon officials said they "understood the motive" for the Croatian attack, which, President Clinton said, "was animated by the Serb attack" on Bihac. The US had given the green light, officials specified, to an attack on Serb forces in and around Bihac, but a red signal to a broader Krajina offensive. In Belgrade, President Milosevic ignored the Croatian Serb leader Milan Martic's appeal for help.[63] The next day, the Croatian army took Knin, and the largest exodus of the war took place, of Serbs from Croatia into Bosnia. In Bosnia, while the government feared that the retreating Croat Serb forces would swell the RSA, Radovan Karadzic announced he was taking over as commander of the RSA from Ratko Mladic; in a show of support, eighteen RSA generals [sic] issued a "declaration of loyalty" to Mladic. A more serious worry for the Bosnian government was that the Krajina refugees would settle the Serb controlled territory, which had been progressively depopulated during the war by a flow of Bosnian Serb refugees to Serbia, and thus provide grounds for an acceptance of partition. These fears were partly substantiated on 9 August, when US Secretary of State Anthony Lake and Under-Secretary Peter Tarnoff went to canvass British, French and German leaders on a US proposal to exchange Gorazde for land around Sarajevo, widen the Brcko corridor, and offer the Serbs the option of confederation with Serbia and the Federation government a "mini Marshall Plan" to rebuild the remains of their country.

On 11 August, Clinton vetoed the move to lift the arms embargo; Senators Bob Dole and Jesse Helms had just tabled a bill to give $100 million in military aid to the Bosnian government. Two days later, Izetbegovic said there could be no exchange of Gorazde. While battles between ABH and RSA troops continued in central Bosnia, Croat forces advanced in the north-west towards Banja Luka and in the south-west towards Trebinje.[64] The international community stepped up pressure on the Bosnian Serbs to comply with the new peace proposals: on 18 August, the UN said it was withdrawing peacekeepers from Gorazde and the enclave would be protected by air power instead, and on 22 August, the US threatened the Serbs with air strikes unless they "made quick and significant progress" on the peace plan. On 28 August, just as the last of the peacekeepers were replaced by the Rapid Reaction Force in Sarajevo, the Serbs shelled the Sarajevo marketplace, killing thirty-seven and wounding eighty. At two a.m. on 30 August, NATO responded with massive air strikes on Serb military targets around Sarajevo, Srebrenica and Gorazde. After two days of air strikes, the SDS appointed President Milosevic to represent the Bosnian Serbs at peace talks. Air strikes were suspended pending a NATO ultimatum to the RSA to comply with the weapons exclusion zone around Sarajevo and halt all attacks on Tuzla, Bihac and Gorazde by 11 p.m. on 5 September. When the deadline expired without RSA response, NATO embarked on a sweeping attack, targeting fifty military sites. The air strikes continued, with interruptions due to bad weather, until 14 September, when the RSA finally pulled back its heavy weapons. By this point, Bosnian Serb missile defence and communications systems had been destroyed.[65]

Bosnian government and Croat forces now began a joint offensive in western Bosnia. Within a few days, they had captured hundreds of square miles between Bihac and the rest of the federation. On 25 September, the foreign ministers of Bosnia, Croatia and the rump Yugoslavia

arrived at a broad agreement in New York on a constitutional framework for a Bosnian confederation, but in Paris President Tudjman
commented, "the problem of how Muslims and Croats will live together
remains open", and referred ominously to growing Islamic fundamentalist tendencies. Within the Bosnian government, there was a growing
rift between Prime Minister Silajdic and President Izetbegovic and Foreign Minister Sacirbey. Silajdic believed that the government should
hold out for a strong multi-ethnic presidency and accused Izetbegovic
and Sacirbey of putting a unified Muslim state above a united Bosnia.

Despite a broad agreement having been reached there was no cease-
fire. Sarajevo, Gorazde and Brcko remained unresolved issues and the
Bosnian government wanted the option of force should the agreement
fall through, as so many had done before. The tensions between Croat
and government forces were also heightened: while the ratio of Federation to Serb controlled territories now pretty well tallied with the 51:49
per cent proposed by the Contact Group, Croat forces controlled some
21.8 per cent of the territory and the Bosnian government held 29 per
cent. A small battle between ABH and Croat forces took place near
Bosanski Petrovac but did not spread; the conflict continued to be chiefly
between ABH and RSA forces, supported by Arkan's Tigers, who had
reappeared in western Bosnia after the fall of Srebrenica.[66]

In early October, the Bosnian government launched an offensive to
open roads out of Sarajevo, which was aided by a NATO bombing of
three RSA surface-to-air missiles which had locked-on to NATO aircraft. On 4 October, the Bosnian government said it would cease fire if
gas and water were restored in Sarajevo by 10 October, and fighting
escalated in west and central Bosnia in anticipation. On 7 October, Federation forces moved towards Doboj, threatening the Brcko-Posavina
corridor, and the RSA shelled refugee camps in Tuzla in retaliation,
inviting NATO air attacks. By this point, much of the fighting was concentrated on important road and rail links between Bihac and Sarajevo,
and between Tuzla and Zagreb, which were largely won by the ABH
and Croat forces. Under intense international pressure, the fighting
waned, and tentative agreements were reached on the reunification of
Sarajevo, a road connection between Sarajevo and Gorazde, and that

Brcko would be placed under international arbitration. Bosnia would comprise two "entities", the Muslim-Croat Federation and the Republika Srpska, each with their own parliaments, armies, police forces and law courts. The stage appeared to be set for partition, but a partition which would be established under international supervision rather than as a result of the divide and rule war fought with Milosevic and Tudjman's support.

The precedent for an internationally supervised ethnic division of Bosnia had already been established by the Federation agreement, which designated a range of European institutions to create a new, ethnically configured administration and executive, and gave UNPROFOR the task of overseeing the military transition to peace (which included integrating the ABH and the HVO). The International Court for Justice in The Hague was to set up the Federation's Constitutional Court and the Council of Europe was to set up its Human Rights' Court; both courts would include a number of foreigners as judges (three out of the nine judges of the Constitutional Court and four of the seven judges of the Human Rights Court would be foreigners). Elections would be jointly monitored by the UN and the CSCE; additionally, the CSCE was to appoint and supervise Human Rights' Ombudsmen.

The allocation of positions by ethnicity, which was to determine both governing and implementing bodies from the Constituent Assembly to the municipal councils and police, also applied to the internationally constituted bodies. The Constitutional and Human Rights' Courts were to have an equal number of Bosniak and Croat judges; the CSCE was to appoint three ombudsmen, a Bosniak, a Croat and an "Other". In effect, this meant that ethnic rights would have primacy over individual human rights; paradoxically, an individual seeking redress would be encouraged to go to his or her ethnic representative. A crucial strand of Milosevic and Tudjman's divide and rule policies, the establishment of ethnic territories and constituencies, would thus be given an institutional frame by the international community. But this would also require the renunciation of divide and rule by Milosevic and Tudjman for the interim; as Tudjman saw it, his agreement to the Federation was a renunciation of divide and rule for only as long as it might take to dim the awareness that partition was the fulfilment of Croat and Serb war aims. With the events of August 1995, Milosevic had completed his own renunciation of divide and rule. It was now left to the international community to complete the shift from divide and rule to divide and quit: a peacetime stabilization of the ethnic partition of Bosnia.

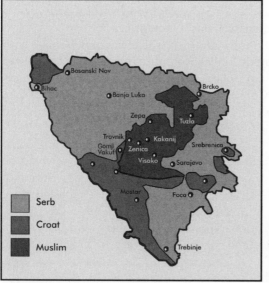

Fig. 3.1 *The front lines in July 1993*
Source: Geography Department, George Mason University, Virginia.

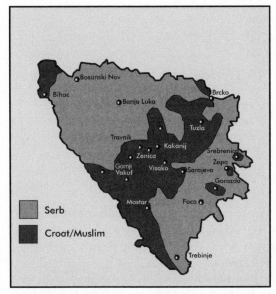

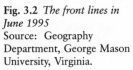

Fig. 3.2 *The front lines in June 1995*
Source: Geography Department, George Mason University, Virginia.

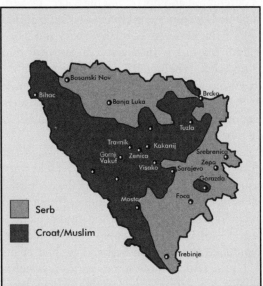

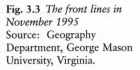

Fig. 3.3 *The front lines in November 1995*
Source: Geography Department, George Mason University, Virginia.

4

. . . To Divide and Fall?

The November 1995 tripartite talks at Dayton took place just after the fiftieth anniversary of the United Nations, at a time when peace seemed at last to be knocking at the door, but it was not clear what kind of peace would be let in. The proposed negotiations had changed into "proximity talks" even before they had begun; preceding weeks had seen evidence of gross UN dereliction and horrifying massacres by Serb forces at Srebrenica, accompanied by continuing ethnic cleansing around Sanski Most and intense jockeying between Bosnian Croats and Muslims to ethnically repopulate regions with a view to political and territorial control. It was not clear whether the Dayton negotiations would halt the process of ethnic apartheid and eventual partition. It was also not clear whether the US led peace plan would be a vital interlude in continued war, a rationalization of partition, or the foundation for Bosnians to take peace into their own hands.

The Dayton talks took some three weeks to conclude. Though the agreements were a rehash of plans which had been on the table since the days of Vance and Owen, and what was eventually signed was drafted by US and UN lawyers well before the talks began, familiar grooves had to be trod before Tudjman could agree to his part of the quid pro quo – getting the Federation started – or Izetbegovic could concede defeat. Milosevic had already abandoned the Bosnian Serbs as he had abandoned the Croatian Serbs, but he had to show some domestic benefits to subdue the rising nationalist opposition within Serbia. After over a week, the talks were still stuck on the functioning of the Federation and on the timetable for lifting the sanctions. On 10 November, a series of new Federation agreements were reached, of which the most significant were to dissolve the institutions of Herceg-Bosna and to locate four federation ministries in Mostar. The four ministries were commerce; traffic and communications; energy and industry; and education, science and culture.[1] Mostar would be the seat of economic power; so Croatia would move a step further towards the colonization of Bosnia which was implied by the Washington Agreement. The agreements also included an annex on the reintegration of the city, that internal customs checkpoints between government and Croatian held territories would be dismantled within a month, and that the ABH and HVO armies would be integrated with US assistance. The task was infinitely complicated by Herzegovinian penetration into Croatia's power structures during the war, at both political and economic levels. Croatia's defence minister, Gojko Susak, was Herzegovinian; the Herceg-Bosna mafia had profited from the sealing of the Krajina border during the war to move into the temporarily crippled Adriatic tourist industry.

In fact, the story of the Herzegovinian mafia illuminates the way in which the process of ethnic war in former Yugoslavia was successively misread by its domestic nationalists as well as the international mediators. The sealing-off of the Krajina, first by the Croat-Serb war and then by the UN peacekeepers, had closed important routes to the coast through Croatia and crippled the tourist industry. This allowed Herzegovinian war profiteers, whose routes to the coast from Bosnia were under HDZ control and thus wide open, to step in. However, the successful Croatian conquest of the Krajina in the summer and autumn of 1995 reopened Croatian routes to the coast and was beginning to bring Croats seeking to revive their tourist industry into conflict with Herzegovinians. Tudjman's support began to split between "Croatia for the Croatians" nationalists and predominantly Herzegovinian supporters of Greater Croatia. In this sense, the more Tudjman supported a second partition (of the Federation), the more his base shifted east and towards consolidating a kind of cross-border control of parts of Croatia by the diasporic Herzegovinian Croats. But the more reliant he became on Herzegovinian support, the more he lost nationalist support within Croatia, and in the municipal elections in Zagreb following the summer offensive, Tudjman lost control of the city to a liberal opposition coalition.[2] The growing internal Croat opposition to Tudjman's "Bosnia policy" offered an important new space to the international community – for example, there would have been considerable support within Croatia for sealing the borders with Herzegovina – but the use of this space would have also thrown the onus on to the international community: if the borders were sealed, both the EU administration and the US would have had to deal directly with the Herzegovinian mafia.

Both the International Tribunal and the Bosnian government were, meanwhile, fighting a losing battle to put the issue of war crimes on the Dayton agenda. On 9 November, when three Serb officers were indicted for the Vukovar killings in 1991, sanctions against oil and gas supplies to Serbia began to be lifted. On 12 November, the Serb authorities in East Slavonia agreed to a one-year UN force to oversee the gradual reintegration of East Slavonia into Croatia, whose tenure could be extended by another year. The agreement was interpreted as a sign of Serb-Croat *rapprochement* which would further cut into the Bosnian government's bargaining space, one consequence of which was that the derision with which the Croats had treated much of the negotiations over the past four years grew increasingly open. On 14 November, the day after the Tribunal indicted six Bosnian Croats for war crimes, including the HDZ chair Dario Kordic and the HVO commander General Blaskic, Tudjman gave Blaskic the job of Inspector-General of the Croatian army. Coming three days after the new Federation agreements were signed, the gesture pointed to the cynicism with which he viewed international agreements. As with previous talks, each party was jockeying fiercely on the ground, not only to improve their prospects in the talks but simply to establish the advantages which the plans offered so that they could not be reneged on.

One of the more ironic moments at Dayton was when the Serbs discovered that their concessions on Sarajevo and Gorazde had whittled the territory under their control from 49 per cent to 45 per cent of Bosnia. Hasty and furious negotiations yielded an agreement that the missing 4 per cent would be made up of land in western Bosnia, around Sanski Most, which was chiefly land held by Bosnian Croat forces. In their turn, the Bosnian Croats hit the roof when they were informed they would have to cede land to the Bosnian Serbs, demanding that a larger proportion should be ceded from Bosnian government control-led territories.[3] While the Bosnians and Croats squabbled over who should cede which villages, the UNHCR reported that ten thousand refugees were forcibly moved to Sanski Most, and the JNA began to repair the Bosnian Serb lines of communication which had been de-stroyed during the NATO air strikes (fearing that once the Dayton Agreement was signed the Bosnian government would effectively pre-vent them from doing so, and Serb controlled territories in west and east Bosnia would be cut off from each other).[4]

Within the talks, dispute now centred on three points: the Serb claim on Sarajevo, the width of the Brcko corridor and the length of the Sarajevo-Gorazde corridor. To some extent, all three had been agreed earlier: Sarajevo was to be reintegrated under the Bosnian government, negotiations over the width of the Brcko corridor were to be put on hold while the region was put under international arbitration, and the length of the Sarajevo-Gorazde corridor was to be sixty miles. The volatil-ity of the latter two agreements, however, was one reason why the talks were prolonged: for the Bosnians, military weakness meant continuing vulnerability, especially for Gorazde and Tuzla, and the Bosnian gov-ernment tried desperately in these last days to wrest a guarantee that their army would be trained and equipped by the US despite European opposition; for the Bosnian Serbs, both agreements left the viability of the Republika Srpska (RS) up in the air. Additionally, they feared that the loss of the Sarajevo suburbs would mean that the seat of government would move to Banja Luka, the only city of Republika Srpska where the Pale leadership had been periodically challenged throughout the war. In exasperation, the US said that if agreements were not reached within a day, the talks would be wound up; on 21 November, the peace agree-ment was signed by all except the Bosnian Serbs.[5] The next day, the UN lifted the arms embargo, which had chiefly affected the Bosnian gov-ernment, and suspended trade sanctions against the rump Yugoslavia.

Within the US, pressure to arm and train the Bosnian army, always strong, mounted further. The Bosnian quid pro quo for accepting partition, the argument went, should be a strong and deterrent force with aid supplied not by Iran but by Pakistan and Poland (which was to be the conduit through which ex-Soviet arms would be transferred to Bosnia).[6]

The text of the agreement which was finally signed on 21 November was an uneasy mix of compromises, reflecting the fact that the agreement was, in any case, temporary. After two years of federation with Bosnia-Herzegovina, Republika Srpska would have the right to review the secession option. Unsurprisingly, the majority of the agreement's clauses favoured the partition process. Under the new constitution signed at Dayton, Bosnia-Herzegovina was to retain a legal continuity but it was going to be a state without a president or prime minister – or, indeed, a defined structure.[7] Instead, there would be a three-member presidency comprising a Bosniak, a Croat and a Serb, who would nominate a chair. The joint presidency and council of ministers would be responsible for framing foreign, trade, customs and monetary policies, but not economic policy. Instead, there was a promise that within six months, the Federation and the Republika Srpska would begin negotiations on common energy policy and use, and co-operative economic projects.

Each entity would have the right to enter into parallel relationships with neighbouring states, and to make agreements with them and with international organizations. Most alarmingly, there was no provision for national defence.[8] The two entities would have separate armies. The only attempt at a common defence system was the promise to establish a Joint Military Commission. Though the Organization for Security and Co-operation in Europe (OSCE) was to head initiatives to preclude the renewal of war through arms control and a military balance, these were to be created not only at the regional level but also between the entities. The proportionate allocation of arms and troops discussed in the agreement (5 Federal Republic of Yugoslavia: 2 Croatia: 2 Bosnia-Herzegovina; within Bosnia-Herzegovina, 2 Federation of Bosnia-Herzegovina: 1 Republika Srpska)[9] could leave Bosnia-

Herzegovina in a fairly weak position. If, for example, the Federation allocation was divided between the HVO and the Bosnian army, and the HVO and RSA forces joined their respective national armies (the Croatian Army and the JNA), the proportions would shoot to 5.6 Federal Republic of Yugoslavia: 2.6 Croatia: 0.6 Bosnia-Herzegovina. The absence of any explicit discussion on building a unified army across Bosnian territory, moreover, also weakened incentives for the Bosnian Croat forces to merge with the ABH.[10]

Though there was a marked tilt towards partition in the Dayton Agreement, it also contained significant options for reintegration. The most important of these was a commitment to the return of refugees, for which a separate commission was set up under the UNHCR. However, the Agreement indicated that the international community had few hopes of this provision taking hold; instead, they laid greater weight on the provisions for a common economic space. Bosnia-Herzegovina was to have one central bank; as noted above, there was also a paper commitment to negotiate co-operative economic projects: theoretically, even if the Pale government disapproved, local authorities could point to the commitment as sanctioning cross-border economic activities. The drawback was that neither the West nor the Islamic countries were willing to come up with the kind of money which would be needed for economic activity to dissolve the lines of partition. Even the minimum required for basic infrastructural repairs and reconstruction which the World Bank had determined was $4 billion had so far only raised pledges of some $1.5 billion. In the absence of a speedy injection of reconstruction aid, the lines of partition were likely to harden in such a way as to make recovery much more difficult, and indeed the first events following the peace agreement were to show that the process of ethnic divide was taking a further turn.

Like the announcement of Indian and Pakistani independence, the Dayton Peace Agreement was marked by conflagration. The reunification of Sarajevo, to which President Milosevic had agreed without consulting the Bosnian Serbs, was an especially sore point. The Bosnian Serb delegation, on hearing of the agreement, protested to US General Clark. "The red line is Milosevic's," General Clark patiently explained. "You can't change it. It's agreed." "It may be Milosevic's line," one of the Bosnian Serbs said, "but it's our road."[11] Despite these intimations of trouble, NATO policy appears to have followed General Clark's advice to the Bosnian Serbs: "it's best to let it alone for now and allow this to sort itself out."[12] On 27 November, when the five Sarajevo suburbs under Serb control began to seethe over the transfer of authority to the Bosnian government, IFOR announced that it would not help with the return of refugees. A large number of the Serbs living in the suburbs were themselves refugees from other parts of Bosnia; according to one resident of Ilidza, "everybody has a hand grenade in his pocket. Remember Somalia? We too will drag the bodies of dead soldiers through the streets."[13]

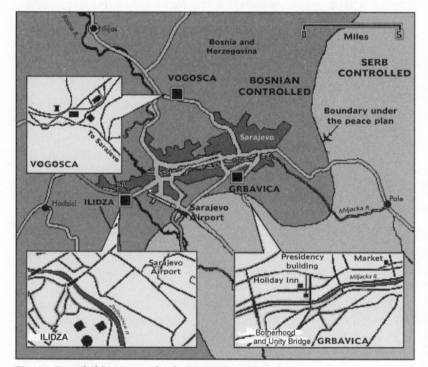

Fig. 4.1 *Reunified Sarajevo under the Dayton Peace Agreement*
Source: New York Times (http://www.newslink.org/nyt).

Under the Dayton Agreement, the transfer of the suburbs was to take place within one and a half months of the IFOR take-over of peace keeping in Bosnia, during which time Republika Srpska would be responsible for withdrawing troops and weapons and demilitarizing the area. The transfer of the suburbs to the Federation government was to be phased over three months; Federation police would not enter the suburbs until the last phase. In the interim, IFOR would "have the right to provide the military security for these transferred areas".[14] The provision was immediately controversial.

The French units, under whose jurisdiction the suburbs of Grbavica, Ilidza, Hadzici, Vogosca and Ilijas fell, began to voice their disquiet at having to patrol the areas, for fear that the sixty thousand Serbs who lived there would revolt and the troops would be drawn in to quell civil unrest. Analysts even predicted a "West Bank scenario" of prolonged conflict over the transfer of the suburbs,[15] and French President Chirac wrote to President Clinton arguing that the articles on Sarajevo's reunification should be amended with additional guarantees for the Serbs living there.[16] The Bosnian Serb leader Nikola Koljevic had already suggested a UN Protected Areas formula for the suburbs, that they should be under international authority for a transitional period.[17] Nevertheless, as unrest mounted in the suburbs over the next three days, NATO was chiefly preoccupied by a wrangle between the US and the Europeans, led by the French, over lifting the arms embargo and the UN role in implementing Dayton. The French demanded that the peace implementation mission should be headed by a civilian, preferably Carl Bildt as the UN appointee; the US resisted any moves to put NATO troops under UN authority.

On 30 November, while Ilidza demonstrated against the agreement to reunify Sarajevo, NATO announced a compromise: the arms embargo would be maintained for six months while arms control talks began under the aegis of the OSCE, after which the international community would work towards creating a balance of forces in the region, using third countries as conduits for arms transfers.[18] The announcement proved premature: under a volley of criticism from both Republican and Democrat senators, led by Bob Dole and John McCain, the US pushed for and won an agreement that the embargo would be kept in place for three instead of six months, but there would be a six-month ban on the sale of heavy weapons. Meanwhile, the US would put together an international consortium of Islamic countries and the US, which would pay for private contractors to train the Bosnian army and for weapons bought from East European countries.

Though news of the presence of Islamic militants in Bosnia had trickled out from time to time since 1994, suddenly there was a flood of articles on *mujaheddin* concentrations in and around Zenica, which were prompted at least in part by the US announcement. In fact, an agreement on the withdrawal of foreign forces had been high on the Dayton agenda.[19] Though the number of militants was not particularly high, their concentration in central Bosnia made the area a flash point. According to the Turkish battalion commander in Zenica, Colonel Ahmet Berberoglu, there were 1,500 to 2,000 *mujaheddin* in the Zenica region, mainly Libyans, Iranians and Algerians who had fought in Afghanistan; many had turned mercenary as the Afghan war dwindled into an internecine battle.[20] One of the ten Islamic charities in Zenica, moreover, was an Egyptian foundation which was banned in Egypt and whose forty employees in Zenica were all wanted for terrorist activities in Egypt.[21] In a small way Bosnia was becoming a haven for terrorists, but the problem of Islamic militants was minor in comparison with the nexus of war profiteers, mercenaries, small arms dealers, and drug and currency mafia which Mostar was riven by, as subsequent reports showed. In fact, the issue of Islamic militants was seized upon by Bosnian Croat nationalists to argue that they could not participate in a government dominated by people "who were no better than Turkish occupiers".[22] In part, the seemingly disproportionate attention paid to the issue was guided also by Western domestic concerns: in late January, for example, US troops in central and north-western Bosnia (a sector including Zenica) tightened security after they received US military intelligence that Islamic militants were planning attacks on them in Bosnia in retaliation for the conviction of Sheikh Omar Abdel Rehman for the World Trade Centre bombing.[23] A week later, the US government was asked uncomfortable questions on their failure to share information on Saudi

Arabia's violation of the international arms embargo by smuggling $300 million worth of weapons to the ABH; to which they replied by citing an October 1994 Congressional ban on sharing intelligence which could be used to interdict arms shipments to the Bosnian government.[24]

Meanwhile, irritated by the French troop commander Jean-Rene Bachelet's comments that Sarajevo would prove non-unifiable without better guarantees for the Serbs, the Bosnian government told the US that they did not trust the French troops to oversee the transfer of authority. Bachelet was recalled, but primarily for having added injudicious remarks about French failures to uphold Gaullist principles, and US imperatives for a pre-election foreign policy success.[25] In Pale, Bosnian Serb leader Momcilo Krajisnik asked NATO commander Admiral Leighton Smith to extend the deadline for the transfer of the Sarajevo suburbs to nine months; the Bosnian government added that they too felt the need to move slowly so as to soothe Serb fears. But in the suburbs, Serbs asked UN officials if they could be given twenty thousand coffins so that they could exhume their dead and take the coffins with them as they left; and after having initially promised to consider extending the deadline for the transfer of the suburbs, Admiral Leighton Smith said he did not have the authority to do so.[26]

Tensions continued to mount: at the absurdly named Bridge of Brotherhood and Unity, opened between government and Serb controlled parts of Sarajevo in the summer of 1994, a Serb checkpoint stepped up harassment of Muslims trying to cross; troops from both the ABH and RSA began to filter back to a critical battlefront in the vicinity of the Jewish cemetery in Sarajevo.[27] By the end of January, Serb snipers had begun firing at IFOR vehicles in Ilidza. IFOR's own attempts to encourage freedom of movement by dismantling checkpoints provided greater freedom of access for crime than for citizens. Travellers along the newly opened roads through Ilidza and Hadzici, where IFOR had dismantled Bosnian Serb checkpoints, started to be abducted by armed gangs, but NATO said IFOR could not provide them with protective convoys.[28] In fact, NATO had prepared a detailed military plan not only to implement freedom of movement but also to provide for the return of refugees as long ago as the Vance-Owen Peace Plan, but once they undertook

IFOR, their main attempt became to limit the mission rather than fulfil its wider mandate.[29]

The problem of lawlessness was compounded by the absence of the international civilian police force, which the Dayton Agreement had stipulated but for which no budget had been drawn up, no funds were available and no plans had been made. In December, the Pentagon voiced concern that though NATO had a thousand-page military plan for the separation of forces and gradual disarmament of the region, no corresponding plan had been developed for the civilian tasks of implementing the agreement;[30] in January, it was reported that US-French bickering had even held up appointments to the civilian mission. The French wanted at least one of the top appointments to go to a Frenchman instead of an American; the US was blocking Bildt's appointment as the UN's head of peace implementation, but was not prepared to induct him on to the NATO Peace Implementation Council either.

Meanwhile, the UN was having great difficulty assembling an International Police Task Force (IPTF) because most countries did not keep reserve police forces (unlike armed forces), and so could not contribute policemen for more than a few weeks at a time.[31] The lack of manpower and funds for the IPTF mission, many UN officials felt, was a sign that the implementation of this aspect of the Dayton Agreement had low priority for the Western governments. In early February, the deadline for the transfer of the suburbs was extended by a month and a half, to provide time for the IPTF to be mustered. Its first task would be to create a mixed Serb-Muslim police force for the suburbs. Until then, the Bosnian Serb police would remain in them. The arrangement was problematic, given the police were armed; according to the Bosnian government, moreover, the Republika Srpska government was putting soldiers into police uniforms. UN reports added that the number of police officers in the suburbs had increased and that many of the original policemen had been replaced with "new and unfamiliar faces". Led by the police, Bosnian Serbs had begun a lock, stock and barrel removal of factories and machinery from the suburbs to the Serb entity.[32]

On 6 February, the Bosnian police arrested six Bosnian Serbs, including two top RSA commanders, whose car had inadvertently strayed on to government territory *en route* to an IFOR meeting. The Bosnian Serbs suspended relations with the Bosnian government, who had offered to turn the arrestees over to the war crimes tribunal, and threatened retaliatory arrests of Muslims and Croats travelling through the suburbs. The mayor of Ilidza, who had co-operated with IFOR, was denounced as a traitor to the SDS. On 9 February, he warned that Pale was planning to stage a crisis by orchestrating the mass flight of the sixty thousand residents from the suburbs in order to drum up pressure to renegotiate the agreement to reunify Sarajevo. In west Mostar, Croat gangs attacked the offices of the EU administrator, Hans Koschnik, and the HDZ municipal council withdrew from the agreement to reunify Mostar. Koschnik himself was given an unpleasant half-hour when the gangs surrounded his car and rocked it.[33]

The issue of the two RSA commanders whom the Bosnian government had arrested, General Djukic and Colonel Krsmanovic, had become so tense that when the Tribunal requested their extradition to the Hague on 10 February, the US dipatched Richard Holbrooke to Sarajevo and Belgrade to negotiate how the request could be fulfilled. Two days later, NATO announced that though they had ferried the two RSA commanders to the Hague, IFOR troops could not themselves arrest accused war criminals because they had not been adequately briefed on who they were. Reportedly, Radovan Karadzic had passed unquestioned through IFOR checkpoints on a trip to Banja Luka. The announcement implied that IFOR was going to take similarly self-protective stances as UNPROFOR had done in the past, with a wider mandate and a much stronger troop presence; it was revealing enough to provoke US Assistant Secretary of State for Human Rights, John Shattuck, to say that NATO commanders had been given records on all fifty-two of the men indicted by the tribunal.[34]

The debate over IFOR's duties continued while conditions worsened across Bosnia. Though the Croat and Bosnian governments had agreed with NATO that foreign forces, including Croatian army troops and Islamic militants, would withdraw from Bosnia in December,[35] on 16 February French troops arrested eleven *mujaheddin*, five of whom were Iranian, and on 17 February, IFOR raided a chalet twenty kilometres from Sarajevo which they said was being used as a terrorist training centre by Islamic militants. The chalet belonged to the Ministry of the Interior and had been used as a training centre by the Yugoslav government. On the same day, senior EU diplomats confirmed reports that Croatian army troops were still in Bosnia, having exchanged their Croatian army insignia for Bosnian Croat insignia. And the Bosnian government reiterated their plea for the return of Croatian Serb refugees or their resettlement outside Bosnia, on the grounds that they were joining the RSA. As rumours that Milosevic might sacrifice Karadzic and Mladic to the tribunal gained ground, RSA commanders launched a boycott of arms control talks. RSA-NATO relations were at such a low point that IFOR gained access to Bosnian Serb arms depots in eastern Bosnia only after threatening air strikes. Two days of talks in Rome, during 17 and 18 February, yielded only an agreement between Presidents Tudjman and Izetbegovic to reunify Mostar, and a joint appeal by Presidents Milosevic and Izetbegovic to Bosnian Serbs to stay in the suburbs.[36]

Most of the Serbs in the suburbs had by now prepared to leave: valuables, including furniture and china, had been sent to relatives outside Bosnia, and they themselves were chiefly awaiting the statement on transfer of authority. On 19 February, when the UN announced that the Federation police would begin to move into the suburbs from 23 February, the Bosnian Serb parliament began a media campaign to induce Serbs to leave the suburbs before the transfer of authority began. The process was to be phased: first Vogosca would pass into the Federation, then, at intervals of six to seven days, Ilijas, Hadzici, Ilidza and Trnovo, and finally Grbavica, Novo Sarajevo and Stari Grad. The transfer was to be completed by 19 March, by when there should be a total of 545 Bosnian policemen in the suburbs under the supervision of 300 international police monitors. The Bosnian Serb police in the suburbs were offered the option of joining the federation police but refused.

In Vogosca, the announcement of the imminent arrival of the Federation police sent residents into a panic: there was a stampede for buses, but UNHCR refused requests to evacuate and said the SDS leaders were bent on creating a fear psychosis amongst the Serbs in the suburbs. Pale radio had begun daily broadcasts urging the Serbs to flee and suggesting they try a scorched-earth policy. On the day the Federation police were to take over in Vogosca, television cameras showed a stream of refugees trudging out of the suburb, leaving burning buildings and streets behind them. By the time the Federation police entered Vogosca, the majority of its ten thousand residents had left. Reports of harassment by both Federation and Bosnian Serb gangs began to be made: the mixed Federation police comprised forty-seven Muslims, thirty Serbs and eight Croats, and there were not enough IPTF monitors to accompany them on every patrol. Meanwhile, the first joint Croat-Muslim police patrol in Mostar was delayed by several hours because the Croat officers failed to turn up and were only persuaded to do so after several hours of frantic negotiation by Koschnik.[37]

As the date for the transfer of Ilijas and Hadzici neared, the same stampede for buses began in Ilijas as had taken place in Vogosca. This time IFOR decided to accept the RSA offer to send trucks to evacuate the Ilijas Serbs. In Ilidza, Bosnian Serbs began digging up the graves of their relatives. In Hadzici, a band of twelve Croats wearing hand-stitched Federation police insignia occupied the police station on the day of the transfer of authority, 6 March, ostensibly to protest the composition of the police force (fifty Muslims, fifteen Serbs and five Croats). They were suspected of having come from west Mostar, and could have been the Croatian army troops wearing federation insignia who had been reported earlier.[38] By 10 March, Ilidza and Grbavica were on fire. The Serb gangs who torched the buildings also organized the flight of residents, threatening those who didn't wish to leave. Local Serb officials warned IPTF monitors that over two hundred buildings were to be burnt in the forty-eight hours leading up to the handover of Ilidza; though French firefighters were sent to swell the contingent of Federation firefighters in the two suburbs, they proved ineffective. In the days following the handover of Ilidza on 12 March, armed Muslim gangs replaced the Bosnian Serb gangs, looting and threatening the three thousand, mostly elderly, Serbs who had remained.

The denouement was at its most graphic in Grbavica: the day before it was to be transferred, gangs armed with gasoline cans dodged IFOR troops in smoke-filled streets. But the division of authority between

IFOR and the IPTF, which allowed IFOR to restrict its mandate while the IPTF lacked the resources and manpower to fulfil its own, meant that even when IFOR troops did try to stop the arson their instructions were to hand the arsonists over to the local police to be dealt with – many of whom were among the arsonists. When Italian troops arrested one gang whom they suspected of four separate arson attacks and took them to the local police station, still in the hands of the Bosnian Serb authorities, the Serb police jeered as the group was marched in and then set the gangsters free. The UNHCR warehouse was fired and it was rumoured that the safe house they had opened for the Serbs who wanted to remain in Grbavica would be fired next. Federation firefighters refused to enter Grbavica because grenades had been thrown at them two days earlier. The few Serb firefighters who were in the suburb refused to help put the fires out. On 18 March, when the Federation police entered Grbavica, so did armed Muslim gangs. Fires continued to rage and the Bosnian police were reduced to bystanders as Muslim gangs roamed Grbavica's streets, looting what they could. In a farewell speech to the Bosnian Serb police as they left Grbavica, Republika Srpska's Deputy Minister of the Interior said that though the Serbs had lost at Dayton what they had defended during the war, future generations of Serbs would reclaim it. Sarajevo, which had so proudly resisted ethnic divide during the war and occupation, was being driven to it by reunification under the peace agreement.

The significance of Sarajevo's *auto de fe* to the future of the Dayton Agreement was underlined both by international mediators and local politicians. Carl Bildt and Haris Silajdic saw the conflagration in the suburbs as testimony that a policy of partition was now being deployed by the SDA, albeit not to the same extent as the SDS and HDZ. Bildt warned that if Sarajevo's reunification failed to maintain a multi-ethnic city, then the prospects for a united Bosnia were dim; Silajdic said Bosnia was now in a situation of *de facto* disintegration.[39] (Relations between Silajdic and Izetbegovic had steadily worsened during and after the Dayton Agreement, and in early February, Silajdic had announced his intention of standing against Izetbegovic in the forthcoming elections.) Within Sarajevo, a new jockeying for power had already begun, which showed the level at which internationally brokered agreements were effective. The question was over the status of the city as defined respectively by the Washington Agreement of 1994 and the Dayton Agreement of 1995. The former had said that as capital, the city would have the status of a district; the latter placed the city within a canton of greater Sarajevo.

The conflict mirrored the tussle over Mostar when the 1994 agreement for an EU administration was signed: as long as the city held a special status, its proportionately larger Croat population could be certain of considerable power; within a larger canton with a proportionately greater Muslim population, Croats risked being outnumbered. Though the Sarajevo Croats were a minority in the city, a greater Sarajevo would make their numbers negligible. The HDZ threatened to boycott the city council if Sarajevo was declared a canton; the SDA held out for a canton. Through February and March, while Serbs fled and the suburbs burned, the city's attention was focused on a series of inconclusive talks between Presidents Izetbegovic and Tudjman on the status of Sarajevo; eventually, the SDA forced the issue by convening a cantonal assembly. The decision caused a further split in SDA ranks: Sarajevo's mayor, Tarik Kupusovic, resigned, saying "the Sarajevo canton is being established through political violence; it has pronounced a death sentence on Sarajevo as an urban environment." It seems that Muslim refugees from eastern Bosnia were being hurriedly resettled in the suburbs the Serbs fled. When it was discovered that fifteen thousand of them were refugees from Srebrenica, the bitter rumour that the Bosnian government had made a tacit agreement with Republika Srpska to exchange the suburbs for the Srebrenica enclave gained a new lease of life.[40]

Nevertheless, it was Mostar rather than Sarajevo which presaged the full gamut of dangers to the Dayton Agreement. Though the Bosnian and Croatian authorities within the Federation signed a twelve-point agreement on 18 April to reorganize the Federation government, unify the police, customs and tax collection, get the multi-ethnic cantons going, and work together in Mostar, the former lacked the power and the latter the will to take on the gangsters who ruled the city. (Indeed, the number of unimplemented agreements on Mostar's reunification which had been signed indicated that the Croats viewed agreements rather as the British viewed inquiry commissions: a useful way of indefinitely shelving action.) In May, a local policeman who arrested one of west Mostar's criminals was so badly beaten for his temerity that he had to be hospitalized; the one unit of integrated police which was all that the EU had been able to muster in its two years of administration was, by EU admission, no more than a showpiece. According to EU police officers, Mostar was becoming "the car theft capital of the world"; in the past eighteen months, they had registered over six thousand vehicles stolen in Italy and Germany, but couldn't reclaim them because the west Mostar mafia were too powerful to cross. In a familiar progression, its two leading lights had both previously worked for the Yugoslav Ministry of the Interior; they now did a roaring trade in forged passports, smuggled alcohol and cigarettes, and the flesh trade to the Netherlands and Germany. The HDZ was in cahoots with them; its newly opened military headquarters was underwritten by one of the mafia leaders, Mladen Naletilic (familiarly known as Tuta). Apparently, local HDZ leaders also levied protection money from stores.[41]

IFOR troops were now beginning to be pushed into actually impeding the return of refugees in order to prevent further violence. On 27 April, when around fifty Muslim refugees from the north-eastern village of Mahala attempted to visit the village, they were fired on by Bosnian Serbs who had been bused into the village. The next day, IFOR troops stopped two buses filled with Muslim refugees seeking to visit the nearby town of Teslic, because there were some 150 Bosnian Serbs dressed as civilians waiting there, whom NATO suspected of being armed with guns and grenades. Teslic, its former mayor Rade Pavlovic said, was being run by hardline SDS police who were helping to expel the few Muslims remaining in the town; though he had asked IFOR troops to provide protection for them, the troops were not permitted to bypass the local authorities.[42] NATO spokesmen said that the task of providing safe escorts for refugees seeking to return was supposed to be undertaken by local officials under the Dayton Agreement; but, as they confessed, even where there were local officials willing to do so, it was difficult for them to find a way around the hardliners. A meeting of local Muslim and Serb officials from the north-eastern village of Koraj, which was held under the aegis of Russian and US troops, had ended without agreement; it was only after further pressure that Serb officials had agreed to permit Muslim refugees a brief visit. After the meeting, a Muslim official had said to one of the Serb officials, "We must find a way to put our extremists, our wild dogs, on chains"; to which the Serb had ruefully replied, "I don't have enough chains to hold all my wild dogs."[43]

Despite the volatility of the situation, the international community decided to push ahead with plans for elections. In late April, the OSCE announced that an additional $53 million would be required for the elections; half of this sum would be put up by the Federation and Republika Srpska. The OSCE would allow only two categories of refugees to cast absentee ballots: refugees living outside Bosnia and displaced people in temporary accommodation. Others, who "appeared to have established permanent residence" in places other than those they were registered in during the 1991 census, would have to register and cast ballots in person. They could register to vote either in the villages they had been driven from, or in their new places of residence. The rules were intended to favour the reintegration option of the Dayton Agreement by making it easiest for Bosnians to vote in their places of pre-war residence. But the absence of any significant change in nationalist controls, especially in Republika Srpska and Herzegovina, meant that both the rules and the intention behind them were largely irrelevant.

According to UNHCR, nine out of ten applications to visit "the other side" were being rejected.[44] This meant refugees were faced with the prospect of either voting in a place which they would be unlikely to return to in the foreseeable future, and in effect wasting a vote, or electing a candidate who might represent their rights to a residence, no matter where. Effectively, this tilted the balance in favour of the nationalists. By late May, registration problems had led the OSCE to warn that they might have to postpone local elections because they had been unable to create a central register to establish who could vote where. In Republika Srpska, the Assistant Justice Minister said that the SDS would not allow independent election monitors into the region, but would form their own election commission.[45] As reports of forcible Serb voter registration in former Muslim villages began to trickle out, the Bosnian government announced that it would withdraw from the elections unless the registration rules were rewritten and Karadzic and Mladic removed from power; the OSCE responded that it was aware of the anomaly of the election rules, but the Bosnian government had agreed to them after a long debate with the SDS and it was too late to change them.

Karadzic had just won a power struggle against the Republika Srpska Prime Minister, Rajko Kasagic, whose popularity in Banja Luka and nose for the main chance had led him to challenge Pale's ascendancy. The problematic viability of Republika Srpska began to be hinted at: "the dispute threatens to split Serb controlled territory into an eastern section under Mr Karadzic in Pale and a north-western region run by a moderate faction based in Banja Luka." Kasagic was a Milosevic appointee whom the SDS had accepted prior to the Dayton talks as a possible link to the international community, but after Milosevic's jettisoning of key SDS demands at Dayton, Kasagic's usefulness was outlived and his threat came to nothing. Karadzic nominated a more hardline replacement for Kasagic; at the same time, he announced he was prepared to resign in favour of Biljana Plavsic, a hardline SDS stalwart from the days of the 1991 coalition government and currently his deputy.

The War Crimes Tribunal was by now at loggerheads with the US: on 21 May, Judge Richard Goldstone "went public" over his anger at NATO's refusal to arrest Karadzic and Mladic; the US replied that their policy was to isolate them.[46] On 2 June, at a meeting between Warren Christopher, Franjo Tudjman and Alija Izetbegovic, it was agreed that presidency and parliamentary elections would be held as scheduled even if Karadzic had not been arrested, provided that he was out of power. Reconstruction aid to Bosnian Serbs had already been made conditional on the removal of Karadzic and Mladic.[47] While Alija Izetbegovic appeared on Bosnian TV to appeal to voters to boycott the elections if these conditions were not fulfilled,[48] the US head of the OSCE civilian implementation, Robert Frowick, instructed his staff to focus on "positive developments" rather than "negative human rights violations". The instruction was in response to a leaked OSCE weekly report which said that the west Mostar police were continuing to expel Muslims. Now it was the Europeans within the OSCE who appeared to be at loggerheads with the US: its Italian head, Francesco Cotti, was reluctant to set an election date, because he feared that a nationalist dominated election would "only bolster ethnic intolerance" and could create new conflicts. Pressure to delay the elections mounted. On 12 June, Human Rights Watch warned that holding elections would solidify ethnic partition; a week later, the Pale board of the SDS nominated Radovan Karadzic to run as president, and at the end of June the SDS Congress re-elected him party president so that he would effectively continue to control Republika Srpska, including the SDS appointed police.[49]

For many refugees, the elections were beginning to pose a choice between underwriting war criminals or sealing partition. As one Muslim refugee from Doboj said in Germany, if he sent an absentee ballot to Doboj (now in Republika Srpska), he would almost certainly sanction the sending of an SDS representative to parliament; but if he voted from somewhere in the Federation, he would seal Bosnia's ethnic partition.[50] By the end of June, it was clear that the Mostar elections, which were going to be held before the all-Bosnia elections because they had been set by the 1994 agreement with the EU, were going to bear out Cotti's fears. No Muslim candidates dared to canvass in west Mostar and no Croat candidates canvassed in east Mostar. The Croat candidates who tried to campaign on a reunification platform in west Mostar were confronted by angry crowds of women and children in mourning, who had been bused in by the HDZ, and who hurled slogans of revenge at the candidates. In both west and east Mostar, local radio and television stations broadcast incendiary nationalist speeches; ironically, the Croatian Peasant Party were denied media access in Mostar, but were broadcast in Republika Srpska.[51] The reservation of municipal seats on an ethnic basis which the 1994 Washington Agreement had provided for, with sixteen seats each for Croats and Muslims and five for Serbs and "Others", said the OSCE election organizer for Mostar, meant that the OSCE was forced to accept a kind of ethnic election rigging.[52]

Predictably, this oversimplified the situation. While the HDZ curtailed opposition campaigning in west Mostar, in east Mostar the SDA entered into a coalition with the Party for Bosnia-Herzegovina, the Liberal Bosniak Organization, the Liberal Party and the Serb Civic Council. The coalition was called the Citizens' List for a United Mostar.[53] But though the imperative to cut into Croat control drove the SDA into coalition in Mostar, matters were very different in areas where partition lines were to be consolidated. Here parties challenging ethnic divide were fiercely resisted, all the more so if the challenge was seen as coming from within. In the Usora-Sanski canton in north-western Bosnia, for example, where there was fierce competition to demographically resettle towns and villages, Haris Silajdic was attacked by SDA policemen while addressing a rally at Cazin held by his Party for Bosnia-Herzegovina.[54] The mayor of the neighbouring town of Sanski Most was the Bosnian army general who had led the autumn 1995 offensives in the area, Mehmed Alagic. The paradoxical choices posed by the political imperatives flowing from the Dayton Agreement were at their most vivid in Republika Srpska, where Milosevic attempted at one and the same time to consolidate Serb resettlement, especially in the more vulnerable border areas, and to pit the Banja Luka SDS against the Pale leadership.[55]

Meanwhile, pressure continued to build on the war crimes issue. On 30 June, the G7 countries threatened to reimpose sanctions on the rump Yugoslavia if Karadzic was not removed from power, and on 5 July, the Tribunal began hearing evidence against Karadzic and Mladic. A debate began amongst US policy makers on the feasibility of a military sortie to arrest the two, but appears to have been shortlived. Instead, the G7 Summit in Lyons created an International Commission for the Missing on 7 July, to be headed by Cyrus Vance. UN war crimes investigators had already begun digging up a mass grave at Cerska, near Srebrenica, which they had identified with the aid of CIA satellite photographs. On 11 July, while Bosnian Serbs "celebrated" the fall of Srebrenica and their leaders told them to think of building an independent Serb state rather than a reintegrated Bosnia, the Tribunal issued international arrest warrants for Karadzic and Mladic, and asked that an inquiry into Milosevic's possible role in war crimes begin. The next day, Richard Holbrooke went to Belgrade to push Milosevic to depose

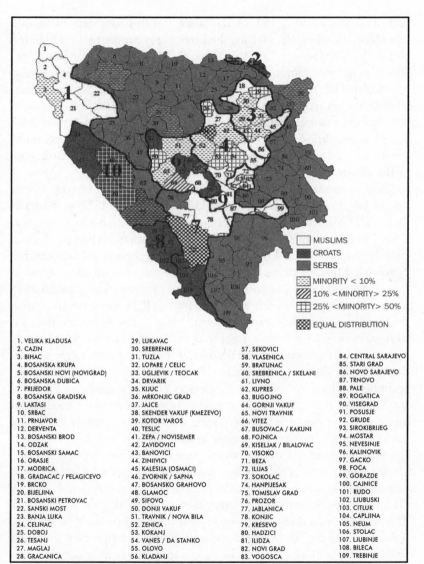

Fig. 4.2 *Bosnia-Herzegovina – ethnic distribution in 1996*
Source: Organization for Safety and Co-operation in Europe (OSCE).

Karadzic and Mladic, and the day after that Bosnian Serbs blew up a UN truck at Doboj. On 14 July, the French government said it planned to ask the UN Security Council to give NATO a wider mandate to arrest indicted war criminals, providing NATO's governing council also agreed; the US troop commander in Bosnia, General William Nash, added that his troops could effect the arrests if ordered to. The next day, Robert Frowick delayed the start of the election campaign until Karadzic and Mladic had stepped down. A party whose officers numbered indicted war criminals, he said, would not be able to participate in the elections.[56]

Tensions continued to rise in Republika Srpska and in Herceg-Bosna. On 16 July, Bosnian Serbs threatened they would take IPTF monitors in Doboj and Modrica, north of Doboj, hostage if Karadzic was arrested. Doboj was becoming as lawless as Mostar: "Bosnian Serb police lurk in pairs behind bushes and trees at the NATO checkpoint on the outskirts of town"; Muslims crossing the checkpoint were beaten and robbed as they moved out of its sight. Crime, in any case, was not considered to be the purview of IFOR troops; it was for the IPTF monitors to control the Bosnian Serb police. But there were still too few monitors, the mission was yet to be properly organized, it lacked funds to even provide monitors with telephones, and their brief was more often to try persuasion than pressure. Additionally, IPTF head Peter Fitzgerald said, training local police forces in public service was a major and gradual undertaking: they had been instruments of state control for too long to adapt easily to the idea that they were employed to protect individual human rights.[57] This problem was, in fact, a key issue which the international community had consistently shied away from because it posed an unpopular, and in many ways impossible, choice: whether to try to retrain people schooled first in authoritarian governance and then by ethnic apartheid, or to risk a potentially colonial takeover of authority and police Bosnia themselves until a new police force could be created. The choice of the former also meant that the international monitors would be little more than a pressure group: because their function was to monitor, they could not even conduct independent investigations into allegations of police misconduct, but could only be present at local police investigations which most witnesses were loath to participate in.

While international pressure for Karadzic's arrest had mounted, the Belgrade magazine *Nin* reported that support for the SDS, which had declined since the Dayton Agreement was signed, had gone up among Bosnian Serbs from 50 to 80 per cent. In Mostar, the results of elections held at the end of June returned a Muslim mayor to the united city council; the Citizens' List had won twenty-one of the thirty-seven seats (this was the total of the sixteen Bosniak and five "Other" reserved seats), and the HDZ the remaining sixteen. The results were further compounded by the fact that in the city municipal elections – in which each of the city's six municipalities elected its own 25-member municipal council – Bosniak and "Other" reserved seats outnumbered Croat seats.[58] Though over 58,000 people had voted, a discrepancy in the votes cast by absentee ballot at Bonn – there were twenty-six ballots too many – was seized upon by Croats to demand that the poll be annulled. The eviction of Muslims from west Mostar multiplied. In fact, the Croat refusal to accept the Mostar election results was guided as much by the Mostar cantonal elections as by the city elections. The threat of the Bosniak majority cantonal assembly was that with its wider regional powers, including over local police forces, it could challenge the hold of the war-created Herzegovinian mafias who were the *de facto* rulers of Mostar. But if the city council itself could be prevented from working, then the cantonal assembly would have little opportunity to act. This would suit the Herzegovinian mafia, who still needed time to consolidate their hold on the Adriatic coast and its rich tourist industry.

Returning to the country-wide elections, in mid-July Holbrooke met with Milosevic, Krajisnik and Serb security chief, Stanisic, in Belgrade to discuss Karadzic's ousting, but the talks proved inconclusive. Meanwhile, over forty-seven political parties had registered to participate in the Bosnian elections, fielding over 25,000 candidates (this included cantonal and municipal candidates). It was reported that while seven thousand Muslims in the federation had applied for a change of their voting residence, some 250,000 had applied in Republika Srpska:

local authorities there were making aid given by UNHCR conditional on registration to vote.[59] Moreover, the authorities in Serbia were refusing to supply Bosnian Serb refugees with forms to register as voters in their home towns, offering change of residence forms instead.[60]

Of the three main opposition parties to the SDS in Banja Luka, two were formed of politicians who had been on the periphery of the Pale controlled SDS: one was a newly formed Bosnian Serb branch of Milosevic's Socialist Party, fielded partly to quench Western pressure to remove Karadzic, led by a well-known pragmatist, Zivko Radisic; the

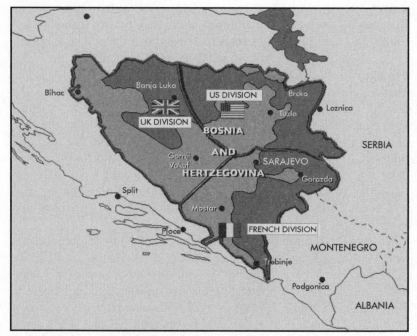

Fig. 4.3 *The Dayton Agreement and IFOR division of responsibilities*
Source: http://www.dtic.dla.mil/Bosnia.

other was a coalition of disaffected politicians, some formerly SDS, called the Democratic Patriotic Bloc, led by Banja Luka's mayor, Predrag Radic. The third and smallest opposition party, the Liberal Party led by Banja Luka's most prominent dissident, Miodrag Zivanovic, was in a broad coalition called the Alliance of Peace and Progress with the Socialist Party, the Social Democrats, the United Left and the New Labour Party. The Alliance made an already weakened SDS so nervous that it sought opposition support for a minimum programme of joint ethnic interests and support for key SDS candidates, in particular presidential candidate Momcilo Krajisnik, but the oppositions' rejection of their offer turned their attention again to intimidation.[61]

In late July, reports of ruling party harassment of opposition parties began to filter through: in Doboj, Bijeljina and Teslic, SDS activists resorted to violence to intimidate Socialist Party supporters; the moderate Bosnian Serb town of Teslic was an opposition stronghold, but its residents were kept in a state of fear by the SDS appointed city council and police, supported by a small band of Serb paramilitaries with whom the local priest, an ardent nationalist, was in cahoots.[62] In Bijeljina, which linked the road from Banja Luka to Serbia, an SDS split between Pale and Banja Luka loyalists had led one faction of the municipal council to ally itself with the Democratic Patriotic Bloc; both they and a recently formed Socialist Party branch were under threat not only from the SDS but from a number of extreme Serb nationalist parties. Arkan's Party of Serb Unity, Seselj's Serb Radical Party and a new party, called the Serb Emigrant's Party, headed by the former president of the self-styled Commission for Population Exchange, were all contesting Bijeljina. The city had been among the first to be attacked by Arkan's Tigers in the spring of 1992 and had suffered systematic ethnic cleansing since. During the war, its strategic position on the route from Serbia had led most of the Pale leadership to open enterprises there; it was also the border customs and tax post for the Bosnian Serb guest-workers in Serbia. Throughout the war, Republika Srpska's economy was propped up by taxes paid here. The SDS split had partly been the result of local resentment at the Pale leadership's war profiteering; in response, the Ministry of Internal Affairs for Republika Srpska was transferred to Bijeljina, and accompanied by roughly a thousand strongmen whose primary task was to protect businesses owned by Pale's SDS members.[63]

Both NATO and the Pentagon were by now sufficiently concerned by the rise in low-level violence to argue that the mission might have to be extended. In late July, General Patrick Hughes, the head of the US based Defence Intelligence Service, said the peacekeepers' deadline would have to be extended by another year to provide a stabilizing force for the peace to take hold. It was possible, he added, that the Europeans might be willing to stay on without US troops, but it would be unwise to treat lightly their threat to pull out when the US did.[64] The comment was an implicit reference to negotiations within NATO to develop a new formula allowing the Europeans to lead missions without US troop commitment, but using the chiefly US provided NATO equipment, intelligence and transport. The formula would present President Chirac with an argument to bring the French into NATO; domestically, he would now be able to say that NATO was *en route* to becoming the European led security force that De Gaulle had stood for. But the US was not ready to give up US command of NATO missions, and this was the issue which had originally led De Gaulle to march France out of NATO. Increasingly, the Bosnian peace-keeping mission had become the theatre of US-French debate on this aspect of NATO's transformation: either the US kept ground troops on an extended mission in Bosnia, or they conceded French demands for European command of NATO.[65]

Tensions continued to rise in the run-up to elections. In Mostar, the continued refusal of Bosnian Croats to accept the results of the municipal elections had precipitated a political crisis both within the Federation and for the Dayton process. The escalation of low-level violence since the announcement of the election results, with tit-for-tat fire-bombing of Muslim mosques and Croat churches in late July, was accompanied by the revival of a demand for partitioning Mostar and recognizing west Mostar as the ethnically pure capital of Herceg-Bosna. At the end of July, Federation Vice-President Ejup Ganic went to request Tudjman's help in pressing the Bosnian Croats to respect the new city council; he was accompanied by the US ambassador to Bosnia, John Menzies, US ambassador to Croatia, Peter Galbraith, and Carl Bildt's deputy, Ambassador

Steiner. The meeting was to press for both the city council to begin operating and for Herceg-Bosna to dissolve itself; the self-proclaimed statelet was an illegal construction, said IFOR-UN press officer Calum Murphy, and Ambassador Steiner had threatened that if the HDZ didn't begin to discipline the Herceg-Bosna mafias, then the IPTF would.[66] The EU administration had already announced that if the vote was not accepted and Herceg-Bosna was not dismantled, it would withdraw; the decision would be taken on 3 August. Tudjman, however, cut the meeting short saying he had a Croatian National Security Council meeting convened; matters were subsequently resolved only at President Clinton's intervention on 2 August, when Tudjman agreed to press the HDZ to allow the united Mostar city council to start functioning and pledged himself to see that Herceg-Bosna began to dissolve itself by the end of the month.[67]

After two years, beginning with the Washington Agreement of 1994, the promises were beginning to sound hollow, but the EU administration's choice was to either confess defeat or swallow the promise with sanguine mien, and they chose the latter. Somewhat rashly, as it turned out: the Bosnian HDZ response to Tudjman's promise of 2 August was to convene an extraordinary meeting at Neum (Bosnia's only coastal town and a critical point of Federation negotiations), which journalists compared to a Mafia gathering called to select a new godfather. The HDZ mayor of west Mostar, Mijo Brajkovic, vowed that "Croats will not submit to EU demands to unite the city . . . No power can make us change that decision."[68] US pressure, in turn, yielded increasingly open defiance; HVO General Ivan Andabak now dismissed US demands for compliance with the Dayton Agreement's provision for a phased integration of the HVO and the ABH within three years as impossible: "It won't happen in twenty years."[69]

In early August, the newly repaired bridge at Doboj, whose opening had been marked by Muslim-Serb conflict, was blown up, a half-dozen Muslim families seeking to return to the town were beaten up, and it was reported that some 1,500 Serbs from West Slavonia were being resettled in the town, while its local residents were told they would be given no more aid unless they registered to vote from Brcko.[70] At the same time, though after Republika Srpska (RS) had appointed an arbitrator to the Brcko negotiations, they boycotted the preliminary meetings of the Brcko Tribunal.[71] The speciousness of holding municipal and cantonal elections had already appeared in the decision to go ahead with elections in Brcko while the region itself was under arbitration; not surprisingly, the vote was being interpreted as a referendum on whether Brcko was to go to the Federation or to Republika Srpska.

Yet another twist in the Dayton Agreement now stood revealed: though the Brcko region was placed under international arbitration, the wording of the Agreement simply referred to "the disputed portion of the Inter-Entity Boundary Line in the Brcko area indicated on the map attached at the Appendix".[72] It now transpired that no map had ever been appended; this meant, Republika Srpska argued, that the Brcko Tribunal had no jurisdiction to proceed. In fact, it seems the Bosnian Serbs had not been shown the full Dayton map: in response to their argument the international arbitrator, Robert Owens, produced "a Dayton map showing the IEBL in the Brcko area and indicating (by footnote) that the location of the line in the Brcko area was subject to negotiation".[73] There is little doubt that the omission was deliberate: mediators must have hoped that by leaving the boundaries vague, the ticklish issue of Brcko would resolve itself by a more indirect process of demographic resettlement or even reintegration.

But – as Bosnia's peculiar telescoping of political time had a habit of ensuring – the announcement of elections put paid to this hope by focusing attention on Brcko. Ultimately, it was the debate over elections in the town which led the OSCE to postpone municipal elections. The debate centred on the status of Brcko town: according to the Bosnian government, the Dayton provisions placed the town itself under international arbitration; according to both the SDS and the majority of the Serb opposition, the town was excluded from the area under arbitration. The Dayton map itself was vague on this point: "the precise segment of the boundary line that lies within the disputed area is not explicitly defined."[74] Before the war began, under the 1991 census, the Brcko *opstina* was 44 per cent Muslim, 25 per cent Croat and 21 per cent Serb; the town itself was 56 per cent Muslim, 20 per cent Serb and only

7 per cent Croat. Now the town was majority Serb, one-third of whom had lived in the town before the war and two-thirds of whom were refugees from the Sarajevo suburbs, Jajce and the Posavina.[75] Though the current city council was SDS dominated, there was a predominantly Muslim city council in exile based in Tuzla, which had set up a co-ordinating committee to establish the Federation's legal right to Brcko soon after the Dayton Agreement in January 1996. The self-appointed mission of the committee was to counter SDS attempts to rig votes through resettlement by registering refugee voters.[76] While the pre-war Serb population of Brcko town was roughly 18,000 (out of a total population of 87,300), OSCE voter registrations showed around 51,200 Serbs had registered to vote there (31,278 of these were refugees in Serbia).[77]

Vote rigging had become so widespread that a pilot UNHCR project to implement the return of refugees, which was promised by the Dayton Agreement, was blocked by municipalities eager to register their ethnicities of choice. Conditions were so bad in the Serb dominated municipalities of Sanski Most, Prijedor and Doboj, and the Croat dominated municipalities of Drvar, Jajce and Stolac, that the UNHCR was considering recommending sanctions against them for violating the Dayton Agreement.[78] The new peace-keeping mission was beginning to find that tentative forays led them into the same dire straits as the UN mission had, with the difference that the UN employed IPTF quite often took the flak for the NATO deployed IFOR's actions. At the end of August, when IFOR troops intervened to stop Bosnian Serb policemen beating up Muslim refugees returning to Zvornik, a mob of six hundred Bosnian Serbs surrounded the local IPTF headquarters, roughing up several officers and destroying several of their vehicles.[79] Faced with a volley of reports of forced registrations, intimidation of opposition candidates and denial of media space to the opposition, on 27 August, the OSCE announced that the municipal and cantonal elections were going to be postponed.

"The real problems, the searing problems of the country," said Robert Frowick, "are centred on the municipalities." The extent of ethnic gerrymandering by the SDS, the HDZ and latterly the SDA was shown, senior EU official Jeffrey Fisher added, by the fact that fifty-five municipalities

were currently partitioned by an ethnic dividing line. But it was pre-
cisely in many of these municipalities that the announcement of the
postponement of local elections was received with most mixed feelings.
Residents suffering under the kind of regime of fear that Teslic suffered
from, for example, had hoped that the international community would
offer them the infrastructural support, including policing, which would
allow them to democratically oust from power the small gangs who
ruled them. Indeed, the postponement of municipal and cantonal elections did nothing to abate the wave of ethnopolitical consolidation:
rather, it shifted the theatre of consolidation to the presidential and
parliamentary elections.

As election campaigns got underway, it became clear that the main
Serb and Croat parties interpreted the Dayton Peace Agreement as providing a peaceful means to the end which they had fought for, and were
using the elections as a proxy war of ethnic partition. In west Mostar,
where the municipal election results were continuing to be challenged,
the threat was so intense that two opposition leaders were under the
protection of EU police and a third had abandoned his candidacy and
fled the region. But, though the new EU administrator, Sir Martin
Garrod, said "any moderate who speaks out can reasonably expect a
bullet in the back of his head", the OSCE regional election head,
Wolfgang Odendahl, said he had seen "no concrete evidence" of intimidation. It was curious, he added, that the moderate opposition parties
were so little in evidence; he would have imagined they would attract
considerable support. As another OSCE official pointed out, this was
putting a none too fine gloss on the OSCE dilemma: "The ruling parties are the government in the places they control. They provide the
election workers; they provide the local officials. If they stop co-operating, it would hamstring us in carrying out our number one mission,
which is to have elections that at least look technically correct."[80]

In a way, the geographically opposite Croat majority towns of Orasje
and Caplina best demonstrated the way divide and rule was translating
itself in the transition to peace: in the north-eastern town of Orasje,
lying between Croat controlled Slavonia and Serb controlled Brcko, the
SDA was able to campaign peacefully though the town was 90 per cent

Croat; a joint Croatian-Bosnian interest in curtailing Serb control over the Posavina corridor had kept the town united throughout the war. On the other hand, in the town of Caplina, which lay south of Mostar on the border with Croatia, from which Muslims had been expelled during the war, the SDA rally could only be held under tight security – and the SDA took the occasion as an opportunity to threaten that if necessary, they would use force to allow Muslim refugees to return.[81]

In Republika Srpska, political contest now devolved on a single issue: whether the Serb entity was going to respect the continued existence of Bosnia-Herzegovina, albeit as a loose federation, or whether it would strive to secede. The SDS was openly campaigning for an independent Serb state; already, by early August, six SDS meetings at which candidates' speeches violated the Dayton Agreement's provisions for joint institutions had been documented.[82] The diasporic Serb nationalist parties which were participating in the Bosnian elections in an alliance with the SDS were even more explicit: addressing a campaign rally of Vojislav Seselj's Serb Radical Party at the end of August, the former paramilitary commander of the "The White Tigers" turned Republika Srpska parliamentary candidate, Slavko Aleksis, said his main concern if elected would be to undermine the institutions of joint government in Bosnia;[83] a week later, addressing a rally held by his Party of Serb Unity in Bijeljina, Arkan said that the period of war for a Greater Serbia was over and, in the peace, the elections constituted the new route to partition and a unified Serb state.[84] As the joint presidential candidate of the Alliance for Peace and Progress and the Democratic Patriotic Bloc, Mladen Ivanic, pointed out, the creation of two entities under the Dayton Agreement lent credence to Arkan's interpretation and meant that moderate opposition groups had a delicate course to steer: they had to simultaneously represent the interests of their constituencies as a national or ethnic group and try to find ways to strengthen the joint institutions of Bosnia-Herzegovina.[85]

In contrast, the Bosnian interest lay in finding ways to ensure that the partition lines did not harden. For the nationalist SDA, this meant both tightening control over the areas they held and registering as many absentee voters in Republika Srpska as they could. In early September, while the SDA kicked off with a rally which opened with Muslim songs and readings from the Koran, at which the Iranian ambassador was the only foreign attendee (he travelled with President Izetbegovic), the SDA dominated municipal court in Bihac began proceedings against Fikret Abdic, who was again contesting the elections; in nearby villages, refugees from Prijedor were assisted to register as voters there.[86] The democratic opposition parties, the Party for Bosnia-Herzegovina, the Joint List of Social Democrats and the United List for Bosnia-Herzegovina, on the other hand, chose an explicitly multi-ethnic and secular platform; though they had suffered some harassment – the Party for Bosnia-Herzegovina, in particular, had had its rallies disrupted and candidates roughed up – and had less media time than the SDA had, they remained the only opposition parties who had the choice of opting for a multi-ethnic and reintegrated Bosnia. As Mladen Ivanic indicated, whatever the personal beliefs of opposition candidates in the Republika Srpska, the Dayton Agreement's recognition of the Serb entity meant that candidates had to represent Serb interests; within the Croat dominated area, as we have seen, non-nationalist opposition was effectively silenced.

The election results reflected these conditions. The nationalist parties dominated both the presidency and the House of Representatives returns. Alija Izetbegovic, Kresimir Zubak and Momcilo Krajisnik were elected to the three-man presidency; significantly however, while Zubak and Izetbegovic won 88 per cent and 80 per cent of the Croat and Muslim vote respectively, Krajisnik won only 68 per cent of the Serb vote. Mladen Ivanic, the moderate opposition candidate, had won 30 per cent. The results of the elections to the House of Representatives gave the SDA nineteen seats, the SDS nine and the HDZ seven. Between them, the opposition parties held seven seats. While the results were similar to those of the 1990 elections, where the three nationalist parties too had won over 80 per cent of the seats, the SDA won three seats from Republika Srpska, and in the intra-entity elections neither party had a two-thirds majority. In the Republika Srpska National Assembly, the SDS won fifty of the eighty-three seats; its allies, the Serb Radical Party, held another seven, but the tally still left the ruling bloc one short of the fifty-eight seats required for a two-thirds majority. The situation was further complicated by the fact that the SDA won six seats. The OSCE, who were responsible for the elections, did not know how these elected candidates would be able to attend Assembly sessions in Republika Srpska; it was not clear who would ensure their safety. In the Federation House of Representatives, the SDA's eighty seats fell far short of the ninety-three required for a two-thirds majority; unless they found common nationalist cause with the HDZ, the joint democratic opposition holding was likely to keep them on the moderate side of nationalism.[87]

By this point, the success of the Dayton Peace Agreement hinged on Mostar and Brcko. After two and a half years of administering the city, the EU had failed both to dislodge the nationalist HDZ and to dissolve the partition of Mostar. In December, the EU withdrew from Mostar; their withdrawal took place amidst renewed sniping in Mostar West. Subsequently an OSCE monitoring mission took their place, and IFOR troops were replaced by the new Stabilization Force (SFOR), which cut the number of NATO troops in Bosnia from sixty to thirty thousand, and extended the NATO mission by another eighteen months to mid-1998. In early February, when east Mostar Muslims visited a Muslim cemetery in Mostar West, they were fired upon by HDZ members; it seems local policemen were involved in the firing. One man died and over twenty others were wounded; SFOR troops did not intervene, but barricaded the bridges between the east and west. HDZ authorities then evicted another hundred Muslims from Mostar West. Ethnic cleansing, it seems, had to be total.[88]

In the same month as the EU withdrew from Mostar, the RS formally attempted to withdraw from the Brcko arbitration, accusing Owens of using the arbitration "as a smoke screen for the imposition of a pre-ordained, unjust decision, all to the harm of the legitimate and vital interests of Republika Srpska". The issue of control over Brcko, both RS and Federation representatives said, was so important that if no agreement was reached, then both would "quit Dayton and resume hostilities". Yet the case of each was based on "the mutually-exclusive demand that each Entity exercise sole control of the Brcko area", which was divided with 48 per cent of the *opstina* controlled by the RS and 52 per cent by the Federation. Only fifteen Muslim families had been able to return to the town since the Dayton Agreement; south of the town, twenty-seven newly-repaired Muslim houses had immediately been destroyed.[89]

In February, days after the Mostar West firing upon and eviction of Muslims, the Brcko arbitration announced its verdict. Brcko would be placed under interim international supervision for a year: the Office of the High Representative would appoint a Deputy High Representative for Brcko, who would supervise the implementation of the Dayton Peace Agreement's provisions for freedom of movement and the return of refugees (the former in liaison with SFOR and IPTF and the latter with UNHCR), and would "strengthen local democratic institutions" in the area. The Deputy High Representative would have authority over the courts and police, who would be required to enforce regulations or orders issued by him even if they conflicted with existing laws. Nevertheless, the current local authorities would remain in place until municipal and cantonal elections were held.

The Arbitration Award essentially put the decision on whether Republika Srpska or the Federation was to control Brcko on hold for another year, in the hope that the interim period would allow the issue to lose its edge. Clearly, Robert Owens believed this would only happen if the international community made a concerted effort to do in Brcko what it had failed to do in Mostar, or indeed, elsewhere in Bosnia: devise and speedily implement a strategy for the return of refugees, economic revitalization and freedom of commercial movement. Brcko was to have an Advisory Council composed of members of the OSCE, UNHCR, SFOR, IBRD and IMF, together with representatives of Bosnia and Herzegovina and local groups. But the Award was not signed by either entity, the representatives of the Federation and Republika Srpska having bowed out of the proceedings while the Award was being formulated.[90] Nor was it clear who was going to provide the troops to man the roads and ensure freedom of movement; and the issue of Brcko town was left open with the intriguing threat that since the Brcko Tribunal was aware "that matters in the relevant area may be so controlled as to prevent satisfactory compliance with the Dayton Accords and the development of representative local government", a later award might conclude that: "the Town of Brcko must become a special district of Bosnia and Herzegovina in which district the laws of Bosnia-Herzegovina and those promulgated by local authorities will be exclusively applicable."[91]

5

Peace Making 1992 Onwards

Like the Bosnian "peace process", new initiatives to deal with the long-standing partitions of Ireland, Cyprus and Israel-Palestine – launched in the same years as the International Conference on Former Yugoslavia – developed similar hitches, and showed that the attempt to accommodate ethnic nationalism politically and administratively would succeed only in inverse proportion to the mandate for such nationalism, paradoxical as this might sound. In other words, ethnic nationalists came closest to agreeing mechanisms for communal power sharing and representation in those regions where there was mounting public pressure against the isolation bred by partition and declining support for ethnic nationalists. As public support for settlement grew, especially in Northern Ireland, the inflammatory potential of ethnic nationalism waned; while this put pressure on ethnic nationalists to compromise, it also meant that the powers of political and administrative mechanisms were themselves gradually narrowing, and implied by extension that communal power sharing was changing from being an end in itself to an interim or transitory means of moving towards citizens' rights based democracy.

Conversely, in those regions where rising public pressure for a settlement was not matched by a narrowing of ethnonationalist scope, such as Israel-Palestine, communal power-sharing formulae either failed to be agreed or they prolonged volatility and intensified conflict. Thus, in both Northern Ireland and Israel, and to some extent in Cyprus, visible public support to move beyond the stalemated partitions or semi-partitions of previous decades had limned the space for new strategies to be deployed in the 1990s; as the ensuing summaries indicate, however, the only region in which some success could be envisaged was Northern Ireland, where the enormous popular mandate for peace, which had accumulated through the 1980s in Northern Ireland, Britain and Ireland, pushed both Britain and Ireland into renouncing Protestant and Catholic homeland claims, and left local ethnic nationalists with little option but to negotiate power-sharing agreements which could make their own political identities redundant over time – as the "framework agreements" for power sharing which were floated in 1995 indicate. Unlike the framework agreements for Cyprus, Palestine and Bosnia, whose emphasis on high-level communal power sharing either limited or ignored issues of economic development and freedom of movement, the Anglo-Irish framework documents not only eschewed national interest but distinguished between high-level and regional or local power sharing, displacing ethnic or communal criteria at the inter-governmental level and accepting them at regional and local levels in Northern Ireland. Significant as this structural distinction was in providing a potential counter to Northern Irish ethnic nationalism, the fact that the major provisions of the Framework Agreements for Northern Ireland concentrated on economic development and freedom of movement as part of a process of EU integration was more significant still.

Both regional economic development and freedom of movement were key to an emerging post-Cold War strategy on ethnic partition which had germinated during the 1980s in Ireland, Britain and Northern Ireland, Cyprus and Israel-Palestine, and to a far more minor extent in India, Bangladesh and Pakistan, and could be seen as part of the wider process of internal challenge for change which accompanied the disintegration of the Cold War. With the fall of the Berlin Wall, the new strategies coalesced into one overall strategy of "renewable peace", that a development centred approach was key to overcoming ethnic conflict and the hostilities of partition (whether in the making or long established). The argument had first been outlined in UN Secretary-General Boutros Boutros-Ghali's *Agenda for Peace* in 1992 and then elaborated in the *Agenda for Development* of 1994. Its key concept was that peace building was vital to successful peace keeping in ethnic conflicts (success being measured by the completion of a peace-keeping mission), and successful peace building depended on combining economic and social reconstruction with the separation of forces and demilitarization.[1]

Though the argument for renewable peace borrowed from the western European experience of economic integration – Spain was often cited as a case in which regional development in the course of integration into the European Community had led to a decline in Basque and Catalonian separatism – the overall strategy of underpinning a peace process by investing in regional development was formulated by the Clinton government in the US, which applied it to differing degrees in Northern Ireland, Cyprus and Israel-Palestine and – as we have seen – attempted it in Bosnia. In turn, the focus on regional development as a means to renewable peace highlighted the need for regional assumptions of responsibility: thus, for example, the US pushed the EU to invest in reconstruction in Bosnia and the Arab states to invest in developing Gaza and the West Bank.[2] The Lyon G7 summit of 1996 stressed "the importance of economic growth and prosperity to underpinning peace and. . . . the need for increased regional economic co-operation and development", as elements of a new strategy for co-operative security and stability.[3]

The emergence of the concept of renewable peace could in itself be seen as an attempt to temper the careless triumphalism of the early years of the Cold War's disintegration, before the recognition that the post-Cold War period might be characterized by the spread of ethnic wars in the East and South had fully dawned. To this extent, the emergence of the concept, with its explicit reference to the North-South development debate (through which the concepts of sustainable development and sustainable democracy had been adopted), was an attempt at a unified international approach to curbing ethnic conflict. From the beginning, the approach devolved upon the initiatives to overcome the hostile legacies of European partition policies, in particular, in Ireland, Israel-Palestine, Cyprus and Bosnia.

Between 1992 and 1996, US President Clinton and his foreign policy team stressed in speech after speech that European reunification and a commitment to pluralist values were the cornerstones of post-Cold War policy:

> our efforts enable us to give North America a deeper partnership with a new Europe without artificial dividing lines. They allow us to work together to contain ethnic conflict and, in the case of Bosnia, to restore peace. They help us maintain stability in the Aegean and work together for a comprehensive settlement on Cyprus.[4]

There were three key elements of the strategy which were new, and which marked a radical addition to the long-established peace-making formulae of high-level negotiations towards ethnic power sharing: supporting civil society both in the struggle against ethnic war and in post-war reconciliation,[5] making immediate use of a window of opportunity, such as a cease-fire or an interim agreement, to put pluralist projects for economic reconstruction and development into place; and prioritizing the role that multi-ethnic enclaves, such as cities, could play in breaking through to an overall settlement.[6]

Despite the US – and to a lesser extent the EU – espousal of the strategy as exemplifying a brave new post-Cold War commitment to renewable peace world-wide, however, the extent to which the strategy was deployed varied according to where the countries were and which ethnic and religious communities were involved. Thus, for example, the US and EU commitment, both politically and financially, to sustaining peace in Northern Ireland was much stronger than their commitments to Cyprus or Palestine; in turn, though the US had a special commitment to an Israel-Palestine peace, the extent to which they were willing or able to act in ensuring that there would be a renewable peace was severely restricted by the intimate relationship between the US and Israel, so that Israel's perceived security needs were allowed to determine the extent of freedom of movement of people, goods and services. The effect of this variation in commitment was that quite often the promise of renewable peace was made hollow by over-reliance on the old formulae of peace making – high-level talks between established ethnic representatives, irrespective of their current levels of political support, or the means by which they hold power (as in the case of Karadzic, Krajisnik and Plavsic, or for that matter, Milosevic and Tudjman) – worse,

the willingness to let windows of opportunity slip by not only undermined the concept of renewable peace, but could restore faltering support
for ethnic and communal leaders (as has happened time and time again
in Bosnia, and might happen again if the SFOR foray into arresting war
criminals is not followed up with the arrest of Karadzic, and tied to the
establishment of an impartial police force). Moreover, the terms of negotiation which the ethnic partition process had set in each country had
a grip which outlived the original conditions in which they had taken
shape, as the halting Northern Irish peace process continues to show.

Notwithstanding the enormous popular mandate for peace in Northern Ireland which had accumulated through the 1980s in Britain, Ireland
and Northern Ireland, it was only after the Berlin Wall fell that the British government explored new channels to settle the stalemated partition
of Northern Ireland. When they did, the strength of the popular mandate
meant that the renewed effort to reach a settlement of Northern Ireland's
partition began at a far more promising level than the negotiations on
Cyprus, Israel-Palestine or Bosnia did. Unofficial contact between the
IRA and the Irish Prime Minister's office to discuss the possible terms of
an IRA cease-fire had been initiated in early 1991 by a group of Catholic
priests, and as official talks between the "constitutional parties" (that is,
excluding Sinn Fein) failed yet again, more attention turned to the unofficial talks, which were themselves spurred by the success of the Labour
Party in the Irish Republic's 1992 elections. In 1993, six months of talks
between John Hume, the leader of the Social Democratic and Labour
Party (SDLP), supported by the majority of Catholic nationalists in Northern Ireland, and Gerry Adams, the leader of Sinn Fein, which commanded
some 30 per cent Catholic support, yielded a set of proposals based on
which the British and Irish Prime Ministers issued a declaration on 15
December 1993, that: the people of Northern and Southern Ireland were
entitled to self-determination, the British government had no "selfish strategic or economic interest in Northern Ireland", and the British and Irish
governments would accept Sinn Fein, and other electoral parties, as legitimate participants in all-party talks for a settlement if they made
commitments to a permanent end to terrorist activities and a commitment to "exclusively peaceful methods and . . . the democratic process".[7]

For the British, who had steadfastly refused to negotiate with Sinn Fein because of its IRA connections, the agreement was a major step forward; ironically, they had in the same period not only led international negotiations with Karadzic, Mladic and Boban in Bosnia (the IRA paled in comparison), but had also pressed the Bosnian government to do likewise.

The British-Irish *rapprochement* had begun almost a decade ago, following the 1980 and 1981 IRA hunger strikes, growing concern that Sinn Fein might supercede the SDLP in Northern Irish Catholic support, and a shift in US policy under President Carter aimed at curbing the supply of arms to Northern Ireland. In 1983, renewed talks between the British and Irish government, combined with the establishment of the New Ireland Forum in the Republic, led Irish nationalists to explore the idea of a shared sovereignty with special provisions for the Ulster Unionists, but the idea was still new and the Unionists had not been involved in the talks. In November 1984, British Prime Minister Margaret Thatcher rejected the New Ireland Forum's proposals; the move was widely protested by an influential new lobby of Irish-Americans, and under US pressure, Thatcher began to move towards an agreement with the Republic.[8] In November 1985, the Anglo-Irish Agreement was signed; under its provisions the British government agreed that Britain would establish permanent structures for consultation with the Irish government, and the Irish government accepted that the decision on whether to remain in the United Kingdom or unite with Ireland had to be made by the people of Northern Ireland as a whole.

Though US President Reagan welcomed the agreement with a grant of $50 million in aid for both parts of Ireland, Unionist opposition slowed the implementation of its provisions for several years. The years following the agreement were marked chiefly by patient efforts to negotiate Unionist acceptance of an Anglo-Irish settlement and when, in 1991, a formula was found in which all-party talks could be held, it was initially based on excluding Sinn Fein. The formula separated the negotiations into three areas: on relations within Northern Ireland, between Northern Ireland and the Republic of Ireland, and between the British and Irish states. The agreement to all-party talks was itself a major advance (in comparison, the Cyprus negotiations continued to aim at proximity talks), but the exclusion of Sinn Fein soon became a sticking point for the negotiations, until in 1993, the Hume-Adams talks opened a new space for a cease-fire and a long-term move away from violence.

The talks took place in the extraordinary atmosphere created by the release of the Opsahl Report, which was issued by an independent enquiry commission established by a new Irish civic coalition, Initiative 92, and headed by Torkel Opsahl, a long-standing member of the European Commission on Human Rights. The Opsahl commission considered some 550 submissions, and concluded that twenty years of direct rule had resulted in a democratic deficit which could only be filled by a power-sharing Northern Irish goverment in which the two communities were seen as political equals ("a parity of esteem"); it also recommended restructuring administrative institutions, in particular the police, so that "nationalists would both want and feel able to exercise their share of responsibility within a context they have historically found inimical".[9] Significantly, this recommendation was similar to the ethnic provisions of the Cypriot and Bosnian federal constitutions but had a radically different meaning in the Northern Irish context, where some seventy years of political exclusion of Catholic nationalists were being ended in a region in which national sovereignty was itself losing importance as the EU took shape. The Opsahl Report was immediately followed by a poll on its recommendations in Britain, the Irish Republic, and Northern Ireland; its most pronounced result was an overwhelming support for its recommendation of power sharing in both the Republic and amongst Catholics in Northern Ireland, which indicated that the issue of partition was beginning to lose its political potency. The immediate impact of the report was so considerable that within a month of its release the Dublin senate debated it; opening the debate, the Irish Foreign Minister, Dick Spring, said that it was the fruit of "an extraordinary experiment in public participation".[10] Civil society was beginning to rise in political importance as nationalism declined.

The Joint Declaration of December 1993 was enthusiastically received by Irish-American supporters of the Hume-Adams proposals, who stepped up campaigns to draw Sinn Fein into the peace process by arranging for Gerry Adams to visit the US. Though their first efforts were disappointed, in February 1994, President Clinton granted Adams a visa to the US; the decision angered the British and when, soon after, an IRA attack on London's Heathrow airport was followed by a Sinn Fein rejection of the Joint Declaration, it seemed as if Clinton's new approach (based on the understanding that the time was right to involve Sinn Fein in negotiations) had merely attested the view that the radical nationalists were not prepared to commit themselves to a peace process. The announcement of an IRA cease-fire on 31 August 1994, however, was partly a consequence of Clinton's move; the British stepped up pressure on the loyalist paramilitaries to follow suit, and on 13 October, the Combined Loyalist Military Command (CLMC) announced that they would join the cease-fire. The cease-fires were welcomed by Britain and the US as offering a special opportunity to apply an evolving strategy of sustaining peace with economic development, which focused on cities as key sites for ethnic or communal integration (the Sarajevo initiative of spring 1994 had been a forerunner which failed because of the continuing reliance on high-level proximity talks).

In December 1994, US President Clinton appointed former Senator George Mitchell as Special Advisor to the President and Secretary of State for Economic Initiatives in Ireland; in the same month US Secretary of Commerce Ron Brown led a delegation of US business executives to Northern Ireland to attend Prime Minister Major's Belfast Investment Conference. The strategy was vigorously pursued in Northern Ireland throughout 1995, at least partly due to US pressure. An Irish-American campaign for "a ban on all commercial transactions by the US government with firms in England and Ireland that practice discrimination in Northern Ireland on the basis of race, religion, or sex" had begun as early as 1984, and between 1985 and 1987 five US states had adopted legislation towards fair employment practices in Northern Ireland. In 1989, the British passed the Fair Employment (Northern Ireland) Act,[11] and from late 1994, when the cease-fires came into effect, the US sought to stimulate investment on fair employment principles as a way of communal integration "from below".

Meanwhile, discussions on power sharing yielded a set of framework

documents in February 1995 which elaborated the ideas of shared sovereignty aired in 1993. The Joint Framework Document, announced by
British Prime Minister John Major and Irish Prime Minister John Bruton
on 22 February in Belfast, proposed that Northern Ireland and the Republic would share an all-Ireland Council, composed of the departmental
heads of the Northern Ireland Assembly and Republican ministers. The
Council would concern itself with "matters with a natural or physical
all-Ireland framework", transport, tourism, industrial development and
the administration of cross-border EU programmes. Britain and Ireland
would establish a new formal structure, such as a standing intergovernmental conference, to implement the Anglo-Irish Agreement of 1985,
under which the two countries acknowledged a joint responsibility for
Northern Ireland; both governments additionally "pledged themselves
to the protection of the rights and identities of both traditions" (that is,
of Protestants and Catholics).[12] The Framework for Accountable Government in Northern Ireland was separately announced on the same
day by Prime Minister Major; it proposed a new, devolved Northern
Ireland Assembly comprised of departmental committees whose heads
would be appointed on the basis of ethnic/communal proportionality;
the assembly and its committees would be overseen by a triumvirate of
two Unionists and a nationalist, whose decisions would have to be con-
sensual, and who would be elected by direct vote.[13] Both framework
documents elicited an immediately hostile reaction from the major Unionist parties, and the Ulster Unionist Party issued its own framework
document calling for the election of a constituent assembly to draft a
new constitution, and said it would be prepared to negotiate with the
British government on the basis of this document. In conciliation, the
British offered that any agreed proposals would be put to referendum
in Northern Ireland.

One of the chief objections of the Unionists to the Framework
Documents was that they placed the administration of cross-border development under an all-Ireland body. The Irish Republic's economic
recovery through EU membership had been one of the causes for a
breakthrough in the Irish stalemate; as the Opsahl process had demonstrated, hopes of regional development had stimulated Northern Irish

support for moving beyond partition's hostile legacies. To this extent, the Opsahl polls showed that the strategy of sustaining peace through economic recovery, and tying investment to integrative employment practices, which had been vigorously pursued in 1994 and 1995, had already opened significant political space for a settlement. In the first-ever visit by a US President to Northern Ireland, Clinton's address to workers at the Mackie Metal Plant in Belfast on 30 November 1995 acknowledged this point: "Here we lie along the peace line, the wall of steel and stone separating Protestant from Catholic. But today . . . you are bridging the divide, overcoming a legacy of discrimination where fair employment and integration are the watchword of the future."[14] Had the Framework Documents adopted the from-below or multi-track principle which the peace-through-development strategy embodied, by independently establishing joint structures for cross-border co-operation instead of placing them under one overall political administration, they might have led to the creation of one overseeing body; instead, the proposal to create one body proved an impediment to any substantive progress on the new proposals.

Despite the broad level of Anglo-Irish agreement which the Framework Documents represented, the issue of demilitarization remained controversial: indeed, it seemed that "punishment beatings", which paramilitaries used "to enforce their Mafia-like discipline within their respective communities" had increased following the cease-fires.[15] A related problem was that while the British government insisted that the decommissioning of paramilitaries was a precondition to all-party talks, the fact that the overwhelming majority of legally held weapons were in Unionist hands was a major obstacle to decommissioning. For the next nine months, progress on the Framework Documents was dead-locked by the British insistence that Sinn Fein could not be a party in the talks until the IRA decommissioned. On 28 November 1995, the day before President Clinton's visit to Northern Ireland, Prime Minis-ters Major and Bruton announced a possible breakthrough: that an international commission headed by Senator Mitchell would look into decommissioning. The announcement implied that decommissioning would be delinked from all-party talks and the Unionists responded by demanding that representation to the all-party talks should be by election instead of nomination. In January 1996, after the international commission recommended that Sinn Fein's participation in the all-party talks should not be made conditional on the prior decommissioning of paramilitaries but should instead proceed side by side with it, the British government accepted the Unionist demand for elections to the all-party talks; in protest, the IRA ended the cease-fire and bombed London's Canary Wharf on 9 February.

By this point, Prime Minister Major's hands were partly tied by his narrowing support within the Conservative party which made him increasingly dependent on the nine Unionist MPs. The loyalists' continuation of their cease-fire despite the IRA's violation further marginalized Sinn Fein. A last-ditch effort to rescue all-party talks by Prime Ministers Major and Bruton in late February by embarking on "intensive consultations" on a broadly acceptable elective process towards all-party talks was inconclusive and the talks, which began on 10 June 1996, did not include Sinn Fein and did not succeed in renewing the IRA cease-fire. The talks soon petered out and were put on hold until after the British elections of May 1997. Despite the grim events of 1996, however, the 1994–95 cease-fire had qualitatively changed the Irish peace process; in the seventeen months that it had lasted, there had been substantive EU and US investment in economic development and cross-border programmes. It was now chiefly a matter of time before the process of EU integration would make the hostilities of partition redundant. Yet the terms set by earlier hostilities still had the power to prolong the waiting time. Though the inflammatory power of ethnic nationalism had waned so considerably, the old recognition-boycott dyad continues to ensure that full peace will come later rather than sooner to Northern Ireland.

In contrast, the process of negotiations towards EU membership for Cyprus was dominated by the hostilities of partition, and indicated that the "strong undivided Europe", which official lips so often paid service to, could live with scattered partitions on its periphery. Indeed, the first phase of post-Cold War negotiations in Cyprus began with the same western European impulse to shrink from potential commitment which had shifted the onus for Bosnia from the CSCE to the UN. In early 1992, reversing its modest negotiating policy of the previous decade, the UN Security Council authorized Secretary-General Boutros Boutros-Ghali to use all "necessary means" to bring about a settlement of the contentious Cyprus partition.[16] The move followed on a series of inconclusive negotiations throughout the 1980s, after the Cyprus government had taken the issue to the UN. In May 1983, the General Assembly called for the withdrawal of Turkish troops from the island, the return of refugees, demilitarization and an international conference for a negotiated resolution of the dispute. In Cyprus, Turkish Cypriots responded with the proclamation of the independent Republic of Northern Cyprus, which Turkey promptly recognized despite the UN's ruling that the proclamation was invalid. The then Cypriot President, Kyprianou, now refused to negotiate with Turkish Cypriot leader Rauf Denktash, and UN negotiations in pursuit of the call for an international conference began as proximity talks with the two leaders. Three months of proximity talks between September and November 1984 resulted in a final agreement that Kyprianou and Denktash would meet in January 1985. The then UN Secretary-General, Perez de Cuellar, spent the next year and a half submitting amended draft agreements which either the Greek or Turkish Cypriot leader rejected.

The chief sticking points were ones which had dogged negotiations since the 1974 invasion: whether Turkish troop withdrawal could be a precondition to agreement on the other issues of refugee return, land rights and weighted representation; what the weightage could comprise and whether a Turkish Cypriot right of veto could be included; whether the 1960 Treaty of Guarantee could be amended to emphasize Cypriot sovereignty or not. In 1986, encouraged by the recently elected Greek Prime Minister, Andreas Papandreou, Kyprianou abandoned UN supervised bilateral negotiations and reiterated the call for an international conference; there matters stood until 1988, when George Vassiliou, an independent candidate supported by the communist AKEL party, won the presidential elections. The result was interpreted as a Greek Cypriot choice for "an individual who had had no active part either in the independence struggle or the bitter inter-communal and intra-communal disputes of the following years".[17] The elections coincided with the start of the Davos process and an improvement in Greek-Turkish relations, and in late 1988, Vassiliou and Denktash embarked on another round of UN supervised negotiations which ended eighteen months later in the same deadlock as earlier talks had, despite Papandreou's loss to Constantine Mitsotakis, who was regarded as more conciliatory than the hawkish Papandreou.

One reason for the 1990 deadlock was Cyprus' application for EC membership, made in July 1990, which Denktash perceived as another means of bypassing Turkish Cypriots by seeking an international solution through a body which had six months earlier, in December 1989, told Turkey its application for membership would not be considered without a Cyprus settlement. In fact, the Vassiliou-Denktash talks had been paralleled by talks between independent Greek and Turkish Cypriot parties and groups; the process had been a part of the UN's quiet diplomacy in the late 1980s, in which the buffer zone running though Nicosia became the venue for meetings between Greek and Turkish Cypriots; with Czechoslovak support, meetings had continued in both Nicosia and Prague. Though the substantial Turkish Cypriot opposition attended these meetings (in the May 1990 elections in Turkish controlled north Cyprus, the opposition had won 44 per cent of the vote but gerrymandering ensured they gained only sixteen out of fifty seats),[18] they were boycotted by the Denktash supported National Union Party.[19] At the same time, work towards revitalization of the divided walled city of Nicosia and its infrastructural reintegration, which had been begun by the representatives of the city's Greek and Turkish Cypriots, first under UNDP and then under UNHCR aegis, continued, again chiefly through meetings in the buffer zone.[20]

By this point, growing pressure for European security to be primarily a European responsibility had begun to underline the anomaly of UN supervised negotiations between three countries who had entered into Association Agreements with the EEC between 1962 and 1972; two of which, Greece and Turkey, were NATO members, and one of which, Greece, was an EC member. In December 1990, the President of the EC Council of Ministers, Gianni de Michaelis, suggested tripartite talks under EC aegis between Turkey, Greece and Cyprus; in February 1991, in response to Perez de Cuellar's appeal for increased European support for the UN's initiatives on Cyprus at the CSCE Paris meeting, the EC announced concerted backing for UN negotiations, and in March US President Bush urged Turkish President Turgut Ozal to take an initiative to break the deadlock. Ozal responded with a proposal in May to Perez de Cuellar for four-part talks between Greeks, Turks, and Greek and Turkish Cypriots.

This was interpreted by Greek Cypriots as a sign that Ozal would wrest concessions from Denktash on the return of Greek Cypriot refugees to the northern zone and acceptance of a territorial settlement of some 27–28 per cent of the island to Turkish Cypriots (as against the 36–37 per cent currently held). In July, UN meetings with officials in Turkey and Greece, and with Vassiliou and Denktash, yielded agreement on the principles of a bicommunal and bizonal federation, its division of powers and institutions, and its ethnopolitical representation through a bicameral legislature with a ratio of 70:30 Greek-Turkish representation in the lower house and a ratio of 50:50 representation in the upper house. But the talks were still deadlocked on the issue of a Turkish-Cypriot right of veto, the actual territorial division, the return of refugees and the withdrawal of Turkish troops, and eventually they foundered on Denktash's final demand that the right of secession be included.[21]

Ozal's proposal had been made with an eye to the EC, but public opinion in Turkey was losing faith in the vision of a Europe which included Turkey, as the EC and US failed to meet commitments of aid and compensation made to Turkey during the Gulf war. Ozal's party lost the October 1991 general elections in Turkey to a coalition for whom a Cyprus settlement did not have the same priority as it had for Ozal; his death soon after meant that the pressure for a settlement which he had rallied in Turkey began to dissipate, and as the Yugoslav and Soviet federations crumbled, Turks and Turkish Cypriots began to ask whether a federation could in fact constitute the safeguard it was intended to.

Though Boutros-Ghali's April 1992 report to the Security Council, which had prompted Resolution 750, had expressed optimism on resolving the deadlock in Cyprus, Turkish Cypriot leaders Denktash and Dervis Eroglu were already voicing apprehension that the federal concept itself was in decline. Pointing to the former Yugoslavia and USSR, the latter said, "federation has ceased to be a solution any more"; coexistence was impossible "for societies which had blood among themselves".[22] To Denktash, any negotiations towards a federation would now have to be prefigured by the recognition of Turkish Cypriot sovereignty, in the form of Swiss-style cantons (a position also being voiced concurrently by Bosnian Serbs and Croats); Cyprus' application for EU membership, made without consulting the Turkish Cypriot leaders, was a disguised form of *enosis* because Greece was a member of the EU while Turkey was not. If the EU accepted Cyprus' application, Denktash concluded, Turkish Cypriots would have to begin a "very new and violent struggle".[23]

Meanwhile, however, under pressure of recession and plagued by conflict in the Kurd south-east and rising Islamic radicalism, the Turkish government was turning away from support for Denktash; Turkish Cypriots, ruling party representatives said, could not continue to be indefinitely "subsidized" by Turkey. Denktash's threat could be read in this context as a sign of his weakening position as much as a statement of intent; certainly Boutros-Ghali's foray into a more robust peace-making style in the Cyprus negotiations was based on the belief that the Vassiliou-Denktash talks had arrived at the point when they could be pushed into a settlement agreement. In intensive negotiations in the summer of 1992, Boutros-Ghali alternatively cajoled and bullied Denktash in particular to agree to a draft "Set of Ideas" which included a map of the territory to be returned to the Greek Cypriot zone, under which Varosha, the once thriving coastal suburb of the city of Famagusta, and the rich citrus-growing area of Morphou would have to be given up by the Turkish Cypriot zone. The map awarded some 28 per cent of the island's territory to Turkish Cypriots, and divagated from Denktash's bottom line of 29 per cent by only 1 per cent; though agreeing to 28 per cent of Cyprus for the 18 per cent Turkish Cypriot population was something of a concession for Vassiliou,

Greek Cypriots had for some years accepted that the traditionally larger land-holdings of the predominantly peasant Turkish Cypriots
entitled them to such a proportion (rather as Bosnians had tacitly agreed
that the pre-war Bosnian Serb land-holdings entitled them to a greater
share of land than their demographic proportion would have entitled
them to).

Denktash's objections were chiefly to the return of the land around
Morphou, which was both fertile and a major supplier of water to the
north, but its agricultural value had diminished with the decline in the
value of citrus growing, and separate clauses on water distribution ensured supply to the north (how make-or-break resource negotiations
could be is indicated by the Israel-Palestine peace process, in which
four years of multilateral and internationally supervised negotiations
on Palestinian access to water resources had yielded only projects to
develop alternative sources). In Cyprus, a graver underlying problem
was the issue of refugees and displaced persons: though the return of
Varosha and the Morphou area would allow a substantial number of
the roughly 160,000 Greek Cypriot refugees to reclaim their homes,
there still remained a substantial population wishing to return to more
dispersed areas in the north. Most of the erstwhile Greek Cypriot areas
had been resettled by mainland Turks, mainly poor peasants themselves,
who would now be displaced and whose return remains a moot point
for both Greek and Turkish Cypriots. The former were unwavering in
their demand that the settlers be forced to return to Turkey; the latter
were concerned that as the numbers of settlers had swelled to roughly
40 per cent of northern Cyprus' population, the Turkish Cypriots' political role was declining. Denktash's own political base by now
comprised substantial support from settlers; as the strength of opposition showed, this was beginning to erode his Turkish Cypriot support.

The "Set of Ideas" which Boutros-Ghali presented to Vassiliou and
Denktash was a kind of forerunner to the Washington and Dayton Agreements for Bosnia. While it drew on many of the provisions for ethnic
representation of the 1960 Cypriot constitution, it departed from it in
a significant way: it specified that Greek and Turkish Cypriots were
"not majority and minority" but "two politically equal communities".

The formula appeared to be a variation on the theme of "parity of esteem" which the Opsahl commission had suggested for Catholics and Protestants in Northern Ireland, but the terminological difference was not merely semantic. As against the Northern Irish move towards coexistence, the Boutros-Ghali document envisaged a situation closer to the equality through separation which the reconstituted "constituent nations" formula for Bosnia implied. It specified that Cyprus would be a bicommunal and bizonal state (in comparison, the Dayton Agreement established a tricommunal and bizonal state in Bosnia); and it divided the powers of the federal state and the zones in much the same way as the Washington and Dayton Agreements would, restricting the former to foreign affairs, international trade and currency, and vesting most rights and duties in the two entities. Though defence of the island was nominally under federal control, the "Set of Ideas" specified that "a numerical balance of Greek and Greek Cypriot troops and equipment on the one hand and of Turkish and Turkish Cypriot troops and equipment on the other hand" would be established, and a timetable would be set for arms reduction and the withdrawal of foreign Greek and Turkish forces. The federal republic would "maintain a federal force", but this would be composed of separate Greek and Turkish Cypriot units which would be respectively stationed in the states administered by members of their ethnic groups.[24] The Dayton Agreement similarly provided the two entities with their own armies and the proviso of an arms balance.

Despite the substantial accomodation to Turkish Cypriot concerns which the "Set of Ideas" offered, Denktash was not prepared to negotiate on a map which he considered to have been foisted upon him;[25] and Vassiliou was not prepared to accept Denktash's proposal that Greek refugee property in the north should be exchanged for Turkish refugee property in the south, arguing that decisions on whether to return or be compensated for property loss should be left to individual refugees to make. Talks were stalemated once again until the summer of 1993, when Boutros-Ghali presented an initiative for confidence-building measures to the newly elected President Clerides and Denktash.

The confidence-building measures proposed beginning with local resolution instead of seeking an overall settlement; their central proposals were to revive the 1977 and 1979 near agreements to permit Greek Cypriot refugees to return to Varosha, and to reopen Nicosia's international airport, located in the Turkish zone. Despite a lukewarm response by Clerides and some stout resistance from Denktash, detailed implementation proposals were presented in March 1994, at the same time as the Contact Group's Bosnia initiative to lift the siege of Sarajevo; the two initiatives had the same impulse of trying to see if a local solution might not open a more promising space for an overall settlement than high-level and restricted political negotiations had. As Boutros-Ghali underlined, "the purpose of this package has not been to substitute for negotiations on a comprehensive settlement of the Cyprus question, but to build confidence between the parties and thereby help create a climate in which such negotiations can succeed."[26]

The package of proposals would have given north Cyprus direct air access instead of having to go through Turkey and would have "substantially punctured" the *de facto* embargo that northern Cyprus' isolation had brought about; the development of Varosha and the Nicosia airport would have brought money and jobs, and, it was estimated, as much as a 20 per cent increase in northern Cyprus' gross domestic product,[27] but by now the imperative of maintaining the north-south divide was overriding for Denktash, and, in an unusually forthright criticism, Boutros-Ghali confessed in May that his "hopes (had) been dashed", essentially due "to a lack of political will on the Turkish Cypriot side".[28] The talks had sunk to such a low that Boutros-Ghali suggested a thorough review of the UN's mission in Cyprus: the five possible options, he suggested, were either to: (1)wind up the negotiations altogether; (2)abandon the "good offices mission" in favour of "coercive measures" against the Turkish Cypriots; (3)revive the 1992 "Set of Ideas" and map; (4)suspend negotiations while considering a fresh approach; or (5)step up pressure for acceptance of the confidence-building package. On US initiative, the last option was tried first and Denktash met with Turkish, US and UN representatives in June 1994 in Vienna. A new agreement was reached by which access to and from Varosha would be restricted to one link road which would be under UN control, but President Clerides rejected the agreement, saying "it would be unrealistic to expect that the people of Varosha will be willing to return to their homes and properties while encircled all around by Turkish forces."[29]

Meanwhile, the processing of Cyprus' EU membership application was bringing its own pressures to bear on the talks. In June 1993, the European Commission had said Cyprus met the criteria for economic and monetary union; and in June and December 1994, the European Council had suggested that Cyprus and Malta should be included in the next phase of EU enlargement. In March 1995, the EU Foreign Ministers' Meeting decided that negotiations for Cyprus' accession would begin six months after the end of the Intergovernmental Conference scheduled in 1996. Partly as a quid pro quo, Greece lifted the veto on Turkey's Customs Union with the EU which it had imposed in December 1994, but this could not allay Turkish fears which had grown as rapidly as Turkey's hopes of EU membership had dwindled, and both Turkey's then Prime Minister, Tansu Ciller, and Foreign Minister Murat Karayalcin declared that Cyprus' entry into the EU without a prior settlement with north Cyprus would leave Turkey with no option but to integrate north Cyprus.

A debate on the terms of EU membership began, on whether it should be linked to a settlement or not. US President Clinton clarified that accession negotiations would "serve as a catalyst in the search for an overall settlement in Cyprus";[30] French President Chirac suggested that, instead, EU membership should be made contingent on a prior settlement, but with the example of former Yugoslavia in mind (especially the debate over recognition), both the European Parliament and European Commission cautioned against such a linkage. Within north Cyprus, the Cyprus Turkish Democratic Association issued a press statement calling on Cypriot leaders, Greece, Turkey and the UN to "facilitate" an active Turkish Cypriot participation in EU membership negotiations, and stated their belief that a peaceful federal solution could only be achieved through this process.[31] The leader of north Cyprus' main opposition party, Ozker Ozgur, at the time serving in a Denktash led coalition government, resigned in protest at Denktash's refusal to participate in pre-accession negotiations with the EU; meanwhile, five thousand Greek and Turkish Cypriots congregated at a UNFICYP gala in the buffer zone.[32]

Despite encouraging signs of Turkish Cypriot support for a settlement, however, the overall political situation continued to deteriorate. Turkey's widening distance from Europe and US support for a Cyprus settlement put further strains on the US-Turkey relationship which had already been strained by post-Gulf War disappointments; Denktash's sudden revelation in early March 1996 that some of the Greek Cypriots missing since 1974 had actually been handed over by Turkish troops to Turkish Cypriot militias for execution exacerbated tensions, and in late March, the US veered to the position that strengthening the *status quo* in Cyprus would prevent a potential slide into conflict.[33] The November 1995 Dayton Peace Agreement for Bosnia had signalled a relinquishment of the reintegrative vision of the early 1990s; as the idea that partition was a lesser evil to renewed conflict revived in its wake, Cyprus began to be cited as an example of successful and stable containment through partition, even as a model for Bosnia.[34]

At the same time, the limits of containment were made clear in August 1996, when a Greek Cypriot demonstration against the *de facto* partition spilled over the buffer zone and two Greek Cypriots were killed by Turkish forces. Outcry against the killings, added to Greek-Turkish tensions over two deserted islets in the Aegean, brought the two countries close to war;[35] and in early 1997, the situation again seemed set to slide into conflict when the Cyprus government threatened to station newly acquired Russian missiles on its borders. The threat refocused international attention on the need for a settlement instead of a preservation of the *status quo*, and the spring of 1997 saw a renewed push for agreement on a bizonal, bicommunal federation. Its first results were a confidence-building measure by which some four hundred Turkish Cypriots visited the south for Bayram; this was followed by a visit of roughly seven hundred Greek Cypriots to the north for Easter. The measure was part of a wider set of negotiations to ease the *de facto* embargo on the north by allowing tourists to cross over for the weekend. This seemingly minor issue hinged on the large and unresolved issue of refugee property – Varosha, for example, had been a thriving resort, the majority of whose hotels were Greek Cypriot owned – and negotiations to allow restricted tourist passage from south to north were accompanied by negotiations which looked for procedures and precedents to the UNHCR Commission for Refugees, which was set up under the Dayton Agreement.

At the same time as the UN under its new Secretary-General, Kofi Annan, renewed initiatives towards a Cyprus settlement, the EU's eastern Mediterranean initiative resulted in a tentative agreement between Greece and Turkey to resolve the Aegean dispute bilaterally, and by implication separate regional security issues. Whether this might, in turn, reduce the domination of regional security concerns over the Cyprus conflict is not yet clear. Though there is some discussion of a reduced Turkish troop participation in a multinational force to ease the transition from partition to a federation, talks are still at a preliminary stage, and much depends on what modifications are made to the Boutros-Ghali "Set of Ideas" both in terms of security guarantees and in terms of freedom of movement and resettlement and property ownership in the North.[36]

Unlike the Irish and Cypriot peace processes' goal of overcoming the troubled history of partition, the apparent goal of the contemporaneous Israeli-Palestinian peace process was to complete the incomplete partition of 1948. Though the UN Security Council had passed innumerable resolutions requiring Israel to withdraw from the territories it had occupied in 1967, recognizing Palestinian self-determination and sponsoring peace negotiations, the first breakthroughs came after the 1982 Israeli invasion of Lebanon and the December 1987 Palestinian uprising known as the *intifada*. Widespread condemnation of the Israeli attack led the US to revive the search for a peace plan which, essentially, it had blocked for the past decade; but Reagan's adoption in 1982 of the plans for truncated and gradual "land for peace", which had been proposed by the Camp David Accords of 1978, came to nothing in the face of continuing Israeli non-compliance with UN resolutions.[37] In December 1983, the UN had called for an International Peace Conference on the Middle East,[38] but Israel had insisted, with US support, that it would only accept bilateral negotiations with neighbouring Arab states (and not the PLO).

The years between 1982 and 1987 were marked by rapid deterioration in the limited rights of Palestinians in the occupied areas. When the then Defence Minister, Yitzhak Rabin, met the *intifada* with force, illegal detentions and deportation, international pressure led US Secretary of State George Schultz to embark on a round of shuttle diplomacy, and for the first time the US accepted the idea of an international peace conference. In July 1988, when King Hussein of Jordan relinquished his claim to sovereignty over the West Bank in favour of the PLO, pressure for PLO recognition grew forceful, and when the Palestinian National Council voted for an independent Palestinian state at its November meeting in Algiers, its implicit recognition of Israel was widely viewed as opening the route to a settlement. When PLO Chairman Yasser Arafat added that the PLO would renounce armed resistance in favour of a peace process, in an address to the UN General Assembly in December 1988,[39] the US announced they would open "a substantive dialogue with the PLO", but repeated their support for bilateral negotiations and the dialogue was slow and halting. During the 1990 Gulf War, the Arab states extracted a US promise to attend to Palestinian rights, and the contemporaneous eruption of the Women in Black and Peace Now initiatives in Israel opened a new space for a peace process. In September 1991, the US initiated unofficial talks with Palestinian leaders to set up a Palestinian Delegation to the international conference scheduled for late October.

From the beginning, negotiations were dogged by the insistence of the ruling Likud Party in Israel that the PLO could not be represented in the delegation; even connections to the wider Palestinian National Council were frowned upon.[40] Yet the talks were to negotiate interim Palestinian self-government arrangements towards a second stage of negotations on the permanent status of the West Bank, including Jerusalem and the Gaza strip. At the international conference which began in Madrid on 3 November 1991, it was agreed that bilateral negotiations would begin between Israel and neighbouring states (Jordan, Syria, Egypt and Lebanon), but Israel refused to allow the Palestinian delegation to participate independently in the conference: instead, they were a part of the Jordanian delegation. In January 1992, however, Israel's deportation of twelve Palestinians on the eve of the third round of negotiations led the Palestinian delegation, headed by Haidar Abdel Shafi, to announce they would boycott the talks. Following UNSCR 726 of 6 January, condemning the deportation, the Israelis agreed to a separate track for Israeli-Palestinian negotiations, and in March, the Palestinian delegation presented a "Palestine Interim Self-Government Authority" plan.

The plan proposed a phased withdrawal of Israeli troops, control over the Palestinian territory's land, water, sub-soil, natural resources, territorial sea, exclusive economic zone and air space; legislative, executive and judicial powers; rights to enter bilateral relations with other states and a strong police force but not an army: it asked that the Authority have the right to ask for a UN peace-keeing force, and suggested establishing a supervisory committee for the interim phase, comprising representatives of the UN, the Authority, and Jordan, Egypt, Syria and Israel. Elections to the Authority would be under UN supervision. As a preliminary to the interim phase, the plan recommended a set of confidence-building measures, including that Israel repeal settler legislation and freeze settlement activity, release political prisoners, allow deportees to return, and refrain from collective punishment.[41]

Israel's initial response to the plan was to offer to restore municipal elections in the occupied territories – which had not been held since the annulment of the 1976 municipal elections results, in which PLO supported candidates had done very well – and to offer Palestinians control over local schools and hospitals (which they already had). While negotations were put on hold pending the Israeli elections of summer 1992, the Palestinian delegation "went public" in a formal meeting with Chairman Arafat; a move which the US interpreted as upping the ante for self-government.[42] Following the election of a Labour government under Yitzhak Rabin, the Israeli delegation presented a counter-proposal to the Palestinian delegation, which made no reference to the territory to come under Palestinian rule, but implied that this might comprise a disparate set of municipalities and villages. The proposal suggested an elected Palestinian Administrative Council to whom powers would be delegated over justice, finance, industry and agriculture, health, education, local police and local transportation. Israel would not only retain control over overall security but would be responsible for all matters concerning settlers; though this meant substantial responsibility in local security, the proposal did not specify either joint or co-ordinated measures with the Council. Israel would also retain control over roads and highways, effectively curbing freedom of movement of people and goods and restricting access to key resources. Instead of the UN led supervisory committee proposed by the Palestinians, the Israeli proposal suggested a "High Liaison and Co-ordination Committee", composed of Israel-Palestinians-Jordan (note the avoidance of the term "Palestine").[43]

The Israeli elections, however, had also brought to power a number of parties in coalition with Labour who were more sympathetic to Palestinian self-government, and the informal talks which had begun between the Mashov group (including members of the Labour left), the Meretz coalition of Israeli social democrats and peace activists, and Palestinian leaders in 1989 – 90, now turned into regular meetings, including informal "proximity talks" in the Hague in the summer of 1992. In the autumn of 1992, as an offshoot of these meetings, low-profile talks in Oslo began under Swedish-Norwegian aegis between an Israeli academic, Ya'ir Hirschfeld, and a PLO nominee, Abu Ala. The talks were presented as academic, and were initially disregarded by most of the negotiators, until the interminable hitches to official progress turned attention on them. In December 1992, when Rabin deported some four hundred Hamas supporters from the occupied territories who were stranded in no-man's land, the official talks were jolted into some movement. At French President Mitterand's intercession, in early 1993, the then Israeli Foreign Minister, Shimon Peres, expressed support for a two-phased return of deportees, which included those expelled in 1967; but Arafat asked for firm commitments which were not forthcoming. Negotiations returned to the US-Israel bilateral agreement that the Hamas deportees would have their sentences halved and would be allowed to return to the occupied territories by December 1993. The French proposals had offered more.[44]

Meanwhile, Rabin's repeal of the law preventing the Israeli government from holding meetings with the PLO appeared to have opened new potential for face to face negotiations, but after a year and a half of presenting proposals to each other, the next round of Israeli-Palestinian negotiations were held in Washington in April 1993 as proximity talks, with the US as intermediaries. Initially, the talks yielded new Israeli concessions on "land for peace" (on the basis of UNSCRs 242 of 1967, and 338 of 1973) and the scope of the Palestinian Authority, but in a sudden reversal, the US presented the Palestinian delegation with a draft Joint Statement which closed the talks and withdrew the tentative agreements on human rights which were in the process of formulation. The PLO instructed the Palestinian delegation to refuse to consider the document, which had been negotiated by the US and Israel; unbeknown to the delegation, the PLO had decided to concentrate its attention on the Oslo process, while using the official Washington negotiations as a testing ground for proposals being developed there. In June–July, Arafat instructed the Palestinian delegation to float a "Gaza-Jericho First" option in the tenth Washington round; the proposal entailed Palestinian acceptance of territorially phased self-government in exchange for an Israeli agreement that Palestinian Liberation Army units could form local police units. This was opposed by a series of Palestinian leaders, including Ashrawi herself, who pleaded that in its current form it would lead to the fragmentation of land and authority, creating the potential for an apartheid-type system in which Israel could rid itself of areas which were difficult to control while retaining control over settlement areas.[45]

From this point on, Palestinian negotiators were on two separate and uncoordinated tracks: while the Palestinian delegation worked on negotiating a sustainable authority whose transitional phase would be linked to the next stage of decisions on permanent status, the secret Oslo negotiations pursued the Gaza-Jericho First option. In early August 1993, a Draft Declaration of Principles was signed in Oslo, accepting Palestinian self-goverment in Gaza and Jericho; its most significant achievement was Israeli recognition of the PLO's right to administer areas of Palestinian concentration, symbolizing both the enormous change since the 1980s in Israeli perception of threat to its security, and opening potential routes to much wider negotiations. The agreement was widely acclaimed and formally ratified under US aegis in Washington on 13 September 1993, with a famous handshake between President Rabin and Chairman Arafat.

At the same time, the Oslo Accords (I and II) were feared to have exchanged substantive self-rule for the trappings of statehood: Arafat, for example, argued that he had acceded to the Accords because he had been tacitly promised such symbols of sovereignty as a Palestinian flag, passports, separate telephone code and stamps. In return, he had allowed most of the substantive conditions of Palestinian self-rule to be left to future negotiations. The Accords did not set a frame for the return or compensation of refugees; they gave Israel an interim period to resolve its settlement plans (and allowed Arab lands to be claimed for settlements during the interim period),[46] and offered no guarantees on Jerusalem; and they left access to vital natural resources and freedom of movement under Israeli control. Indeed, the second phase of devolution of Palestinian cities, under Oslo II, was envisaged as leading to a gradual cantonization of the West Bank, with five large and unconnected Palestinian "cantonal clusters" around Nablus, Ramallah, Bethlehem, Jericho and Hebron, with a possible corridor to Gaza and Rifah by an elevated rail and motorway system.[47]

In February 1994, the Cairo Agreement set a timetable for Israeli withdrawal from Palestinian towns, and in May, a second Cairo Agreement was signed on Gaza and Jericho. The agreement stipulated a strong Palestinian police force, more akin to paramilitary than civil police, with an intelligence branch and mobile land forces, and naval and air elements. Following the agreement, more than nine thousand former PLO regulars and irregulars were deployed in Gaza and Jericho. While the Cairo negotiations were underway, rising settler violence against the Oslo Accords, in particular the Hebron massacre of 23 March, intensified Palestinian pressure to remove settlers from highly populated Palestinian areas (there were 450 Israeli settlers in Hebron and 100,000 Palestinians), ban extremist settler groups and disarm the highly armed settler population. Rabin outlawed the extremist settler groups Kach and Kahane Hai, but said that the issues of the settlements and the disarming of settlers would have to be subject to future negotiations. Within Israel the consensus was that the public mandate for the peace process was partly contingent on defending the settlements.[48]

Although Arafat's entry into Gaza in July 1994 was triumphal, Israel's follow through on demarcating the boundaries of the Palestinian Authority restricted Gaza's access to water and trade routes, and Israel's ability to close its borders to the roughly seventy thousand Palestinians working in Israeli areas, which was frequently used by the Israeli government to pressurize Palestinians, caused unemployment to rise steeply. Israel's control over roads and highways, moreover, was used to collectively punish Gaza for terrorist acts committed by Hamas,[49] responsibility for whose control had inexorably shifted to the Palestinian Authority following the Cairo Agreement. Indeed, a substantial portion of US aid was for counter-terrorist equipment and training. A new cycle of violence began, but in September 1995, important details of a West Bank settlement were agreed which laid out a phase by phase Israeli redeployment out of key West Bank areas, the transference of civil authority in Palestinian cities from Israel to the Palestinian Authority, the modalities of elections to a Palestinian Council, the roads which Israelis or Palestinians would control, the arms which the Palestinian police would hold, and the rights of the more far-flung or isolated settler groups to live within Palestinian territories but vote in Israeli elections. The agreement also made a significant concession to Palestinian sovereignty by agreeing that the new Palestinian entity would be able to sign bilateral agreements with other countries on cultural, economic and scientific issues.[50]

Two months later, Prime Minister Rabin was murdered by a Jewish fundamentalist; a nation in mourning pledged itself to the peace process, but terrorist attacks by a Jewish visitor and Hamas militants in February and March 1996 swung Israelis to an intensified sense of insecurity, and in the summer 1996 elections, a right-wing coalition led by Benyamin Netanyahu won. The Palestinian authority responded to the Hamas suicide bombings with a widespread crackdown on militants of both Hamas and Islamic Jihad, but the arrests were made with little attention to legal procedure and considerable human rights violations, and Palestinian grievances grew at the spectacle of Palestinian police firing on Palestinian demonstrators. Netanyahu's aggressively nationalist rhetoric and political dependence on radical Zionist parties slowed negotiations considerably, and as talks over the transfer of Hebron deteriorated, it began to look as if the remaining transfers would not only be indefinitely delayed but that the territories to be transferred might shrink.[51]

In response to renewed US pressure, Netanyahu began redeploying Israeli troops out of Hebron in early January 1997, and made a commitment to withdraw from the three remaining Palestinian cities by mid-1998; he also agreed to begin talks on borders, resources and the status of Jerusalem.[52] The transfer of Hebron entailed a partition of the city, with Palestinian authority over the bulk of it and Israel retaining authority over the enclaves of Jewish settlers; although initially Palestinian and Israeli police worked smoothly side by side, the arrangement also meant a very visible, armed police presence.[53] At the end of January, when Likud and Labour reached a draft agreement on a joint Israeli peace plan, it became clear that Palestinians would have the right to national but not territorial partition. Key clauses of the agreement were that Israel would annex the majority of Israeli settlements while the more far-flung settlers would retain Israeli citizenship and freedom of movement to Israel; Jerusalem would be the unified capital of Israel within its present municipal borders; refugees would not be allowed to return to Israeli territory but would be cared for by an international organization "in which Israel would play an important role, with the goal of financing and carrying out projects for compensation and rehabilitation of the refugees in their places". The issue of whether Palestinian refugees could return to Palestinian territories was postponed to future negotiations.

The draft had taken close to four months of biweekly meetings to prepare, and caused dissension both within Labour and Likud.[54] While it signalled Likud's first public acknowledgement of Palestinian rights to self-rule, the limits it set on territorial contiguity, the return of refugees and the status of Jerusalem also showed how much further negotiations had to go.[55] In March 1997, Netanyahu again escalated pressure on the negotiations by approving a plan to build a new Jewish settlement in Arab east Jerusalem; at the same time, the Israeli cabinet voted to transfer 9.1 per cent more of the West Bank to Palestinian control, chiefly villages around Jenin, Bethlehem and Hebron (which were classified under Area B of the Oslo II map). Arafat had expected a much larger transfer.[56] The decision on east Jerusalem drew an unusual public rebuke from President Clinton, though the US used its veto to block a Security Council resolution on the issue; a week later, the US Consul General was among representatives of Russia, Europe, Japan and the Arab states at an emergency meeting called by Arafat on the Jerusalem housing plan, to which Israel was pointedly not invited.[57] Arafat warned that the peace process might break down on the issue; when violence erupted a week later in the West Bank following a Hamas suicide bombing in Tel Aviv, Netanyahu blamed Arafat for giving Hamas "a green light". At the end of March, as violence mounted in the West Bank and Gaza, the Oslo peace process was in tatters. The step by step build-up of trust, which the Oslo peace process had been centred on, had been pre-empted by events, many of which could have been forecast by the inherent flaws of the process itself.

In practice, the Gaza-Jericho First policy put the Palestinian Authority in an untenable position. With Israeli control over key infrastructure, especially roads and borders, the Palestinian Authority's jurisdiction was restricted, and in the absence of freedom of movement between the West Bank, Gaza and Jericho, the West Bank grew further apart from both Gaza and Jericho.[58] With little to secure, the Palestinian Authority's overbloated security forces turned to internal security, a move which encouraged the inherent authoritarian tendencies of an organization nurtured by exile and interdiction: with the shocking consequence that the Authority actually announced, at the end of April 1997, that the death sentence would be imposed on Palestinians selling land to Israelis in east Jerusalem. In fact, the issue of east Jerusalem pointed to a quite separate flaw in the Oslo peace process. The policy of "thickening the settlements" which Netanyahu espoused meant, in the case of Jerusalem, that Palestinians would not only lose a vital economic lifeline, but also that the north-south connections, which were necessary to prevent the Palestinian areas from becoming a collection of "Bantustans", would become much more difficult to make. Indeed, Israel's post-Oslo actions pointed towards the ultimate creation of an invisible Palestine within a bispatial structure whose upper tier would comprise an Israel with highways overpassing Palestine to the rest of the Arab world, and whose lower tier would comprise impoverished and disparate Palestinian territories.[59]

But perhaps the biggest flaw in the Oslo Accords was their reliance on process, which in practice made the implementation of peace conditional on immediate events within Israel. Ironically, the events of 1997, the revelations of the widespread use of torture by Israeli security forces, the corruption scandal involving trusted Netanyahu associates and the debate on whether to indict him, the resignation of his (relatively) moderate Finance Minister and the abortive move to bring Sharon into the peace negotiations, and the growing friction between more and less orthodox Jews on the issue of conversion, all showed that Israel's internal democratization processes need not complement the peace process; indeed, given the time factor, the former could in fact prove inimical to the latter. Thus, as enquiries into corruption and torture rocked the Netanyahu government, Labour and the left parties concentrated their energies on displacing the Likud coalition. In effect, this left the peace process to the mercies of the government, that is, to a shaky political coalition whose short-term needs almost dictated an escalation of conflict with the Palestinians. As the US, the Arab states and the Europeans consider Netanyahu's proposal to move immediately to the "final status" talks which were envisaged as the end of the Oslo process, it is beginning to look as if the incomplete partition of Palestine will remain just that, but the failure to complete a process which is underway infinitely multiplies the potential conflict.

By 1997, as the faltering peace processes in Ireland, Israel-Palestine, Cyprus and Bosnia sank to new lows, the hope of a transformed, post-Cold War commitment to democracy and renewable peace began to crumble. There had, from the start, been a tension both between and within each of them: the goals of strengthening market democracy were very different from the goals of renewing peace through regional development, and though the two goals were uttered in the same breath, the former was focused on the relatively peaceful countries of central Europe, while the latter centred on conflict-ridden ethnic partitions at Europe's peripheries in the Balkans and Middle East.

Inevitably, investment in the latter had been a tiny fraction of invest-ment in the former.[60] At a general level, the problem was that readiness to invest was contingent on some assurance of potentially stable peace, but the political reliance on ethnonational negotiations allowed at best a simmering peace, restricted the potential for regional economic de-velopment and subordinated its capacity to create conditions in which the hostilities of partition could be bypassed. Indeed, the Eurocentric nature of the project imposed its own limits on the endeavour.

As the Israel-Palestine peace process indicated, the goal of subduing partitions in the quest for renewable peace was chiefly restricted to Europe, on the assumption that the European values of pluralism and citizenship were embedded in European democracy. How true this as-sumption was was unclear. As the debate over the Maastricht Treaty of 1991 to 1992 showed, there was more division than consensus over who was to be included in the new Europe and what European integra-tion entailed; a feature of the period was that while several of the Scandinavian countries voted against joining the EC/EU, within EU coun-tries like Britain, larger and larger numbers of people expressed the desire to emigrate to the Pacific and even Africa. As the 1990s played out, it became clear that the "peaceful, undivided and democratic Eu-rope" which had been a refrain of the early post-Cold War years was less an adaptation of the vision of a Europe stretching from the Atlantic to the Urals – and more a reconfiguration, whose chief goal was to eradicate the "old divisions of the Cold War"[61] rather than to undo the ethnic or communal divisions which lay at the heart of Europe.

The two, however, could not be so easily separated. The vision of a "Europe, whole and free", expressed by the 1991 NATO summit in Rome, had been accompanied by the establishment and rapid enlarge-ment of the CSCE to include the former Warsaw Pact countries and the new countries of the former Soviet Union. Though the original plan was that the CSCE and NATO would provide a new European security architecture of which the CSCE would be the civilian and NATO the military wing, its first test, the conflict in former Yugoslavia, had led the EU to pass the buck from the CSCE and NATO to the UN. At the time, the dominant EU feeling appears to have been uncertainty as to whether

NATO was in a position to play its first active security role, or whether indeed active peace keeping was a desirable role for NATO in the first place. In the event, the UN's role was to pick up the slack while NATO prepared itself for multi-functional peace keeping. The 1991 NATO summit had also established the North Atlantic Co-operation Council, to plan and implement military co-operation between NATO countries and the former communist states, and UNPROFOR in Croatia and Bosnia provided the early testing grounds for co-operation between western and eastern European troops (in particular, from the Czech Republic and Poland). In 1994, when the Partnership for Peace was founded at the NATO summit in Brussels, it was again UNPROFOR in Bosnia which was the mechanism through which Russian and western European military co-operation could be tentatively explored. In this first form, the stationing of Russian troops on the Serb controlled side of the Sarajevo partition line appeared to symbolize a greater comfort with Europe's traditional ethnic and communal divisions than with European unification, and by 1997, it seemed that the first post-Cold War decade would end in the two-tier Europe which had been forecast in the late 1980s, of richer and poorer, and more and less stable countries.

Nevertheless, there are indications that the new walls of Europe are no longer going to be defined by ethnoterritorial partition (indeed, the spread of information technology, which was cited as aiding in the erosion of the Cold War, had already made territorial partition metaphorically redundant). NATO's gradual process of transformation through the Bosnian war, from a security shield to a multi-functional force capable of flexible deployment, and its testing of enlargement mechanisms through UNPROFOR and then IFOR, had also led to an extension of its presence in Bosnia. Though the new NATO Stabilization Force (SFOR) could either stabilize the Bosnian partition or help Bosnia to find a slow route out of partition, the inherent instability of the Serb entity implied that the latter strategy might gradually come into its own. Recent commitments to the arrest of war criminals and the return of refugees again imply that Bosnia will be the turning point of partition theory, though how far the commitments will be honoured remains to be seen. The Irish peace process and the Cyprus accession talks, moreover, indicated that there was a turn away from viewing partition as a lesser evil.

As we have seen, the extent of this turn remains qualified by culturalist assumptions that a partition at the heart of Europe is less acceptable than partitions at its periphery; it has also been qualified by the highly uneven application of programmes for renewable peace, and over reliance on the power sharing formulae which had underwritten ethnic partition in the first place. As the first post-Cold War decade nears its end, it is unclear whether the turn away from partition will end by substituting a form of cantonization for partition, or whether it will concentrate on supporting multi-ethnic or reintegrative programmes. What is clear is that a substitution of cantonization for partition is likely to be successful only as a way out of long-existing but still volatile partitions, where cantonization signifies the relinquishment of sovereignty or homeland claims, as it would in Northern Ireland or Cyprus. Elsewhere, as the case of Bosnia implies, cantonization can be as much an impetus to war as partition; indeed, its half-way nature when espoused as an alternative to partition can only prolong low-level conflict – as the Bosnian Croat hostility to the cantonal formulae of the Croat-Bosniak Federation illustrates.

Sadly, the recognition of truisms of this sort does not easily translate into international action. Communities shattered by ethnic, communal and internecine conflict can only be rebuilt over a slow period of time and at considerable cost, and governments are not prone to altruism. Even the very real needs of the US and Europe to wrest some sort of proclaimable success for intervention in Bosnia may not lead any of the concerned countries to invest the kind of time and resources that the stabilization of that country requires. Yet, grim as this sounds, if the international community can even learn that proposals to cantonize or partition are more likely to inflame and prolong ethnic conflicts than to solve them, it will be no mean achievement in the history of peace making. Knowing what not to do is nowhere near as good as knowing what to do, but it is an important step in that direction and – crucially – it can save a lot of lives.

Notes

CHAPTER 1 A LESSER EVIL

1. Michael Williams, "Polling for Partition", *Index on Censorship*, 4:1996; David Rieff, "Prelude to Partition", *The New York Times*, 14 August1996. Henceforth *NYT*.
2. *The Charter of Paris for a New Europe*, Paris, 21 November 1990, re-printed in *The SIPRI Yearbook*, Appendix 17B, Copenhagen 1991, pp. 603–13.
3. Boutros Boutros-Ghali, "Empowering the United Nations", *Foreign Affairs*, Winter 1992–93, p. 89.
4. Walter Goldstein, "Europe After Maastricht", *Foreign Affairs*, Winter 1992–93, pp. 117–20. Goldstein, in fact, discusses EU expansion as comprising first the possible extension of membership to Malta, Cyprus and Turkey, and then perhaps to Poland, Hungary and the Czech Republic. As we now know, Malta and Turkey are out of the running for the nonce.
5. For a discussion of contemporary security ideas on refugee flows, see Myron Weiner, "Bad Neighbours, Bad Neighbourhoods: An Enquiry into the Causes of Refugee Flows"; Alan Dowty and Gil Loescher, "Refugee Flows as Grounds for International Action"; Barry R. Posen, "Military Responses to Refugee Disasters"; all in *International Security*, 21:1, Summer 1996, pp. 5–112.
6. Sadako Ogata, *The State of the World's Refugees, 1993: The Challenges of Protection*, New York, Oxford University Press 1993.
7. E. J. Hobsbawm, *Nations and Nationalism Since 1780: Progress, Myth, Reality*, Cambridge, Canto Press 1991, p. 164; Mary Kaldor and Radha Kumar, "New Forms of Conflict", in *Conflicts in Europe*, Helsinki Citizens' Assembly Publication Series No. 7, Prague 1993, pp. 12–5.
8. It is in this context that Samuel Huntington's *The Clash of Civilizations* can be read as making a profound point – that of illustrating the West's

propensity for casting disputes in civilizational terms, which serves the dual purpose of allowing either an abnegation of resposibility or providing a rationale for intervention. Samuel P. Huntington, *The Clash of Civilizations*, New York, Simon and Schuster 1996.

9. Penderel Moon, *Divide and Quit*, London 1961.
10. As Home Secretary Risley frankly confessed in 1904, divide and rule was an important motive in the plan to partition Bengal. Sumit Sarkar, *Modern India*, Delhi, People's Publishing House 1983, p. 107.
11. Radha Kumar, "The Troubled History of Partition", *Foreign Affairs*, 76:1, Jan.–Feb. 1997.
12. Norman Davies, *God's Playground: A History of Poland*, Oxford, Oxford University Press 1991, vol. 2, chs. 2–4, 19, esp. map 12, p. 395.
13. In the main, self-determination was limited to one or two regions in Europe; other territories were to "be accorded the freest opportunity for autonomous development". Harold Nicolson, *Peace Making, 1919*, New York, Universal Library 1965, pp. 39–41.
14. The German and Austrian frontiers were limited on these grounds, while ethnic criteria were jettisoned when Transylvania was handed to the Rumanians and the Banat divided between Rumania and Serbia.
15. Ibid., pp. 192–3. Nicolson also recounts the following anecdote of the 1919 Paris Peace Conference:

> Crowe is cantankerous about Cyprus and will not allow me even to mention the subject. I explain . . . that we are left in a false moral position if we ask everyone else to surrender possessions in terms of Self-Determination and surrender nothing ourselves. How can we keep Cyprus and express moral indignation at the Italians retaining Rhodes? He says, "Nonsense, my dear Nicolson. You are not being clear-headed. You think that you are being logical and sincere. You are not. Would you apply self-determination to India, Egypt, Malta and Gibraltar? If you are *not* prepared to go as far as this, then you have no right to claim that you are logical. If you *are* prepared to go as far as this, then you had better return at once to London." (p. 246)

16. John J. Mearsheimer, "Shrink Bosnia to Save It", *NYT*, 31 March 1993.
17. Reginald Coupland, *Palestine Royal Commission Report*, 1937.
18. Susan L. Woodward, *Balkan Tragedy: Chaos and Dissolution after the Cold War* Washington, The Brookings Institution 1995, pp. 7–8, esp. f. 6.
19. Thus, for example, the influential political scientists John Mearsheimer and Stephen Van Evera argue, in an uncanny echo of Coupland, that the 1992–94 US reluctance to support a Bosnian partition reflected: "a dogmatic American faith that other multi-ethnic societies can harmonize themselves, that ethnic groups elsewhere can learn to live together as America's immigrants have . . . But US policymakers must be willing at times to decide that some states cannot be sustained and should instead be disassembled." John J. Mearsheimer and Stephen Van Evera, "When Peace

Means War", *The New Republic*, December 1995. See also, John J. Mearsheimer and Robert A. Pape, "The Answer: A Three-Way Partition Plan for Bosnia and How the US Can Enforce It", *The New Republic*, 14 June 1993.

20. Chaim Kaufmann, "Possible and Impossible Solutions to Ethnic Civil Wars", *International Security*, 20:4, 1996, pp. 136–75. Mr Kaufmann actually suggests that after an international military take-over, the international forces should intern "civilians of the enemy ethnic group" and "exchange" them after peace is established, but few other proponents of population transfer display a like imperviousness to the authoritarian connotations of such a scheme.

21. For an especially lucid exposition of the dangers of half-hearted and attemptedly impartial intervention, see Richard K. Betts, "The Delusion of Impartial Intervention", *Foreign Affairs*, 75:4, Sept.–Oct. 1995.

22. Chaim Kauffman.

23. For a summary of the process, see T. G. Fraser, *Partition in Ireland, India and Palestine*, London, Macmillan Press 1984, pp. 131–76.

24. Ayesha Jalal, *The Sole Spokesman*, Cambridge, Cambridge University Press 1994.

25. T. G. Fraser, p. 131.

26. Interestingly, the proposal was made at a time when the demographic ratio of Catholic: Protestant was at its lowest in the Ulster region (in Belfast the Catholic population declined from 34 to 23 per cent between 1861 and 1911, chiefly due to male outmigration). At another level, the communal conflict in Ireland was stimulated partly by British settlement policies from the seventeenth century on, which created a kind of multi-religious demographic belt between England and the predominately Catholic rest of Ireland. A. C. Hepburn, *A Past Apart: Studies in the History of Catholic Belfast, 1850–1950,* Belfast, Ulster Historical Foundation 1996, pp. 137–51. This history, strikingly, combines the Palestinian conflict root of a wide resettlement policy with the former-Yugoslavia conflict root of resettlement to form buffer zones (the Croatian and Bosnian *krajinas*).

27. Ibid., p. 32. For an analysis of the process, see also E. Phoenix, *Northern Nationalism: Nationalist Politics, Partition and the Catholic Minority in Northern Ireland, 1890–1940*, Belfast 1994.

28. South African leaders had played an important mediating role in the Anglo-Irish conflict; indeed, the proposal for an Irish Free State had been made at the intercession of South Africa's General Smuts.

29. The issue proved controversial and many nationalists subsequently withdrew their support for it. In Bengal, for example, Muslim leaders who had initially accepted the allocation of 40% of the seats in the provincial legislature to Bengali Muslims, despite the fact that Muslims comprised over 50% of Bengal's population, soon shifted to demands for proportional

representation. Leonard Gordon, "Divided Bengal: Problems of Nationalism and Identity", in Mushirul Hassan, ed., *The Partition of India*, Delhi, Oxford University Press 1993, pp. 287–8.

30. In a fascinating development, some 20,000 Muslims from Sind and the North West Frontier Provinces (NWFP) left the shores of British India in a protest *Muhajirin* trek to Afghanistan, whose new ruler, Amir Amanullah, had fought a brief war with British India in June 1919 and was said to have negotiated with Bolshevik Russia. Sumit Sarkar, *Modern India*, p. 198.

31. Interestingly, little substantive research has been done on these proposals; while contemporary historians of India's partition have dwelt on the League's proposals for a federation of Muslim and Hindu majority states as an alternative to partition which the Congress opposed, few have asked the far more interesting question of why the multi-ethnic federal proposals were not given more attention.

32. Whether, however, a federation of communally defined states would have been stable and viable is a moot point; arguably, it might have prolonged communal conflict and brought it to more and more intimate levels. Indeed, if the Bosnian case – in which attempts to establish just such an ethnic or communal power-sharing arrangement merely accelerated the process of war and breakdown – can be treated as a retrospective example, then the evidence would incline one to the latter view.

33. Penderel Moon, *Divide and Quit*; Sumit Sarkar, *Modern India*; V. P. Menon, *The Transfer of Power in India*, Calcutta 1957; Mushirul Hassan, *The Partition of India*.

34. *The Origins and Evolution of the Palestine Problem, 1917–1988*, The United Nations, New York 1990, p. 24.

35. Harold Nicolson, pp. 185–8.

36. See for example, Amos Elon, *The Israelis: Founders and Sons*, New York, Bantam Books 1972. For the demographic transformation of Palestine, see Janet Abu-Lughod, "The Demographic Transformation of Palestine", in Ibrahim Abu-Lughod, ed., *The Transformation of Palestine*, Evanston, Northwestern University Press 1971, pp. 153–61.

37. The Congress eventually accepted the partition option after the Holocaust.

38. *The Origins and Evolution of the Palestine Problem*, pp. 48–55.

39. Significantly, the minority report was submitted by the Indian, Iranian and Yugoslav members of the UN Committee (UNSCOP).

40. Michael Attalides, *Cyprus*, Edinburgh, Q Press 1979; Christopher Hitchens, *Cyprus*, London, Quartet Books 1984.

41. Michael Attalides, pp. 103–32.

42. In fact, when the British threatened partition in 1956, it was Radcliffe, who had drawn the partition boundaries for India, who was asked to do the same for Cyprus.

43. These were trapped Muslim enclaves surrounded by the Serb nationalist

army (RSA), to whom international aid could only be sporadically provided because the RSA used its power to interrupt aid convoys as leverage
in the political negotiations.

44. These events are detailed in Chapters Two and Three of this volume.
45. See Chapter Five of this volume.
46. *Report From the Select Committee on Cyprus*, London, Her Majesty's
    Stationery Office 1976, p. 18.
47. Ibid., p. 14.
48. The partition of Ireland embroiled the British in Northern Ireland indefi-
    nitely, as we have seen; in Palestine, the British decided simply to quit and
    the UN partition plan was pre-empted by the Zionists; in Cyprus, the Brit-
    ish attempted to quit without dividing and ended with a *de facto* division,
    and a continuing British presence with the UN.
49. *NYT:* 25 August 1996; 29 August 1996.

CHAPTER 2 DIVIDE AND RULE

1. Laura Silber and Allan Little, *Yugoslavia: Death of a Nation*, TV Books
   1996, p. 205.
2. Whose figures have to be treated warily, as the census was carried out in
   volatile circumstances.
3. Tom Gjelten, *Sarajevo Daily: A City and Its Newspaper Under Siege*, Harper
   Collins, New York 1995, pp. 88–9.
4. According to David Owen, the Serbs discovered in their attacks on Vukovar
   that capturing larger towns or cities in modern warfare extracted a terrible price and so turned to "the medieval siege, putting citizens under barrage
   and psychological pressure but not launching a frontal attack". This was
   the tactic adopted with Sarajevo. David Owen, *Balkan Odyssey*, Harcourt
   Brace and Company, New York 1995, p. 84.
5. Silber and Little, pp. 244–7.
6. Nandita Haksar and Uma Chakravathy, *The Delhi Riots*, Delhi, Lancer
   International 1987.
7. Izetbegovic distinguished between the JNA proper and the reservists; the
   latter, he said, had caused havoc in the republic.
8. Susan L. Woodward, *Balkan Tragedy*, The Brookings Institution, Washington 1995, pp. 279–80.
9. The primordialist position covers a range of opinion, from the racist/
   civilizational view held by Croatian nationalists and voiced by John
   Mearsheimer and Stephen Van Evera, to the tribalist view expressed by
   the term "Balkan madness", which is more widely espoused in Europe
   than in the US.
10. In this view, economic and political factors would have primacy over
    social and pyschological ones. For example, Susan Woodward does not deem it

necessary to explore the rise and form of ethnic nationalism in the Balkans, even though it is linked to the decline of the Cold War. See Susan L. Woodward.

11. Michael A. Sells, *The Bridge Betrayed: Religion and Genocide in Bosnia*, Berkeley, University of California Press 1996; Roy Gutman, *Witness to Genocide*, New York, Macmillan 1993; Mark Thompson, ed., *Forging War: The Media in Serbia, Croatia and Bosnia-Hercegovina*, Article 19, London 1994.

12. The SDA won 33.8% of the seats, the SDS 29.6% and the HDZ 18.3%. Of the remaining 38 seats, 18 were won by reform communists and 13 by the Anti-Markovic alliance. The ethnocommunal breakdown of deputies elected in the 1990 Bosnian elections was: 39.5% Muslim, 35.4% Serb, 21.6% Croat, 3.3% Yugoslav. Lenard J. Cohen, *Broken Bonds: Yugoslavia's Disintegration and Balkan Politics in Transition*, Boulder, Westview Press 1995, p. 146.

13. Silber and Little, pp. 206–7.

14. David Owen, p. 186.

15. Silber and Little, pp. 209–10. According to the Bosnian constitution of 1974, however, Muslims, Serbs and Croats were constituent nations, and so ethnic representation was written into the elections.

16. The Conference on Security and Co-operation in Europe (CSCE), *The Referendum on Independence in Bosnia-Herzegovina*, Report of the Helsinki Commission delegation to Bosnia-Herzegovina, 12 March 1992, p. 6.

17. An analysis of the different party programmes in the Yugoslav elections of 1990 shows that in a republic-wide breakdown, support for parties with programmatic commitments to ethnopolitical or communal identities was highest in Croatia (40.4%), followed by Macedonia (36%) and Serbia (33.3%), and lowest in Slovenia (14.8%). In Bosnia, support for liberal-democratic and ethnopolitical programmes was the same (23.2%), while support for Yugoslav unity was higher than in any other republic (13.9%, followed by 4% in Macedonia and Montenegro). Lenard J. Cohen, p. 166. Nevertheless, the Macedonian elections had the most pluralist result, with a predominantly social-democratic coalition coming to power, headed by Kiro Gligorov, whose first cabinet included members of all the minorities.

18. And was later implicated in a scandal comprising oversubscription to the company.

19. Lenard J. Cohen, p. 161, fn. 16.

20. Janusz Bugajski, *Ethnic Politics in Eastern Europe*, New York and London, M. E. Sharpe 1995, pp. 34–5.

21. On 25 March 1991, Tudjman and Milosevic met at the Karadjordjevo hunting lodge. The meeting had been arranged by Stipe Mesic and Boro Jovic, advisors respectively to Tudjman and Milosevic. According to Mesic:

I warned Boro Jovic it is the Serbs in Croatia, who have been supplied with weapons and are being pushed into a tragedy by Belgrade, who will suffer the most. He responded without hesitation: "Listen, we are not interested in the Serbs of Croatia. They are your citizens, do whatever you want with them, impale them, we don't care. We are interested in Bosnia Herzegovina, we want 66% of that territory, we will take it."

(Lenard J. Cohen, p. 208)

22. Lenard J. Cohen, pp. 130, 134.
23. Ibid., pp. 212–3.
24. Warren Zimmerman, "The Last Ambassador: A Memoir of the Collapse of Yugoslavia", *Foreign Affairs*, March–April 1995, p. 16.
25. David Owen, pp. 31–3.
26. Ibid., p. 33.
27. On 29–30 May, EC President Jacques Delors and Luxemberg Prime Minister Jacques Santer visited Belgrade, and the former promised to request $4.5 billion for Yugoslavia in return for economic reforms aimed at turning it into a free market and political reforms aimed at maintaining its territorial unity. Susan L. Woodward, p. 160. The offer was too little too late: the market reforms would have had to build on the failed structural adjustments and depended on financial centralization while the political reforms were open to decentralization.
28. On 3 June 1991, in a last ditch effort to save Yugoslavia, Izetbegovic and Gligorov proposed a "Community of Yugoslav Republics", with common market and common defense and foreign policy institutions, though each republic would also maintain its own armed forces and embassies. The proposal was first rejected and then conditionally approved by Serbian President Milosevic, and was also approved by Croatian President Tudjman and Slovene President Kucan, though the approval of the latter was disingenuous as the Slovenes were already preparing to declare independence on 26 June. Given this, the proposal came too late.
29. Lenard J. Cohen, p. 217.
30. Silber and Little, p. 213.
31. Lenard J. Cohen, p. 241, Silber and Little, p. 214.
32. Silber and Little, pp. 291–2.
33. Ibid., pp. 214–6.
34. Janusz Bugajski, p. 34.
35. Silber and Little, pp. 306–7.
36. It has been argued that as Germany's announcement came six months after the war began in Croatia, the Germans cannot be held responsible for (indirectly) worsening the conflict. However, the announcement was made while Croats and Serbs were discussing a cease-fire and the creation

of UN Protected Areas in the Krajina, and while Lord Carrington was negotiating a series of domestic and bilateral agreements between the Croat and Serb leaderships. Its impact was to weaken Carrington's bargaining position with the Croats and intensify Serb fears.

37. Silber and Little, pp. 199–200.
38. Lenard J. Cohen, p. 239.
39. Interview with Jiri Dienstbier, then chair of the CSCE, 19 October 1992.
40. It is probable, too, that the French quid pro quo for acquiescence had a greater role in European security.
41. European public opinion appears to have supported the German decision. A poll conducted in December 1991 showed that the percentage polled who were in favour of preserving Yugoslavia's territorial integrity were 18% in Germany, 20% in France and 17% in Britain. As against this, support for "respecting democracy and self-determination (including possible independence)" was 63% in Germany, and 73% in France and Britain. *Eurobarometer,* no. 36, December 1991, p. A41.
42. CSCE Report, p. 10.
43. Ibid., p. 11.
44. Ibid., pp. 13–4, 20.
45. Susan L. Woodward, p. 281.
46. Cited by A. Jayaratne Wilson, *The Break Up of Sri Lanka: The Sinhalese-Tamil Conflict,* Honolulu 1958, p. 85. This makes ironic reading in the context of the Bosnian war and the international peace plan.
47. Lee Bryant, "Bosnia-Herzegovina", *WarReport,* Nov.–Dec. 1992, p. 12.
48. Susan L. Woodward, p. 281, fn. 12.
49. The referendum turn-out was roughly 63% of eligible voters, as the overwhelming majority of Serbs did not vote, but though Serb opposition to independence had been the reason for the EC's suggesting a referendum in the first place, the outbreak of war had convinced them that withholding recognition would be worse than granting it.
50. Zoran Pajic, "Where Do You Go From Here", paper presented at the Helsinki Citizens' Assembly Meeting on "The State of Europe", London, 6–7 July 1995.
51. This issue is muddled by the fact that the majority of JNA troops posted in Bosnia were Bosnian Serbs, who turned from the JNA to the RSA.
52. Silber and Little, pp. 219–43.
53. Ibid., pp. 307–8.
54. Lenard J. Cohen, p. 276.
55. Ibid., pp. 289–96.
56. David Owen, p. 49.
57. Silber and Little, p. 251.
58. STC/2/2, Geneva: ICFY, 27 October 1992, pp. 4–5.
59. UNSCRs 758 (1992); 761 (1992); 770 (1992); and 776 (1992).
60. Radha Kumar, "Report of Municipal and Citizens' Delegation to Sarajevo,

26–29 November 1992", Helsinki Citizens' Assembly, Prague, 10 December 1992.

61. David Owen, p. 114.
62. In early April 1992, for example, UNPROFOR commander General Mackenzie:

> told Carrington that we (the UNPROFOR commanders) thought the Bosnian presidency was committed to coercing the international community into intervening militarily, and was therefore in no mood to honour a cease-fire – we recommended that Carrington advise the president that he would not receive military intervention and consequently should negotiate a solution with Dr Karadzic and the Bosnian Serbs.
>
> (Silber and Little, p. 253)

63. David Owen, pp. 82–3.
64. Three Serb majority, three Muslim majority, two Croat majority, one combined Muslim-Croat majority and a multi-ethnic province around Sarajevo. Owen says he and Vance chose to call the regions provinces rather than cantons so as to avoid a reference to the failed Cutileiro proposals of 1991, but, as the Washington Agreement of 1994 was to show, this was regarded as semantic sophistry by the SDS, HDZ and SDA. Ibid., p. 63.
65. Ibid., p. 62.
66. Ibid., pp. 90–9.
67. Ibid., pp. 78–9.
68. Ibid., p. 116.
69. Ibid., pp. 133–43.
70. This was not, however, the first time that the UNHCR had found itself assisting in the forcible expulsion of population: in late September 1992, UNHCR vehicles had transported Muslims from Banja Luka and Prijedor. Ibid., p. 55.
71. Silber and Little, pp. 266–75.
72. Ibid., pp. 279–82.
73. David Owen, pp. 137–9.
74. Silber and Little, pp. 297–9, David Owen, p. 143.
75. Dion Van Den Berg, *Municipal Peace Zones*, Helsinki Citizens' Assembly Report, The Hague, October 1992.
76. Silber and Little, pp. 294–7.
77. David Owen, pp. 164–76.
78. Radha Kumar, *Helsinki Citizens' Assembly Report*, 1992.
79. UN S/26260 of 6 August 1993, "Report of the Co-Chairmen of the Steering Committee on the Activities of the International Conference on the Former Yugoslavia", p. 2.

80. From the beginning, negotiations over the maps straddled an uneasy relation between ethnic demography and land distribution by ethnic composition in Bosnia. While Muslims comprised some 44% of the population, Serbs 33% and Croats 17%, a majority of Muslims were concentrated in towns and a majority of Serbs lived in villages.

81. UN S/26337 of 20 August 1993.

82. David Owen, pp. 189–216.

83. Milos Vasic and *Vreme* staffers, "A State Without Bread: The Banja Luka Uprising", *Vreme*, 20 September 1993, pp. 14–7.

84. Silber and Little, pp. 304–6; Liljana Smajlovic, "Buddies in a Clinch", *Vreme*, 11 October 1993, pp. 25–7. Smajlovic also interprets the falling out as a portent of the emergence of a Muslim state in Bosnia.

85. Joint Statement issued by President of the Croatian Republic of Herceg-Bosna, Mate Boban, and President of the AP Western Bosnia, Fikret Abdic, Zagreb, 21 October 1993, *Declaration issued by President Dr Radovan Karadzic of the Republika Srpska and President Fikret Abdic of the Autonomous Province of Western Bosnia of the Republic of Bosnia*, Belgrade, 22 October 1993.

86. Silber and Little, pp. 300–1.

87. David Owen, pp. 227–30.

88. An EU administration for Mostar was agreed following Croat opposition to a UN administration.

Chapter 3 Divide and Quit

1. *NYT*, 12 January 1994.

2. Department of Public Information, UN, "The United Nations and the Situation in Former Yugoslavia", Reference Paper Revision 4, p. 19.

3. David Owen, pp. 319–23.

4. Ibid., pp. 269–70.

5. Ibid., pp. 227–56.

6. UN S/1994/291 of 11 March 1994, "Report of the Secretary-General Pursuant to Security Council Resolution 900 (1994)". Resolution 900 (1994) dealt with lifting the siege of Sarajevo and the appointment of a "senior civil official to draw up an assessment and plan of action for the restoration of essential public services in the various *opstine* of Sarajevo".

7. Silber and Little, pp. 313–8.

8. Some analysts feared that the new division of responsibilities might lead to: "a partition of Bosnia between a Croat dominated part allied to the West and a Serb dominated part allied to Russia . . . this could be the beginning of a new East-West division of Europe, running through the middle of Bosnia-Herzegovina. The bridge of Brotherhood and Unity would indeed become the new Orwellian Berlin Wall." Mary Kaldor, "An Alter-

native Political Approach in Bosnia-Herzegovina", *HCA Quarterly*, no. 9, Spring 1994, p. 11.

9. Silber and Little, p. 327.
10. Ibid., pp. 324–34.
11. Radha Kumar, "Sarajevo Report, April 1994", Helsinki Citizens' Assembly, Prague, 2 May 1994.
12. Muhamed Sacirbey, "Bosnia: What Hopes for Multiculturalism? – Government", *WarReport*, no. 27, June–July 1994, p. 13.
13. Damir Juric, "Tudjman's New Radicalism", *WarReport*, no. 44, August 1996, p. 4.
14. Negotiations in Vienna on the draft Federation agreement had, by 13 March, settled on four Croat dominated cantons and five Bosniak dominated ones. Lee Bryant, "The Croat-Bosnian Accord", *WarReport*, no. 25, March–April 1994, p. 25.
15. David Owen, p. 304.
16. Zoran Daskalovic, "Croatia: Holding on to Bosnia", *WarReport*, no. 25, March–April 1994, p. 24.
17. Radha Kumar, "Report of One-Day Workshop on Refugees and Displaced Persons, 9 May 1994", Helsinki Citizens' Assembly, Sarajevo, 11 May 1994.
18. *Memorandum of Understanding on the European Union Administration of Mostar*, Brussels, 10 June 1994, art. 2.
19. "Activities Report", *HCA Quarterly*, no. 8, Autumn 1993, p. 27.
20. Vlado Azinovic, "Monthly Report", Helsinki Citizens' Assembly, Sarajevo, October 1994.
21. Indeed, Muhamed Sacirbey justified this conclusions: "Serbs in Bosnia-Herzegovina are now appropriately categorized – along with Romanians, Slovaks, Czechs, Jews, etc. – as "others" in a Bosnia-Herzegovina which remains committed to pluralism." The comparision was invidious: the numbers of Romanians, Slovaks, Czechs and Jews in Bosnia-Herzegovina was negligible. Muhamed Sacirbey.
22. Sejfudin Tokic, "Bosnia-Herzegovina: What Hopes for Bosnian Multiculturalism?", *WarReport*, no. 27, June–July 1994, p. 12.
23. Though, as Tokic says, the SDA could not be classified as a uniformly Muslim nationalist party; many secular SDA politicians were elected, and the choice of Haris Silajdic as Prime Minister indicated that the pluralist image was preferred. Sejfudin Tokic.
24. Radha Kumar, "Dying in Sarajevo", *Index on Censorship*, April–May 1994, pp. 186–7; "Report of Two-Day Workshop on Human Rights, Minority Rights and Collective Rights", Sarajevo, 25–6 June 1994, Helsinki Citizens' Assembly, 29 June 1994.
25. Zoran Daskalovic.
26. UNSCRs 942 (1994) and 943 (1994) of 23 September 1994.
27. By this point, there were only 1,000 Muslims left in Bijeljina. European

Community Military Monitors, Special Report, "Expulsions from Bijeljina and Janja", CC Tuzla to HQ ECMM CHUM, 22 September 1994.

28. *NYT,* 16 October 1994.
29. UNSCRs 958 (1994) and 959 (1994) of 19 November 1994.
30. *NYT,* 16 October 1994.
31. *NYT,* 24 November 1994.
32. *NYT:* 25 November 1994; 30 November 1994; 1 December 1994.
33. *NYT,* 1–6 December 1994.
34. *NYT,* 7–14 December 1994.
35. *NYT:* 21 December 1994; 24 December 1994.
36. "The position of Hans Koschnik, the new EU Administrator, is very difficult. As he says, Mostar is not a protectorate but an administration. He is not a Protector but an Administrator. His only power is to negotiate." Tony Bloomfield, "The European Union Administration in Mostar", Helsinki Citizens' Assembly UK, November 1994. There was, however, an element of sophistry in the argument: the *Memorandum of Understanding on the EU Aministration in Mostar* specified that the WEU would "supervise" police functions such as the "guarding of sensitive areas . . . protection of civilian property". Article 13.
37. Tony Bloomfield.
38. Radha Kumar, "Sarajevo and Mostar Report", Helsinki Citizens' Assembly, Sarajevo, 10 November 1994.
39. *NYT:* 5 February 1995; 18 February 1995.
40. *NYT,* 13 August 1995.
41. *NYT,* 16 July 1995.
42. *Associated Press,* 29 June 1995.
43. Robert Block, "Betrayal of Srebrenica", citing a leaked report of a Dutch government investigation, *The Independent,* 30 October 1995.
44. *NYT,* 13 July 1995.
45. See William Safire, "The Time Has Come", *NYT,* 13 July 1995; Anthony Lewis, "Weakness as Policy", NYT, 14 July 1995.
46. *NYT,* 14 July 1995.
47. Tihomir Loza, "From Hostages to Hostiles", *WarReport,* no. 43, July 1996, pp. 28–9.
48. *NYT,* 16 July 1995.
49. *NYT,* 17 July 1995.
50. *NYT,* 18 July 1995.
51. *NYT,* 19 July 1995.
52. *NYT,* 20–21 July 1995.
53. Letter from the Croatian foreign minister, Mate Granic, to the UN Security Council, *NYT,* 21 July 1995.
54. *NYT,* 20 July 1995.
55. *NYT,* 26 July 1995.
56. *NYT,* 22 July 1995.

57. *NYT*, 23 July 1995.
58. *NYT*, 13 July 1995.
59. *NYT*, 24 July 1995.
60. *NYT*, 26 July 1995.
61. *NYT*, 27 July 1995.
62. *NYT*, 30 July 1995.
63. *NYT*, 1–5 August 1995. The UN, Russia and Britain condemned the Croatian attack.
64. *NYT*, 5–18 August 1995.
65. *NYT*, 19 August–15 September 1995.
66. *NYT*, 23–29 September 1995.

CHAPTER 4 . . . TO DIVIDE AND FALL?

1. Additionally, every fourth session of government and parliament had to be held in Mostar. *NYT*, 11 November 1995.
2. Though Tudjman responded by attempting to annul the results, as Milosevic was to later annul municipal election results in Serbia, eventually he had to give way.
3. The dispute was eventually resolved by a phone call from President Clinton to President Tudjman. *NYT*, 23 November 1995.
4. *NYT*, 13–18 November 1995.
5. *NYT*, 20–22 November 1995.
6. William Safire, "Biting Bosnia's Bullet", *NYT*, 23 November 1995.
7. The new constitution dropped the definition of Bosnia-Herzegovina as a republic, but did not substitute another definition: "the Republic of Bosnia and Herzegovina, the official name of which shall henceforth be Bosnia and Herzegovina". UN SC A/50/790, S/1995/999 of 30 November 1995, Annex 4, *Constitution of Bosnia and Herzegovina*, Article 1(1), p. 59.
8. Ibid., pp. 59–70.
9. Taking the determined holdings of the Federal Republic of Yugoslavia (FRY) as the baseline, the FRY would be limited to 75% of the baseline and Croatia and Bosnia-Herzegovina would be limited to 30% each of the baseline. The allocation for Bosnia-Herzegovina was further subdivided into 2:1 (2 for the Federation and 1 for Republika Srpska). Ibid., Annex 1–B, *Agreement on Regional Stabilization*, pp. 44–5.
10. Indeed, under the new constitution each of the three-member presidency would have control over the armed forces; an arrangement which could be viewed as a tacit acceptance that while the Serb member would control the RSA, the Bosnian would control the ABH and the Croat the HVO. Mient Jan Faber, "The Dayton-Ohio Agreement and a Civil Society Response", paper presented to the Helsinki Citizens' Assembly, Prague, January 1996, p. 1.

11. *NYT*, 23 November 1995.
12. Ibid.
13. *NYT*, 27 November 1995.
14. UN SC A/50/790, Annex 1–A, *Agreement on Military Apects of the Peace Settlement*, p. 13.
15. *NYT*, 27 November 1995, citing Michael Clark, director of the London-based Centre for Defence Studies.
16. *NYT*, 3 December 1995.
17. *NYT*, 26 November 1995.
18. *NYT*, 27–30 November 1995.
19. UN SC A/50/790, Annex 1-A, Article 3, p. 10.
20. *NYT*, 1 December 1995.
21. *NYT*, 3 December 1995.
22. *NYT*, 13 February 1996.
23. *NYT*, 24 January 1996.
24. *NYT*, 3 February 1996.
25. *NYT*, 3–4 December 1995.
26. *NYT*, 24 and 31 December 1995.
27. *NYT*, 2 December 1995.
28. *NYT*, 3 December 1995.
29. David Owen, p. 168.
30. *NYT*, 2 December 1995.
31. *NYT*, 3 December 1995.
32. *NYT*, 4–5 February 1996.
33. *NYT*, 6–10 February 1996.
34. *NYT*, 11–13 February 1996.
35. And NATO reported that the withdrawal had begun soon after. *NYT*, 20 December 1995.
36. *NYT*, 15–19 February 1996.
37. *NYT*, 20–28 February 1996.
38. *NYT*, 3–7 March 1996.
39. *NYT*, 11–19 March 1996.
40. Senad Avdic, "The City's New Siege", *WarReport*, no. 44, August 1996, p. 37.
41. *NYT*, 1 May 1996.
42. *NYT*, 1 June 1996.
43. *NYT*, 29 April 1996.
44. Ibid.
45. *NYT*, 2 June 1996.
46. *NYT*, 19–22 May 1996.
47. *NYT*, 12 May 1996.
48. "Bosnia Media Monitoring Report", *WarReport*, no. 43, July 1996, p. 23.
49. *NYT*, 3–30 June 1996.
50. *NYT*, 25 June 1996.

51. Zelko Ivankovic (Vice-President of the Croatian Peasants' Party), "Breaking the Monoliths", *WarReport*, no. 44, August 1996, p. 36.
52. *NYT*, 30 June 1996.
53. Mirsad Behram, "Back From the Brink", *WarReport*, no. 44, August 1996, p. 6.
54. *NYT*, 4 September 1996.
55. Milos Vasic, "Milosevic's New Men", *WarReport*, no. 44, August 1996, p. 28.
56. *NYT*, 31 June–16 July 1996.
57. *NYT*, 17–27 July 1996.
58. International Crisis Group Report, *Mostar Election Day: Technical and Legal Analysis*, Sarajevo, 8 July 1996.
59. *NYT*, 17–18 July 1996.
60. *Nasa Borba*, 31 July 1996.
61. Miodrag Zivanovic, "Against the Odds in Republika Srpska", *WarReport*, no. 44, August 1996, p. 35.
62. *NYT*, 17–31 February 1996.
63. Milan Cvetinovic, "A Frontier Town Prepares to Vote", *WarReport*, no. 44, August 1996, pp. 39–41.
64. *NYT*, 25 July 1996.
65. This was the chief bone of contention at the NATO Foreign Ministers' meeting in Berlin on 3 June 1996. *NYT*, 5 June 1996.
66. Press officer, Calum Murphy, IFOR-UN daily news briefing, Sarajevo, 1 August 1996.
67. *NYT*, 2–3 August 1996.
68. Mirsad Behram, p. 5.
69. *NYT*, 31 August 1996.
70. *NYT*, 2–3 August 1996.
71. UN S/1997/126, "Arbitral Tribunal for Dispute over Inter-Entity Boundary in Brcko Area", p. 7.
72. UN SC A/50/790, p. 49.
73. UN S/1997/126, p. 9.
74. Ibid., p. 15.
75. Suzana Andjelic, "The Corridor to New Conflict?", *WarReport*, no. 44, August 1996, pp. 6–7.
76. *Proceedings of the Municipality Council*, Brcko, Tuzla, January 1996.
77. *NYT*, 23 August 1996.
78. Interview with UNHCR protection officers, Banja Luka, 3 August 1996.
79. *NYT*, 31 August 1996.
80. *NYT*, 4 September 1996.
81. *NYT*, 8 September 1996.
82. Press officer, Calum Murphy, IFOR-UN daily news briefing, Sarajevo, 1 August 1996. Indeed, the democratic opposition coalition, the United List for Bosnia-Herzegovina, had filed a complaint with the Elections Appeal

Sub-Commission to protest SDS violations of the Dayton Agreement in late June, and Robert Frowick later responded by threatening to disbar the SDS from the elections, but the threat was made two days before campaigning was to end. In the international negotiations, meanwhile, the SDS began to push for the renegotiation of the Dayton Agreement's provisions for the return of refugees.

83. *NYT*, 1 September 1996.
84. *NYT*, 12 September 1996.
85. Press Conference of the Alliance of Peace and Progress, Banja Luka, 12 July 1996.
86. *NYT*: 2 September 1996; 12 September 1996.
87. *NYT*, 22 September 1996, citing OSCE figures for election results.
88. *NYT*, 10–11 February 1997.
89. UN S/1997/126, pp. 11,15–6, 20–1.
90. The lack of domestic agreement does not, in fact, necessarily mean that the award is of little consequence. In the India-Pakistan partition, the British head of the boundary commission, Cyril Radcliffe, decided on the north-western border between India and Pakistan without agreement by the Sikh, Hindu and Muslim representatives to the commission; the Radcliffe line was not subsequently contested and is the official border between the two countries.
91. Ibid., pp. 46–7.

Chapter 5   Peace Making 1992 Onwards

1. UN A/47/277–S/24111, UN Secretary-General Boutros Boutros-Ghali, *Agenda for Peace*, UN A/48/935, *Agenda for Development*. See also UN A/50/60–S/1995/1 of 3 January 1995, "Supplement to an Agenda for Peace: Position Paper of the Secretary-General on the Occasion of the Fiftieth Anniversary of the United Nations", pp. 1–5.
2. Joan E. Spero, US Under-Secretary of State for Economic, Business and Agricultural Affairs, "The New Transatlantic Agenda: Setting the Course for US Co-operation with Europe", *US Department of State Dispatch*, vol. 7, no. 23, 3 June 1996, pp. 12–4. Joan Spero relates economic and security architectures, and argues that the new agenda combines economic diplomacy with traditional foreign policy.
3. "Lyons Summit Chairman's Statement: Toward Greater Security and Stability in a More Co-operative World", *US Department of State Dispatch*, vol. 7, supplement no. 2, June 1996, pp. 29, 34.
4. John C. Kornblum, "A Tour Through the New Atlantic Community", *US Department of State Dispatch*, vol. 7, no. 41, 7 October 1996, p. 6.
5. Secretary Christopher, "International Women's Day: Celebrating Remarkable Achievements", *US Department of State Dispatch*, vol. 7, no. 12, 18

March 1996, p. 12. See also President Clinton, "The G7 Summit: Achieving Key Objectives", "We will contribute $5 million to the work of the Bosnian Women's Initiative. After a past in which so many men were killed in the fighting, Bosnia's future may depend more than ever on its women. We will provide training and loans to help women find jobs and create businesses so they can support their families and get their nation going again". Ibid., supplement no. 2, p. 20. The recognition of the special role of women in economic and social reconstruction was again partly a by-product of the development debate, which had highlighted the successes of targeting women in micro-credit enterprises (for example, in Bangladesh).

6. "During the war Sarajevo became a symbol . . . this city – like Banja Luka, Mostar [*sic*] and Tuzla – has been a symbol of multi-ethnic co-operation." Secretary Christopher, "Implementing the Dayton Agreements: New Partnerships", *US Department of State Dispatch*, vol. 7, no. 7, 12 February 1996, p. 7.

7. Kevin Boyle and Tom Hadden, "The Peace Process in Northern Ireland", *International Affairs*, vol. 71, no. 2, 1995, pp. 271–2.

8. Adrian Guelke, "The United States, Irish Americans, and the Northern Ireland Peace Process", *International Affairs*, vol. 72, no. 3, July 1996, p. 531.

9. Robin Wilson, "The Opsahl Report: A Civil Society Response to the Conflict in Northern Ireland", *HCA Quarterly*, no. 8, Autumn 1993, p. 7.

10. Ibid., pp. 7–8.

11. Adrian Guelke, pp. 527–8.

12. Ibid., p. 46.

13. *A Framework for Accountable Government in Northern Ireland* and *A New Framework for Agreement*, 22 February 1995, Stormont, Belfast, Northern Ireland.

14. President Clinton, "Waging Peace in Northern Ireland", Remarks to the employees and community of the Mackie Metal Plant, Belfast, Northern Ireland, 30 November 1995, *US Department of State Dispatch*, vol. 6 no. 49, 4 December 1995, p. 9.

15. Richard Holbrooke, "A Framework for Peace and Justice in Northern Ireland", *US Department of State Dispatch*, vol. 6, no. 14, 3 April 1995, p. 45.

16. UNSCR 750 of 10 April 1992.

17. Mary Southcott, "Cyprus Elects a New President", *Friends of Cyprus Report*, no. 31, Summer 1991, p. 9.

18. Kevin Watkins, "A Window of Hope for Cyprus", *Friends of Cyprus Report*, ibid., p. 5.

19. Mary Southcott, p. 13.

20. Mary Southcott, "Prospects for Cyprus", *Friends of Cyprus Report*, no. 32, Autumn 1991, p. 3.

21. UN S/23121 of 8 October 1991, "Report of the Secretary-General on His Mission of Good Offices in Cyprus", paras. 17–19.
22. Suha Bolukbasi, "Boutros-Ghali's Cyprus Initiative in 1992: Why Did It Fail?", *Journal of Middle Eastern Studies*, vol. 31, no. 3, July 1995, p. 469.
23. Ibid., p. 470.
24. UN Secretary-General, "Set of Ideas on an Overall Framework Agreement on Cyprus", Sections 1(Overall Objectives), 2 (a) (Constitutional Aspects), 3 (Security and Guarantee).
25. A territorial agreement, he contended, would weaken his bargaining position on other issues. Suha Bolukbasi, pp. 472–3.
26. UN Secretary-General, "Letter Submitted to the Security Council", 28 June 1994.
27. UN S/1994/629 of 30 May 1994, "Report of the Secretary-General on His Mission of Good Offices in Cyprus", paras. 48, 54.
28. Ibid., para. 53.
29. Letter from President Clerides to the UN Secretary-General, 5 July 1994, *Friends of Cyprus Report*, no. 37, Autumn 1994, p. 18.
30. *NYT*, 26 April 1995.
31. *Friends of Cyprus Report*, no. 38, Autumn 1995, p. 19.
32. *Friends of Cyprus Report*, no. 39, Autumn 1996, "Diary of Events", back page.
33. On 26 March, after a meeting with President Clerides in Nicosia, Assistant Secretary of State John Kornblum announced that "without some change in Ankara's position on fundamental issues . . . it might be better for this effort [US push for a settlement] not to take off." Ibid.
34. George Kenney, *The Nation*, October 1996.
35. Tozun Bahcheli and Nicholas X. Rizopoulos, "The Cyprus Impasse: What Next?", *World Policy Journal*, Winter 1996–97, pp. 27–39.
36. This summary of events in April 1997 is based on interviews with government officials, UN representatives, researchers and peace activists in Nicosia between 16 and 24 April 1997.
37. On the travesties which the Camp David agreements represented and the critical ways in which they set the terms for future negotiations, see Edward Said, *The Question of Palestine*, New York, Vintage Books 1980, pp. 182–238. Said also illuminates the complex and frequently tragic problems which regional engagements can entail: while Palestine has been *the* key issue for Arab identity through much of the twentieth century, the vicissitudes of great power and Middle Eastern relations have often led Arab states to complicity in diplomatic erasures of the Palestinians.
38. UN General Assemby Resolution 38/58 C of 13 December 1983.
39. The UN had to move the General Assembly to Geneva because the US refused to grant Arafat a visa, and the Assembly's resolution that the term "Palestine" should now be used in UN documents was vetoed by the US. "The Origins and Evolution of the Palestine Problem", pp. 269–71.

40. Hanan Ashrawi, *This Side of Peace*, New York, Simon and Schuster 1995, pp. 108–11.
41. UN A/47/115 S/23680 of 4 March 1992, Document presented by the Palestinian Delegation (Palestinian side of the joint Palestinian-Jordanian Delegation to the Israeli Delegation) on 3 March 1992.
42. Hanan Ashrawi, pp. 212–3.
43. Israeli proposal presented to the Palestinian Delegation, Washington DC, 21 August 1992.
44. Hanan Ashrawi, pp. 238–9.
45. Ibid., pp. 249–53.
46. Jemal Tutunji and Kamal Khaldi, "A Binational State in Palestine: the Rational Choice for Palestinians and the Moral Choice for Israelis", *International Affairs*, vol. 27, no. 1, January 1997, p. 41.
47. Jan de Jong, "Palestine After Oslo: Borderlines Between Sovereignty and Dependency", in *Beyond Rhetoric: Perspectives on a Negotiated Settlement in Palestine, Part Two*, Washington DC, The Centre for Policy Analysis on Palestine, August 1996, pp. 14–6.
48. Jemal Tutunji and Kemal Khaldi, pp. 47–8.
49. *NYT*, 2 February 1997.
50. *NYT*, 26 September 1995.
51. *NYT*, 10 January 1997.
52. *NYT*, 19 January 1997.
53. *NYT*, 22 January 1997.
54. *NYT*, 26 January 1997.
55. Ahmed Khalidi, "No Longer the Unthinkable", *NYT*, 11 February 1997.
56. *NYT*, 8 March 1997.
57. *NYT*, 16 March 1997.
58. The latter was, in any case, a "governorate", though why the Palestinian Authority chose such a colonial nomenclature is mystifying.
59. This assessment is based on interviews with Legislative Council members, human rights groups and independent analysts in the areas of the Palestinian Authority and Israel between 8 and 16 April 1997.
60. For example, the US spent over $11 billion in market investment in central and east Europe, including the former Soviet Union, in the 1990s, but was hard put to it to find $200 million for reconstruction in Bosnia. Its efforts to raise regional investment in sustainable peace had garnered European pledges of less than $1 billion for Bosnia, and it had had similar difficulty in raising funds from the Arab states for Palestinian reconstruction and development programmes.
61. *Report to the Congress on the Enlargement of the North Atlantic Treaty Organization: Rationale, Benefits, Costs and Implications*, The Bureau of European and Canadian Affairs, US Department of State, 24 February 1997, p. 3.

Glossary of Acronyms

ABH	Army of Bosnia-Herzegovina
APWB	Autonomous Province of Western Bosnia
CIA	Central Intelligence Agency
CLMC	Combined Loyalist Military Command (Northern Ireland)
CSCE	Conference on Security and Co-operation in Europe (renamed Organization for Security and Co-operation in Europe in 1995)
EC	European Community
EEC	European Economic Community
EU	European Union
FRY	Federal Republic of Yugoslavia
HDZ	Croatian Democratic Union
HOS	Croatian Party of Rights
HVO	Croatian Defence Council
IBRD	International Bank for Reconstruction and Development (the World Bank)
ICFY	International Conference on the Former Yugoslavia
IEBL	Inter-Entity Boundary Line
IFOR	(United Nations) Intervention Force

IMP	International Monetary Fund
IPTF	Intenational Police Task Force
IRA	Irish Republican Army
JNA	Yugoslav National Army
MBO	Muslim Bosniak Organization
MP	Member of Parliament
MUP	Croatian Ministry of Internal Affairs
NATO	North Atlantic Treaty Organization
OSCE	Organization for Security and Co-operation in Europe
PLO	Palestine Liberation Organization
RS	Republika Srpska
RSA	Republika Srpska Army
SDA	Muslim Party for Democratic Rights
SDLP	Social Democratic and Labour Party (Northern Ireland)
SDS	Serb Democratic Party
SFOR	(NATO) Stabilization Force
UN	United Nations
UNDP	United Nations Development Programme
UNFICYP	United Nations (Peace-Keeping) Force in Cyprus
UNHCR	United Nations High Commissioner for Refugees
UNPA	United Nations Protected Area
UNPROFOR	United Nations Protection Force
UNSCOP	United Nations Special Committee on Palestine
UNSCR	United Nations Security Council Resolution
USSR	Union of Soviet Socialist Republics
WEU	Western European Union
WTO	Warsaw Treaty Organization (Warsaw Pact)

Index